PALESTINE AND THE PALESTINIANS IN THE 21ST CENTURY

PALESTINE *and the* PALESTINIANS IN THE 21ST CENTURY

edited by

ROCHELLE DAVIS *and* MIMI KIRK

INDIANA UNIVERSITY PRESS

Bloomington & Indianapolis

This book is a publication of
Indiana University Press
Office of Scholarly Publishing
Herman B Wells Library 350
1320 East 10th Street
Bloomington, Indiana 47405 USA

iupress.indiana.edu

Telephone orders   800-842-6796
Fax orders   812-855-7931

Library of Congress Cataloging-in-Publication Data
Palestine and the Palestinians in the 21st century / edited by Rochelle Davis and Mimi Kirk.
    pages cm
  Includes bibliographical references and index.
    ISBN 978-0-253-01080-3 (cloth : alk. paper) — ISBN 978-0-253-01085-8 (pbk. : alk.
paper) — ISBN 978-0-253-01091-9 (ebook) 1. Palestinian Arabs—Politics and government—
Congresses. 2. Palestinian Arabs—Western Bank—Congresses. 3. Palestinian Arabs—Gaza
Strip—Congresses. 4. Arab-Israeli conflict—Congresses. 5. Israel—Politics and government—
Congresses. I. Davis, Rochelle, editor of compilation. II. Kirk, Mimi, editor of compilation.
III. Piterberg, Gabriel, [date] author. Zionist colonization of Palestine in the context of
comparative settler colonialism.
    DS113.6P324 = 2013
    956.95'3044—dc23
                            2013034075

1 2 3 4 5 18 17 16 15 14 13

Contents

Acknowledgments

The editors would like to thank first and foremost the Center for Contemporary Arab Studies (CCAS) at Georgetown University, which hosted the initial conference from which this volume emerged and which subsequently supported the volume in all its stages of development. Special recognition goes to former CCAS director Michael C. Hudson, who cochaired the conference and who edited a volume on Palestine twenty years earlier (*The Palestinians: New Directions*) from the first CCAS conference on Palestine, which inspired this one. The support of the current director, Osama Abi-Mershed, has been crucial to this volume's publication. We are also grateful to associate director Rania Kiblawi, multimedia and publications editor Steve Gertz, former CCAS director the late Barbara Stowasser, public events coordinator Maggie Daher, and information officer Nick Hilgeman for their critical help. Nick especially stepped in at a late stage to help wrap up the volume; his meticulous and speedy work is particularly appreciated. We also thank Rebecca Barr for her essential help with the proof process and index. Warm thanks particularly go to Rebecca Tolen, sponsoring editor at Indiana University Press, for her support and guidance. The IUP team, including managing editor Angela Burton and copyeditor Eric Levy, made the process of completing the volume a seamless one. Two reviewers provided very helpful comments and made the chapters and overall volume better at a crucial stage. Zan Studio in Ramallah allowed us to use their 2010 remix of Franz Kraus's 1935 Visit Palestine poster as the cover for the paperback edition. The remixed image symbolizes the change that has come for Palestinians living in Palestine in the twenty-first century, where the wall prohibits their access to Jerusalem. Our thanks to the Palestine Poster Project Archive for facilitating our use of this cover image.

The participants in the conference made it an invigorating and provocative milieu in which to talk about Palestine and Palestinians in the twenty-first century. And while a number of them did not contribute papers, we thank them for making us think deeply about many diverse subjects.

Rochelle Davis and Mimi Kirk are especially grateful that they worked so easily and competently with each other across multiple continents and with good humor. They appreciate the contributors' hard work, persistence, and patience throughout the long process of editing this volume.

PALESTINE AND THE PALESTINIANS IN THE 21ST CENTURY

Introduction

ROCHELLE DAVIS

The first decade of the twenty-first century witnessed both significant ends and noteworthy beginnings for Palestinians. In this volume, specialists on Palestinian politics, history, economics, and society examine the continuities that bind the twentieth to the twenty-first century. The contributors address these junctures with an analytical eye on the effects of colonial rule and on the political and ideological trends following the 1948 and 1967 wars, bringing a close reading of history into crucial and critical scholarship on the present. They also consider what the future may hold based on the evidence provided by ongoing political, social, economic, and legal developments. The rigorous scholarship in this volume offers a well-grounded perspective from which to recommend informed solutions to bring a just and peaceful future to Palestine and Israel.

At the outset of the twenty-first century and as the decade progressed, it became clear that the political agreements that had underpinned post–Oslo Accord Palestinian-Israeli relations were no longer being observed. Israeli policy under prime ministers Ariel Sharon and Benjamin Netanyahu moved sharply to the right. The launch of the second Intifada (2000) shifted Palestinians' resistance to Israelis in a way that adopted a new and violent character. The decade saw an increase in the repressiveness of Israeli occupation policies, including completion of the major portions of the separation wall,[1] continued confiscation of Palestinian land in the West Bank and East Jerusalem and the building of settlements,[2] extrajudicial executions,[3] and arrests of political activists.[4] These policies solidified the settlement, water, and road networks that by design also inhibit Palestinians' access to their farmland, to enough water to live on, and to unhindered movement.[5] The decade also witnessed the rise and then the sharp decrease of Palestinian suicide bombings,[6] as well as the widespread use of nonviolent resistance to land confiscations.[7] At the same time, the Palestinian Authority (PA) in the West Bank and Hamas in Gaza infringed on residents' freedoms of expression and assembly, targeting civil society organizations in general and human rights organizations in particular.[8] This internal repression, coupled with the willingness of the PA to continue to appear at the negotiating table when called by the United States and Israel, has diminished its legitimacy in the eyes of many Palestinians.

The first decade of the twenty-first century also witnessed the beginning of new internal divisions among Palestinian political groups. Following the death in 2004 of Palestinian Authority president Yasser Arafat, the longtime head of the Palestine Liberation Organization (PLO) and the Fatah movement, new political forces mobilized to take over the leadership role. The Islamic Resistance Movement (Hamas) agreed to participate in the national legislative elections that took place in 2006. Its entry into the political mainstream signaled its acceptance at that time of the political framework in which the Palestinian Authority and the Palestinian Legislative Council existed and was seen as a move toward widespread democratic representation. Israel and the international community responded by penalizing the Palestinians for voting for Hamas, creating new cleavages and more opportunities for internal repression.[9] Accompanying these political shifts, Palestinian society has witnessed a rise of religious groups and local civil society organizations, and these ties are increasingly important as bases for social identification, reflecting a weakening of the major political parties in the PLO and their associated organizations such as women's and student groups and labor committees.

After 2001, the international community called for or set up no fewer than eight negotiation processes between Palestinians and Israelis, none of which produced tangible changes. While peace, stability, and democratic rule have long been the desired outcomes of these negotiations and elections, it seems evident that for Palestinians they have instead resulted in increased instability, internal political conflict, and continued Israeli occupation of the West Bank. While Israel unilaterally withdrew troops and settlers from the Gaza Strip in 2005, it remained in control of all borders, trade, and sea access, with the exception of the Gaza border with Egypt. Both the 2002 Israeli re-invasion of the West Bank[10] and the 2008–2009 and October 2012

Israeli assaults on Gaza continue to define the way that Palestinians see and feel the power of the Israeli state over their lives. These experiences make them wary of another decade of negotiations and what it might lead to, while at the same time Palestinian political leaders fail to work together or form common goals. Palestinians enter the second decade of the twenty-first century, it seems, with different leaders and different social movements, but many of the same challenges, concerns, and desires. This volume addresses this era through the lens of these transitions and examines deeply some of the major issues that concern land, economics, elections, political leadership, legal paradigms, and possibilities for the future.

Currents from the Twentieth Century

For Palestinians, one of the continuities that circumscribe and define their relationship to Palestine is the origin of the Israeli state as a colonial project. The volume opens with a chapter by historian Gabriel Piterberg, who deconstructs the hegemonic narrative that emerged through the Zionist colonization of Palestine. Piterberg points out that this narrative, which includes the privileging of the consciousness of the settlers at the expense of the Palestinian Arabs, became deeply ingrained in the thoughts of prominent Zionists before the founding of Israel in 1948. He further argues that "the creation of a nation-state out of a settler society is not just a foundational event but a continuing process."

Also referencing colonial control, economist Leila Farsakh studies the economies in the West Bank and Gaza, specifically Palestinian development, by examining the economic record of the Oslo years (1993–2000). She notes that during this period the Palestinian economy experienced pauperization rather than development, building her argument from detailed data and using the theoretical work of economist Yusuf Sayigh.

In continuing the historical current, Tamim al-Barghouti describes a pattern of war, peace, or appeasement, and then civil war or dissent, in the ranks of the Palestinian national movement over a period of more than fifty years. He argues that factions that compete to represent the Palestinian people have a history of initially struggling against the occupying power but then making concessions to it to gain its recognition. The result is that the national movement continually shifts from a position of strength with those it represents (war) to one of lost legitimacy (peace or appeasement, then civil war or dissent).

Taken together, these three chapters provide a means of understanding how policies enacted during the colonial period and into the 1950s and 1960s form the structures of action and thought as well as the paradigms through which political positions, legal arguments, and economic development and decision-making are framed and engaged with by Israelis and Palestinians, among many others, in the present.

Continuities into the Twenty-First Century

The first decade of the twenty-first century witnessed political events that signaled a weakening of Palestinian leadership in the PLO and the rise of Hamas. The ensuing political conflicts between Fatah and Hamas diverted Palestinian political energies and created internally divisive stands and attacks. External actors exacerbated the split; even after Hamas agreed to participate in legislative elections in the West Bank and Gaza in 2006 (and won the majority of the seats), Israel and the Quartet (the United Nations, the United States, the European Union, and Russia) continued to label it a terrorist organization and refused to engage it as a political player unless it met certain requirements, including the acceptance of previous agreements. One result was that all aid money from these countries to the PA was suspended, and the economy of the West Bank and Gaza nosedived as the PA found it difficult to pay salaries, among other economic issues. These countries' stance vis-à-vis Hamas continues to this day. Many found hope in the Saudi initiative to bring Fatah and Hamas together in 2007, and the Palestinian Legislative Authority formed a unity government that included all of those elected—including those officials whom Israel had arrested and put in administrative detention.[11] In June of that year, however, fighting broke out between Fatah and Hamas, resulting in an unprecedented political/administrative division: Fatah officials took over governing the West Bank and Hamas officials took responsibility for the Gaza Strip. This allowed the West Bank under Fatah leadership to return to the international fold and accept international aid money from the United States and others that had suspended it when Hamas was in the government. At the same time, Israel tightened its blockade of Gaza and coerced the Egyptian government to do the same. The overthrow of the Mubarak regime in Egypt in 2011 has changed the Egyptian-Gaza relationship, but living conditions in Gaza remain difficult and Gazans' lives are circumscribed by borders that they and the goods they produce and need are rarely allowed to cross, except illegally through underground cross-border tunnels. One consequence is the creation of a thriving black market in Egypt's Sinai to take goods into Gaza, which is possible because of the absence of Egyptian authorities. This creates a compromised security situation for all living there due to the subsequent rise in the trafficking of arms, gasoline, and humans.

On the Palestinian political front, in April 2011 Hamas and Fatah agreed to form an interim government, but as of the beginning of 2013, no progress had taken place. Legislative elections that were scheduled for May 2012 did not occur,[12] and the continued internal divisions and strife along with the international blockade of Gaza and the unwillingness of the international community to engage with Hamas have left Palestinians with many questions about national unity and international sanctioning. And while the Arab uprisings that began in early 2011 have fostered the hope that positive changes are ahead for everyone living in the Middle East, they have also served to emphasize to Palestinians their own statelessness and lack of freedoms.

In this section, chapters by scholars As'ad Ghanem, Sara Roy, and Susan Musarrat Akram examine political cycles, election results, paradigm shifts, and legal developments in the ways that the Palestinian-Israeli conflict is conceptualized. Together they paint a picture of national and international politics in the region in this period. As'ad Ghanem writes of the 2006 Palestinian legislative elections in which a more disciplined Hamas defeated Fatah, which was seen as corrupt and submissive to the United States and Israel. The splitting of the national movement into the Gaza Strip (Hamas) and the West Bank (Fatah), according to Ghanem, "has prevented and will continue to prevent a Palestinian consensus that would permit progress in the political process." Ghanem's chapter illustrates in detail the cycle proposed in al-Barghouti's chapter, as Fatah, the party of Yasir Arafat and for decades the most popular of Palestinian political parties, lost some measure of popularity and legitimacy. Ghanem shows that Fatah failed to understand how to both mobilize and rein in Fatah members in the face of growing support for Hamas.

Sara Roy, a scholar and expert on Gaza, writes in her chapter about the direness of the political situation by outlining recent paradigm shifts, such as the acceptance—even erasure—of the idea of occupation. She describes the situation such that "the occupation has been transformed from a political and legal issue with international legitimacy into a simple dispute over borders. In this regard, Israel has successfully recast its relationship with Gaza from one of occupation to one of two actors at war, a recasting the international community has also come to accept." Roy argues that this recasting must end, along with the occupation and suffering of the Palestinians, particularly those in the sealed-off Gaza Strip. As is well documented, the blockade of Gaza has produced a humanitarian crisis for its residents, and Amnesty International has classified these acts as collective punishment.[13] Roy's argument is well illustrated by the events of December 2008 and January 2009, when Israel launched an offensive against the Gaza Strip and the Hamas government. The twenty-three-day attack resulted in the massive destruction of buildings, roads, institutions, and other infrastructure, as well as the death of 1,380 Palestinians, most of them civilians, and 13 Israeli soldiers. Despite the one-sided attack, popular parlance described it as a "war." In the aftermath, UNICEF estimated that more than 70 percent of Gazans were living in poverty in the summer of 2009, "with an income of less than $250 a month for a family of up to nine."[14] Four years later, the situation is still dire, dominated by the continued economic blockade, and thus poverty and political and economic disenfranchisement continues to be the status quo.

Legal scholar Susan Musarrat Akram echoes Sara Roy's analysis of the paradigm shifts in international discourse about the status of the West Bank and the Gaza Strip. Akram discusses the exclusionary paradigms that have been adopted about Palestinian refugees. In her chapter, she reviews how despite the many international peace agreements—such as in Rwanda and Bosnia-Herzegovina—that have required the implementation of refugee rights, those rights are continually excised from or deliberately made ambiguous within the framework of Palestinian-Israeli negotiations. Thus, Palestinians living in the diaspora—in Jordan, Syria, Lebanon, Egypt, and beyond—have been almost entirely excluded from any discussions about the future of Palestine and Palestinians, while, with the exception of those living in Jordan, they continue to live without passports or the rights of citizens.

The second part of this section addresses the shifting identifications of Palestinians in the twenty-first century as they conceive of themselves as a national community and as belonging in various types of groups, be they religious, secular, or political, broken down along class and gender lines. Two authors, Islah Jad and Loren D. Lybarger, elaborate on how Palestinians, both as individuals and in groups, identify with secular and religious groupings in complex ways. In her chapter on Palestinian women's movements, Jad argues that nationalist and Islamist political platforms share common ground vis-à-vis their gender ideologies, with both using Islam as a means of gaining support. These ideologies, Jad argues, are not based on religious texts, but are fashioned as a "modern" means of political mobilization. Complementing this work, Lybarger's analysis builds on ethnographic fieldwork he conducted among three groups: a politically divided family in a Gaza refugee camp; an Orthodox Christian youth group in Bethlehem; and members of a small mosque in a Bethlehem-area refugee camp. He found that these actors possess multiple affiliations, rather than a solely secular/nationalist or Islamist identity. As such, "various and conflicting interpretations of nation and religion . . . emerge." Ultimately Lybarger argues that neither religious nor secular identities (nor a combination of the two) can offer any real hope of ending the crisis. He asks, "Could exile be a permanent condition? Could it be tolerated?"

Lybarger and Jad thus examine in complementary ways the overlaps between contemporary Palestinian nationalism and Islamism. Combined with the chapters on the shifting political landscape among Palestinians, this section touches on social issues and identification practices that enrich the interpretations and understandings of Palestinian issues in the twenty-first century.

Trajectories for a Future

The years following this first decade of the twenty-first century have proved to be much the same as those that preceded it, continuing the status quo of military occupation, resistance, and international support and aid. On the international front, the Palestinian Authority launched a campaign for increased international recognition, preceded by its declaring itself the Palestinian *National* Authority in contrast to the designation of Palestinian Authority as outlined in the Oslo Accords. It failed to achieve a hearing in the Security Council to become a full member state at the UN in 2011, and then shifted its case to the General Assembly, which voted overwhelmingly to grant it the status of non-member observer state in November 2012. The PLO had held permanent observer status since 1974, and this shift in the body representing the Palestinians at the UN—from the PLO to the PA—as well as the upgrade in status indicate that the PA has taken on the mantle for all Palestinians and not just those in the West Bank, who elected them. This unilateral act angered many Palestinians and continued the Oslo Accord-era political processes that exclude the millions of Palestinian refugees in the diaspora from any form of representation in the international arena.

Those supporting the PA's move, however, argue that acquiring non-member observer state status allows for the possibility of the PA's joining the International Criminal Court (ICC) as well as other UN agencies. Israel and the United States, both of which strongly opposed this move and rallied other states to vote against it, fear the international legitimacy garnered by such status as well as the potential international instruments of law to which the Palestinians could have access regarding human rights and crimes against humanity. Applying to become a member of the ICC is something that the PA has yet to pursue.[15]

U.S. president Barack Obama has continued to talk about the need for a two-state solution to the conflict while nothing is done to achieve it. Despite repeated declarations to the contrary, the United States has continued to allow illegal Israeli settlement-building in the West Bank to continue unabated, and the slightest criticisms by U.S. administration officials that the settlements are not helpful for peace efforts have been met with denunciations by a large chorus of Israel supporters in Congress. The U.S. administrations of George H. W. Bush and Bill Clinton more than twenty years ago had more teeth and more willingness to bring the two sides together.

Obama's visit to Israel in March 2013, the first of his presidency, may signal his interest in addressing the issue and working toward a two-state solution. Regardless of what the political outcomes of the visit are, there is consensus among scholars that new visions for the future for Palestinians and Israelis must be considered. To that end, the final section of this book addresses possibilities for the future vis-à-vis U.S. policy and regarding a shared state. Political scientist Michael C. Hudson examines U.S. policy toward Palestine under the Obama administration and the possibility that an American administration cognizant of the new realities of the Palestinian-Israeli conflict could contemplate a change of course. Lawyer Noura Erakat supplies a kind of response to the chapters by Akram and Hudson by formulating a strategy by which activists can frame international law within a domestic context to appeal to the U.S. government, thus using a known and well-established framework to promote justice for the Occupied Territories. She proposes that activists emphasize civil and political rights as enshrined in the Constitution; frame grievances in the form of violations of U.S. domestic law, such as the Foreign Assistance Act, which prohibits assistance to any government that consistently violates internationally recognized human rights (as Israel did in the Gaza offensive of 2008–2009); and stress the United States' long-standing policy of condemning Israeli settlement expansion.

Using the recent history of Ireland as a model, Ali Abunimah's chapter details former U.S. special envoy for Middle East peace George Mitchell's successful 1998 negotiations between unionists and republicans in Northern Ireland as an example of how to create a single, just state. "The experience in Northern Ireland indicates that unequal power relationships produced by settler colonialism and ratified by partition are durable and are likely to generate resistance as long as they exist," he writes. "Ending a conflict requires a sustained and deliberate effort to dismantle existing relationships and replace them with ones that are more equal and just—in other words, effective decolonization." Saree Makdisi's chapter echoes Abunimah's vision. He advocates for a single state in which all citizens enjoy equal rights, regardless of their religious preference. He argues that the current Palestinian-Israeli system (separation based on religion) has no place in the twenty-first century and guarantees endless conflict. In his view, its opposite—"secular and democratic cooperation between people"—offers a real chance for peace.

Notes

1. This wall separates the towns and cities in the West Bank from Israel. It does not, however, follow the 1967 border between the West Bank and Israel, but rather cuts into the West Bank and separates villages from their farmland and divides contiguous populations. It has been condemned by the International Court of Justice in a nonbinding advisory opinion delivered on 9 July 2004.

2. B'Tselem, "By Hook and by Crook: Israeli Settlement Policy in the West Bank," July 2010; Office for the Coordination of Humanitarian Affairs, "The Humanitarian Impact on Palestinians of Israeli Settlements and Other Infrastructure in the West Bank," July 2007.

3. According to the Palestinian Center for Human Rights, between December 2000 and June 2007, the overall number of Palestinians killed by Israelis in

extrajudicial killings/assassinations was 664. Of those, "434 . . . were specifically targeted, the other 230 having been killed in the process of the attacks," http://www .pchrgaza.org/special/position_extra.html.

4. B'Tselem, "Without Trial: Administrative Detention of Palestinians by Israel and the Incarceration of Unlawful Combatants Law," joint report with Hamoked—Center for the Defence of the Individual, October 2009; United Nations Economic and Social Council, "Economic and Social Repercussions of the Israeli Occupation on the Living Conditions of the Palestinian People in the Occupied Palestinian Territory, Including Jerusalem, and of the Arab Population in the Occupied Syrian Golan—Note by the Secretary General," 3 May 2006, http://www.un.org/en/ecosoc /docs/report.asp?id=1127; United Nations Information Service, "Israel's Land Confiscations, Home Demolitions, Exploitation of Natural Resources Main Causes of Crisis in Occupied Arab Territories, Second Committee Told," 28 October 2005, http://www.unis.unvienna.org/unis/pressrels/2005/gaef3121.html.

5. Hagit Ofran and Lara Friedman, "West Bank 'Settlement Blocs,'" Peace Now, May 2008, http://peacenow.org.il/eng/content/west-bank-%E2%80%9Csettlement -blocs%E2%80%9D; Amnesty International, "Israel and the Occupied Palestinian Territories: Enduring Occupation. Palestinians Under Siege in the West Bank," 4 June 2007; United Nations Information Service, "Israel's Land Confiscations."

6. Israel Ministry of Foreign Affairs, "Victims of Palestinian Violence and Terrorism since 2000," http://www.mfa.gov.il/MFA/Terrorism-+Obstacle+to+Peace /Palestinian+terror+since+2000/Victims+of+Palestinian+Violence+and+Terrorism +sinc.htm.

7. A 2009 documentary film, *Budrus,* chronicled the nonviolent resistance movement there: http://www.justvision.org/budrus; Donald Macintyre, "Ni'ilin: The West Bank Focus of Unarmed Demonstrations and Civil Disobedience," *Independent* (London), 31 July 2008, http://www.independent.co.uk/news/world /middle-east/niilin-the-west-bank-focus-of-unarmed-demonstrations-and-civil -disobedience-881584.html.

8. Hugh Naylor, "Hamas and Fatah Hammered for Human Rights Abuses Against Their Own People," *The National* (UAE), 19 May 2011, http://www .thenational.ae/news/worldwide/middle-east/hamas-and-fatah-hammered-for -human-rights-abuses-against-their-own-people.

9. Graham Usher, "The Democratic Resistance: Hamas, Fatah, and the Palestinian Elections," *Journal of Palestine Studies* 35, no. 3 (Spring 2006): 20–36.

10. Called "Operation Defensive Shield," the 2002 re-invasion is suggested to be the largest military attack in the West Bank since 1967. See "Operation Defensive Shield (2002)," Ynetnews, 3 December 2009, http://www.ynetnews.com/articles /0,7340,L-3685678,00.html.

11. Tim Butcher, "Hamas and Fatah Agree Unity Government Deal," *Telegraph* (London), 8 February 2007, http://www.telegraph.co.uk/news/worldnews/1541992 /Hamas-and-Fatah-agree-unity-government-deal.html.

12. "Interview: Holding Palestinian Elections on [sic] May 'Impossible': Official," Xinhuanet News, 12 January 2012, http://news.xinhuanet.com/english/world /2012–01/12/c_131357060.htm.

13. Amnesty International, "Suffocating Gaza—The Israeli Blockade's Effects on Palestinians," 1 June 2010, http://www.amnesty.org/en/news-and-updates/suffocating -gaza-israeli-blockades-effects-palestinians-2010–06–01.

14. UNICEF, "Growing Poverty in Gaza Pushing Children to Work," 22 July 2009, http://www.unicef.org/infobycountry/oPt_50318.html.

15. "Q&A: Palestinians' Upgraded UN Status," 30 November 2012, http://www .bbc.co.uk/news/world-middle-east-13701636.

PART 1

Colonial Projects and
Twentieth-Century Currents

1. The Zionist Colonization of Palestine in the Context of Comparative Settler Colonialism

GABRIEL PITERBERG

To deeply understand Zionism and the state of Israel, one must engage with the field of comparative settler colonialism. The expansion and conquest by Europe that began in 1500 produced two kinds of related but clearly distinguishable forms of colonialism. One was metropole colonialism, in which Europeans conquered and ruled vast territories but administered and exploited them without seeking to make them their home; British India is a good example. The other type was settler colonialism, in which the conquest by European states brought with it substantial waves of settlers who with the passage of time sought to make the colonies their national patrimony. This process entailed a relationship with the indigenous people that ranged from dispossession to elimination, or from slavery to cheap labor, depending on the land and labor formations of a given settler society. Settler colonialism can be said to have begun in earnest with the English—and later Scottish-Presbyterian—settlers in Ireland in the second half of the sixteenth century, and continued with the settler colonies in what would become Virginia and New England in the seventeenth century. It is within the burgeoning field of comparative settler colonialism that I seek to place the Zionist colonization of Palestine and the state of Israel.[1]

The achievements of the comparative study of settler colonialism have been at once scholarly and political. Many settler projects gave birth to powerful nation-states, which have asserted their hegemonic narratives nationally and internationally. The comparative field not only acutely refutes these narratives through evidence and interpretation; it also creates a language that amounts to a transformative alternative to the way in which these settler societies narrate themselves. Three fundamentals of hegemonic settler narratives are thus undermined: (1) the uniqueness of each settler nation, (2) the privileging of the intentions and consciousness of settlers as sovereign subjects, and (3) the putatively inconsequential presence of natives in regard to the form and contours of settler societies.

To take uniqueness first, there is something deeper in the comparative approach than what the act of comparing obviously entails. This something is akin to what Benedict Anderson calls, in a separate but intimately related context, the modularity of nationalism. Comparative studies of settler nations undercut the claim to uniqueness not because they find all settler nations identical; in fact, many of these comparisons result in underscoring historical specificity as much as similarity. What they do, however, is offer a language that identifies a white settler trajectory and renders it reminiscent of other white settler trajectories. This is true not only for studies whose explicit purpose is to make a comparative argument (e.g., a study of the United States and South Africa as white settler projects), but also for those that are solely concerned with one case (e.g., a study of Zionist Israel as a white settler project that brings to bear upon this single case the conceptual language of comparative settler colonialism).

The exponents of comparative settler colonialism neither are oblivious to intentions nor suggest that intentions do not matter. In his masterful book on the United States and South Africa, *White Supremacy,* the late George Fredrickson attributes much explanatory importance to the fact that the Dutch East India Company's intention in creating the Cape colony in the mid-seventeenth century was to have a secure trading post on the way to the Indian Ocean, whereas the intention in establishing the English colonies in Ireland at the end of the sixteenth century and in what would become Virginia and New England in the early seventeenth century was to create pure settlements and exclude the local population. The idea is therefore not to ignore intentions. Yet, one must acknowledge that a persistently structural and predominantly material investigation overwrites intentions and, crucially, emphasizes results. This kind of examination could, for example, substantially change the way many consider the ethnic cleansing during the 1948 war in Palestine. Instead of the rather obsessive concern with whether or not there was an Israeli master plan to cleanse Palestine of Arab presence, one might ask whether the structural logic embedded in settler nationalism, which the notion of a Jewish nation-state implies, explains the cleansing. One might also ask whether cleansing-as-result is not, empirically and ethically, as important as cleansing-as-intention (or the absence thereof).

The third fundamental—whether the presence of indigenous people is consequential to how settler societies were shaped—is possibly the most subtle fundamental and the one that exposes the exclusionary, or segregationist, nature of white liberalism and perhaps also of multiculturalism. The more liberal versions of hegemonic settler narratives may admit that along the otherwise glorious path to nationhood bad things were done to the indigenous people and, where applicable, to enslaved Africans. They may even condemn these "bad things" and deem them unacceptable. At the same time these narratives, by the very way in which they are conveyed, deny that the removal and dispossession of indigenous peoples and the enslavement of others is an *intrinsic* part of what settler nations are—indeed, it is the most pivotal constituent of what they are—rather than an *extrinsic* aberration of something essentially good or an extrinsic issue that requires attention and action. The point is not whether settler nations are good or bad, but the extent to which the act of exclusion in reality is congruous with the hegemonic rendering of that reality. The exclusionary fundamental that inheres in these white hegemonic narratives lies not in the denial by the sovereign settlers of the wrong they did to those whom they disinherited or enslaved (though this happens too), but in the denial that the interaction with the dispossessed is the history of who the settlers collectively are. What is denied is the extent to which the nonwhite world has been an intrinsic part of what is construed as European or Western history.

The comparative study of settler societies is not a subaltern studies project. It does not seek to salvage the voice of the dispossessed victims of settler colonialism and reassert it, nor does it adhere to a postcolonial methodology or register. In fact, most of these works' chief subject matter is the settlers themselves more than the metropoles or the indigenous peoples. But this subject matter is described in terms of its incessant interaction with the peoples who were either dispossessed and removed or used for labor. In this type of analysis, by definition there cannot be a history of the institutions and ideologies of the settler societies that is not simultaneously a history of settler-native relations. The history of white supremacy throughout Fredrickson's oeuvre is not a trajectory within the larger American or South African histories; in a very consequential way the history of white supremacy *is* the history of these settler societies.

Similarly, this work cannot include a history of private property (as the subject of legal studies and political theory) in early modern England that is not at the same time a history of land-looting first in Ireland and then east of the Appalachians. Analogously, and to be dwelt on in greater detail below, there cannot be a history of the cooperative settlements and settlement-theories, which is one trajectory in the hegemonic Israeli narrative, that is separable from another trajectory in that narrative, namely the "Arab Problem"; for what shaped the cooperative settlements and made some theories more pertinent and applicable than others was precisely what the Zionists called the Arab Problem, or the consequential existence of indigenous people who, from a settler vantage point, posed a problem. For example, Arabs (and for the most part, Mizrahi Jews) are completely absent from kibbutzim. This absence is the single most important fact in the history of the kibbutzim, for it tells the story of inclusion and exclusion.

One of the most important things to bear in mind when examining the nature of the Israeli occupation, the wall, the Nakba, and so forth, is that the creation of a nation-state out of a settler society is not just a foundational event but a continuing process. It is worth remembering the observation by Australia-based scholar Patrick Wolfe: "The determination 'settler-colonial state' is Australian society's primary structural characteristic rather than merely a statement about its origins. . . . Invasion is a structure, not an event."[2]

Three fundamentals of hegemonic settler narratives were mentioned above: the uniqueness of each settler nation, the exclusive primacy accorded to the settlers' subjectivity, and the denial that the presence of the colonized has been the single most significant factor in determining the structure and nature of the settler society. The Zionist Israeli narrative is a particular case of that general depiction. Its three fundamentals accordingly are: the alleged uniqueness of the Jewish nation in its relentless search for sovereignty in the biblically endowed homeland; the privileging of the consciousness of the Zionist settlers at the expense of the colonized, as well as the privileging of the intentions of colonization by the settlers rather than the consequences for the indigenous Palestinians; and the denial that the presence of the Palestinian Arabs on the land destined for colonization was the single most significant factor that determined the shape that the settlers' nation took.

This third fundamental is articulated in the way Zionist scholars and others who followed present the history of Palestine from the beginning of Zionist settlement in the 1880s until 1948 and beyond. They present the dual society thesis, meaning that two completely separate and self-contained en-tities emerged in Palestine: the Jewish Yishuv and Palestinian Arab society. Each developed according to its own trajectory, which is explicable—in the former case—by a combination of European origins and Jewish essence. Each trajectory is depicted as unrelated to the other, with the only meaning-ful relations being those of a struggle between two impregnable national col-lectives (if the national authenticity of the Palestinians is not altogether de-nied).[3] It cannot be sufficiently stressed that what is denied is not the mere presence of Arabs in Palestine, but rather the fact that their presence and re-sistance were consequential to the very essence of the Zionist colonization project and the Israeli nation-state. This thesis is clearly the ultimate schol-arly articulation of the empty land concept.

One of the most original scholars of the Israeli-Palestinian conflict, the Israeli historical sociologist Gershon Shafir, demolishes the dual society para-digm. He brings to bear the language and method of comparative settler co-lonialism upon the early phase of Zionist colonization (1882–1914) and later upon the nature of the Israeli state. He masterfully demonstrates that al-though it contains certain historically specific features, Zionism is nonethe-less perfectly comparable to other settler projects, and what shaped the na-ture of Zionist colonization, including its institutions and state formation, was the settler-indigene struggle rather than intrinsic ideologies and the at-tempts to realize them. Adhering to a different concept—relational history—Zachary Lockman argues the same. Relational history is a concept Lockman borrows from Perry Anderson and adapts to his own research. By relational history Anderson meant a history "that studies the incidence—reciprocal or asymmetrical—of different national or territorial units and cultures on each other," a history "that is the reconstruction of [such units'] dynamic inter-relationships over time." The result is that unlike Shafir, whose sole focus is the Zionist settlers, Lockman looks at the interaction between Arab and Jewish railway workers in Mandatory Palestine.[4]

My work complements studies such as Shafir's and Lockman's by add-ing a dimension whose subject matter and themes they do not examine. The comparative study of settler societies has been for the most part concerned with land, labor, and legal and political institutions. My interest is that of the literary and intellectual historian, who is concerned with interpreting human consciousness, imagination, and ideas, and with placing them in their material context. My work therefore shows that the framework of set-tler colonialism is applicable not only to the base (to use somewhat loosely

Marxist terminology)—to land and labor—but also to the superstructure, to themes such as ideology, literary imagination, the use of the Old Testament, and scholarly knowledge. Below I show how deeply the sense of being part of a settler project was ingrained in the thought and consciousness of two prominent Zionists from the pre-1948 period.

Chaim Arlosoroff's "Exercise" in Comparative Settler Colonialism

While scores of pro-Zionist scholars have been at pains to suppress the degree to which the presence of the Palestinian Arabs was intrinsic to the nature of the Zionist project, and the extent to which the Zionist project was a settler-colonial project, a no less committed Zionist inadvertently manifested awareness of precisely that which would be later denied. This Zionist was Dr. Chaim Arlosoroff (1899–1933), by far the intellectually brightest politician of note within labor Zionism; it has been speculated that had his death not been untimely he would have eclipsed Ben-Gurion. Arlosoroff is best—almost only—known for his assassination in Tel Aviv on 16 June 1933; the assassins remain unidentified. He was then the maverick of Zionist politics, one of the leaders of the main labor party, Mapai, and head of the Political Department of the Jewish Agency, and was thus basically a foreign minister. Arlosoroff was amidst discussions with the Nazi leadership that aimed to enable emigrating German Jews to salvage at least some of their wealth, provided their destination was Palestine. The right-wing Revisionist[5] agitation against the negotiations and Arlosoroff personally peaked at that time, though it has not been conclusively shown that the killers were Revisionists.[6]

Chaim Viktor Arlosoroff was born in 1899 in Ukraine to well-off middleclass parents who spoke both Russian and German. He studied Hebrew at home with a private tutor. The family fled to Königsberg in Germany in the wake of the 1905 revolution and during World War I settled in Berlin. There Arlosoroff became engrossed in two worlds: German letters and culture through the gymnasium he attended, and Zionism through the Hapoel Hatzair (the Young Worker) party. The latter was an anti-Marxist and, for the most part, nonsocialist party. It was inspired by Tolstoy's cult of return to nature and tilling the land, which was preached by the early laborite settlers' father figure, A. D. Gordon. At the end of the war he studied economics at Berlin University. In 1919, at the age of twenty, he published his first work, *Jewish People's Socialism* (*Der jüdische Volkssozialismus*), which in a way amalgamated his intellectual and political sources of inspiration: Marx, Kropotkin, Russian Narodnik moods, and German romanticism. In 1923 he submitted his doctoral dissertation on Marx's concept of class and class struggle, and was offered a university position by his advisor, Werner Sombart. He declined the offer, and in 1924 Arlosoroff immigrated to Palestine.[7]

In 1927 Arlosoroff published a remarkable essay in Hebrew, which he entitled "On the Question of Joint Organization" (Le-she'elat ha-irgun ha-meshutaf). It appeared in Hapoel Hatzair's daily and was included in the collection of his works published shortly after his assassination.[8] Let me first explain the context of joint organization.

Although the Zionist settlers were successful in creating an exclusively Jewish labor market in their own economic sphere, they could not do so in the part of the economy controlled by the British Mandatory state. In the state-run railway and postal services there developed a vigorous mixed labor market of Arab and Jewish workers, who sought to unionize. The increasingly marginalized—but nonetheless lively—left-wing parties in the Histadrut, or Federation of Laborers, tried to challenge the Histadrut's Zionist nature and Ben-Gurion's iron hand through the railway workers union, which was jointly Arab-Jewish and could therefore be used as an alternative power base to the exclusively Jewish labor Zionist wing of the Histadrut. They called for a universally inclusive Histadrut based on class instead of Jewishness. By the late 1920s Ben-Gurion defeated them in two steps: (1) he first supported a joint organization but, crucially, one based on separate national divisions—Arab and Jewish. By doing so, he subverted the true purpose of joint organization, which was meant to be joint on class and labor criteria rather than on an ethno-national criterion; (2) he brought the railway union into the Histadrut (so that it wouldn't exist as an independent power base) and, striking ruthlessly at an opportune moment, expelled the left from the Histadrut altogether.[9]

The essay that contains Arlosoroff's contribution to the joint organization debate demonstrates in an original way how instinctive the consciousness of white settlers had become. For Arlosoroff there is one, and only one, criterion by which the worthiness of joint organization should be judged:

> Can the joint organization nullify the competition between the expensive and modern Hebrew labor and the cheap and primitive Arab labor

and [thereby] create more amenable conditions for the collective of Hebrew workers in their war for the conquest of labor . . . ? The answer to
this question—rather than a pre-conceived doctrine—will determine our
verdict on the method of joint organization.[10]

This clear formulation vindicates, first of all, Zeev Sternhell's thesis that
what labor Zionism offered in both practice and ideology was nationalist
socialism, almost completely devoid of any humanistic and universalist appeal or content.[11] Arlosoroff attributes no value whatsoever to joint organization, even in its pure settlement garb of autonomous ethnic sections, unless it could be shown to contribute to colonization (of labor in this case),
immigration (by guaranteeing wages that were commensurate at least with
the more modest European economies), and settlement. Developing a detailed analysis based on substantial economic data, he argues that joint organization would not only fail to enhance the Zionist colonization of Palestine,
but in certain respects would even hinder it. Concerning wages, Arlosoroff
questions the assumption that joint struggle would necessarily result in an
upswing of labor generated by the Mandatory state. He maintains that in
such struggles there is no uniform result and that wages would always depend on the nature of "an actual national economy and its objective capacity."[12]

Arlosoroff first offers a hypothetical analogy to illustrate the futility of
joint organization in Palestine. This analogy involves the migration of a few
tens of thousands of American or Australian workers to Poland. When these
American workers unionized, they would instantly face the competition of
cheaper labor from the indigenous Polish workers. "What would we say if
these American workers seriously suggested to solve the problem by uniting with the Polish workers in order [to obtain] an American wage-level?"
Arlosoroff asks. "We would say that such a suggestion was to no avail."[13] Arlosoroff's point is that interethnic joint organization could perhaps work in
certain national economies, but not in the type of economy Palestine represented. In the Palestinian case, he points out, two economies are simultaneously very different yet porous: "the native economy" (mesheq ha-aretz)
and "the settler economy" (mesheq ha-hityashvut). The former is a primitive
Eastern economy, whereas the latter a relatively advanced European one.[14]
In the hypothetical analogy, the arriving American workers, like their Jewish
Zionist counterparts, represent the more developed economy, and the local

Polish workers, like the Palestinian Arabs, represent the primitive economy. The main point Arlosoroff is making is that the more advanced settler workers would not be able to successfully compete with the more primitive workers in the labor market without accepting the latter's low wages, nor would joint organization push wages up to the level required by the advanced settler workers. The absence of reasonably well-paid employment would be, in this analysis, a kiss of death for the immigration of more settlers.

Clearly, Arlosoroff puts his weight behind the complete rejection of joint organization with Arab workers. He uses an analogy in the latter part of the essay to introduce his preferred course of action, but this time the analogy is real:

> I think it is worth trying to find an equivalent to our problem in the annals of settlement of other countries, and to explain our situation by deduction. This is not easy. There is hardly an example of this [the Zionist] endeavor of a colonizing people [ʿam mityashev] with European level of needs, which does not resort to enforcement measures and its purpose is to transform a country, in which there is a low level of wages . . . into a site of mass immigration and mass settlement.[15]

Arlosoroff proceeds with settler-colonial examples that do not involve the interaction of settler-workers and native workers in the labor market. The United States was not an adequate comparison, he writes, and neither were New Zealand and Australia, "since they nipped this problem in the bud through a fervent policy of 'White Australia'" (a set of policies, practices, and institutions whose purpose was to curtail non-white labor in Australia from 1901 to 1973)[16] He then asserts that South Africa is

> almost the only case in which there is sufficient similarity in the objective conditions and problems so as to allow us an analogy. To prevent misunderstanding in advance, it should be stressed that we know full-well also the difference of the factors at work in the two countries' conditions, and that we do not wish to attempt here [to create an analogous] political construction, but only to compare to one another the polar points in the two countries' economy.[17]

In comparison to Palestine, Arlosoroff maintains, in South Africa a labor market emerged in the late nineteenth century and the early decades of the twentieth century that consisted of a minority of white workers who were unable to compete with the vast majority of Asian and African work-ers and whose material expectations and needs were much higher. These gaps, Arlosoroff says, were greater than between Jews and non-Jews in Pal-estine; thus the problem was even more serious in South Africa than in Pal-estine. Eventually the solution came with the Color Bar laws, which were in-troduced as a result of the political weight of the South African labor party and trade unions. These laws excluded all non-Europeans from skilled, su-pervisory, and better-paid labor, and preserved that domain for Europeans only. Arlosoroff remarks that "it is not important whether we reject this politics . . . or justify it. . . . It is important here to highlight the economic rea-sons and social relations that led, rightly or wrongly, to the promulgation of Color Bar laws."[18]

Arlosoroff's conclusion issues from the South African analogy and from an article by Lord Sidney Oliver in which he recommends an absolute sep-aration—"segregation" he calls it—of whites and blacks.[19] Arlosoroff asserts that in the forthcoming decades the only way to achieve the fulfillment of Zionism would be to completely forsake any notion of joint organization (joint anything, really) and stiffen the separation into two economies: one modern, well paid, and conducive to an enhanced immigration of settlers, and the other undeveloped and low paid, which would enable the settlers to continuously exclude the indigenous workers from their labor market.[20]

Arthur Ruppin: A Note on the Genealogy of Early Zionist Settlement

The kibbutz, according to common knowledge, originated from an aston-ishing socialist experiment with an ideology the settlers (pioneers, or *chalut-zim*) had acquired in Europe. Even someone as astutely prophetic and sober as Hannah Arendt thought that the kibbutzim were marvelous.[21] That this rendering accords the settlers not only a central role but also hyperagency is hardly surprising, for these settlers were members of the Second and Third Aliyas, that is, the ruling political elite of the Yishuv (from the 1920s on), the World Zionist Organization (WZO) and Jewish Agency (from the 1930s on), and the state of Israel (1948–1977). I wish to question this story and offer a threefold correction by tempering the claimed hyperagency of the settlers by underscoring the pivotal role played by the German Jewish settlement experts; by showing that the decisive factor in the creation of the kibbutzim was the conditions and desire of colonization; and by showing that even in terms of ideational flow from Europe to Palestine, what we have are ideas of colonization and race rather than socialism.

In the mid-1980s two geographers of the Hebrew University, Shalom Reichman and Shlomo Hasson, published a revealing article on the formative influence of the pre–World War I German Reich's colonization project in the Posen (Poznan in Polish) province in the east Prussian marches upon the early phase of the Zionist colonization effort in Palestine.[22] The wider background of the project was the crisis of German agriculture and the attendant *Landflucht* (land flight). As such, Prussia took a large area of the east Prussian marches, or the Ostmark, in the partitioning of Poland in the late eighteenth century. In the latter decades of the nineteenth century three of the Ostmark provinces—Eastern and Western Prussia and Silesia—had a German majority; only the fourth, Posen, had a Polish majority of roughly 60 percent. The Germans also identified Posen as a center of Polish nationalism. The purpose of the state project was to effect a demographic transformation in Posen, and the Ostmark more generally, by dispossessing the Polish majority of its hold on the land and settling Germans in their stead.

The process began in 1886 with the promulgation of the Colonization Law by the Prussian Diet, and the creation of the main instrument to implement its intention, namely, the Colonization Commission (*Ansiedlungskommission*). The Commission's main task was to purchase large portions of land, especially from the big German and Polish landowners, and financially facilitate the establishment of small- and medium-sized German colonies. A fund of one hundred million marks was provided and was refilled regularly over the next two decades.[23] "The German method of settlement," Reichman and Hasson elaborate,

> was intended to produce a new space that on the one hand would check the geographical expansion of the Poles and on the other would strengthen the German presence in the area. To attain this goal the German Colonization Commission embarked on a comprehensive program that included land purchasing, planning and development, land parcelling, selling and renting land to German colonists, and provision of administrative services and guidelines for new colonists.[24]

Of crucial importance was the Commission's attitude toward labor. The Commission subdivided the large estates it had purchased into two types of colonies. One was the farm, in which each settler received an area of ten to fifteen hectares, and the other was the working people's colony, where settlers were apportioned allotments of one-half to one and a half hectares for garden produce and were employed in nearby cities. As for the farm, "the main principle underlying the choice of this size was that it would provide for the subsistence of one family without the help of hired labor. This was intended to prevent the employment of Polish labor in areas settled by Germans."[25] The German colonization project was ultimately unsuccessful, for although it purchased substantial tracts of land and settled large numbers of Germans, it could neither transform the Ostmark's, especially Posen's, demography nor remove the Poles. The latter, creating their own institutions, fought back effectively, and the former's immigration to the area and settlement in it was offset by emigration from it.

The German project and the Colonization Commission had a formative impact on the Zionist project in four related ways: it irrevocably discarded the French model that had been introduced by the Rothschild experts, a model that required cheap indigenous labor, was based on private land ownership, and insisted upon profitability; it accorded primacy to national colonization over economic profitability; it accorded primacy to (an equivalent of) the state and its bureaucracy over the market and private capitalists; and it implanted in the WZO what Shafir perceptively calls the pure settlement frame of mind.[26] The agents of this formative impact were two German Jewish settlement experts, Franz Oppenheimer (1864–1943) and, perhaps the single most important individual for the Zionist settlement in Palestine, Arthur Ruppin (1876–1943). One might also add the botanist Otto Warburg (1859–1938), head of the Zionist Executive Committee and chairman of the Palestine Land Development Company (PLDC).

Ruppin was born in Posen, though his family moved away when he was a child. A crisis in his family's finances forced Ruppin to leave school at the age of fifteen. He nonetheless managed to enroll in university, and studied law in Berlin and Halle, but considered it a practical necessity. His real passion lay in political economy and social studies, and his hope was to become an expert for the betterment of society through public (i.e., state) service. His political leanings combined social democracy and social Darwinism. As a good German Hegelian, Ruppin firmly believed in the ultimate guidance of the state, as well as the foundational place of the peasant and agriculture in the national edifice. In the 1900s he was increasingly drawn to Zionism and,

given his immense organizational gift, soon became a prominent techno-
crat. In 1907 he immigrated to Palestine, and in 1909 established the PLDC
and also headed the Palestine Office, in which capacities he was answerable
to Warburg in Germany.[27] Ruppin was a founding member of Brit Shalom
(an organization mainly consisting of intellectuals who promoted bination-
alism as a political framework for Palestine, in which Jews would not attain
a demographic majority) in the 1920s but left it rather early.

Ruppin's role in the colonization of Palestine was so pivotal that Zionist
historiography—even post-Zionist scholarship—has called him "the father
of Jewish settlement in the land of Israel." In addition to settlement, he was
also responsible for the historical alliance within Zionism between the nationalist bourgeoisie and the labor movement, and for the agreement with
the Nazis on the transfer of German Jews and their capital, in which Arlosoroff too was involved. While a leading Zionist, he was engaged in intensive
scholarly research and was considered an international authority on the social scientific study (including statistics) of the Jews.

Before proceeding with the impact of the German colonization project
in the Ostmark, it is important to briefly dwell on Ruppin's other passion,
namely, race and social engineering.[28] Ruppin's *weltanschauung*, a term on
which he himself insisted, was social Darwinism, and its early formation occurred within a budding interdisciplinary paradigm that became known as
eugenics or racial hygiene (*rassenhygiene*).[29] One of his main mentors was a
central promulgator of the new paradigm in Germany, the blond, blue-eyed
biologist Ernst Haeckel, who Ruppin described in his diary as "the marvel-
lous German type." Haeckel's mission was to disseminate "Darwinism as a
weltanschauung."[30]

From Ruppin's early work in the early 1900s it is clear that he adhered to
a rigid biological determinism of race, whereby "we are connected to our
predecessors not through the spiritual tradition but through the continuity
of the primordial substance that exists in our body."[31] His reflections on the
super-man (*übermensch*) made him conclude that such a man should develop only among those similar to him,[32] from which the move to the purity
of race needed just a nudge.

Ruppin concerned himself for the rest of his life with the correction
and betterment of "the Jewish race" because of his beloved German nation
and homeland's anti-Semitic rejection of him. His poem entitled "Without
Homeland," which Ruppin penned at the nadir of his painful realization,

conveys this rejection and swift passage to Zionism.[33] It cannot be sufficiently emphasized that Ruppin's path was typical of other Central European nominal Jews: not from Judaism to Zionism, but the other way around.

Ruppin's mission was now to transform the Jewish race by renewing the purity it once knew. Here he explicitly followed Houston Stewart Chamberlain. Chamberlain (1855–1927) was a British popularizer of philosophy and history who at an early age became enchanted with German culture. He was an admirer of Wagner, whose daughter he married. His ideas on pan-German nationalism as well as his anti-Semitic pronouncements were read by Ruppin. One of the main challenges Ruppin took on was how to eradicate the Jews' "commercial instinct," which was seen as responsible for their excessive fondness of mammon and subsequent rupture from the soil. On this question he adopted the thesis of the pro-Zionist economist Werner Sombart (as mentioned, Arlosoroff's advisor in the 1920s), whom he had met at Berlin University. The key for dealing with the "commercial instinct," which Ruppin related, crucially, to the "Semitic element," was to preserve racial purity and eschew racial mixture (*rassenvermischung*).[34] This was systematized in Ruppin's *The Sociology of the Jews*, which appeared first in German and was promptly translated into Hebrew in the early 1930s,[35] a period in which Ruppin also met for a conversation on race with Himmler's mentor, Professor Hans F. K. Günther.[36] Ruppin's diagnosis was that the original Jewish Volk (*urjude*), which had belonged to Indo-European tribes, had deteriorated because of the increasing presence of the Semitic element in its body, through intermingling with the Oriental type in particular. The Semitic component in the Jewish race gradually became dominant, extricated the Jews from nature, from their soil, and from their productive-agricultural way of life, and infused into them the insatiable "commercial instinct" as early as the First Temple era (i.e., long before the first century AD).[37]

Ruppin's plan to remove the Semitic component—or at least reduce its presence—from the Jewish Volk, since that component was dysgenic, was predicated upon identifying a human reservoir that could renew a purer, more Indo-Germanic Jewish race, one whose contact with its original soil would release "the springs of natural sensation" (*naturempfinden*). That reservoir, Ruppin determined, was East European Jewry, within which non-Semitic elements were discernible. Ruppin asserted that the Middle Eastern and Sephardi Jews did not exhibit the same signs of eugenic renewal that was evident in their East European race-relatives and, worse, they were experiencing a palpable biological degeneration. He never tired of categorically underscoring the superiority of the Ashkenazis over the Mizrahim and Sephardim in creativity, mathematical skills, hygiene and, above all, in a bio-mystic force called *lebenszähigkeit* (roughly, life-tenaciousness), with which the Volk could successfully navigate through the *daseinskampf* (struggle for survival). Ruppin's ultimate conclusion was that the Jewish type par excellence—the Ashkenazi Jew—was closer to the Indo-Germanic races than the Semitic ones.[38] This belief was not solely Ruppin's. As I point out elsewhere, there were other bourgeois Jews and non-Jews—real, like George Eliot and Gershom Scholem, and fictional, like Daniel Deronda—from western and central Europe to whom East European Jews seemed "authentic."[39]

So obsessed was Ruppin with race that just a few days before his death in 1943, with the Judeocide in Europe peaking, he began to write an introduction for a study on the Jewish race based on a taxonomy of noses. His samples were noses and facial features of various Zionist figures.[40]

Ruppin was not just a theoretician but also an active settler–colonial official who could implement his research. From the outset his Palestine Office worked vigorously to create a community of settlers that would consist of human beings of a higher type (*höherer menschentyp*). He applied a strict process of selection for the candidates for immigration when they were still in their countries of origin. Statistics from two years (1912–1914) show that the rate of those who applied for immigration and were rejected by Ruppin exceeded 80 percent. Even those who had been selected but contracted serious illnesses or were severely injured while in Palestine were sent back by the Palestine Office to their ports of departure. One of the foremost scholars of this topic, Etan Blum, writes,

> Ruppin's methods of operation were part of his comprehensive culture planning, in the framework of which he established a network of training farms and agricultural settlements, in order to facilitate a pincer movement: the control of land acquired by the Zionist movement, and the creation, through intensive selection, of "the human matter" that would form the dominant racial component of the old-new Jewish race, a component he called "the Maccabian Type."[41]

Evidence for how the German colonization project in Posen and Eastern Prussia informed Ruppin is both explicit and structural. On several occasions Ruppin stated his indebtedness to the German venture. In the PLDC foundation prospectus of 1909 Ruppin explained that "in its work the Company will assume the methods used by the German 'Land Bank,' the Polish 'Ziemsky Bank' [a countercolonization bank] and the Prussian Colonization Commission, which are engaged in a colonization process in the east Prussian provinces." Not only were the tasks and methods of the PLDC formulated along the lines of the German Colonization Commission model, but even the sizes of farms were similar to their Posen equivalents: fifteen to twenty-five hectares per farmer-settler and one-half to one and a half per settler who dwelled in a working people's colony and was employed in a nearby city.[42] Like Ruppin, Warburg, the PLDC Chairman, was unequivocal: "We do not propose new ways, new experiments whose nature is unknown. We assume instead the Prussian colonization method as it has been practiced in the last ten years by the Colonization Commission."[43]

Reichman and Hasson offer a meticulous survey of the structural ways—both conceptual and actual—in which the Posen model guided Ruppin and the thrust of the WZO settlement drive before the First World War.[44] One of the most crucial features they unwittingly uncover is what Shafir calls the WZO experts' pure settlement frame of mind. Reichman and Hasson write from a clearly Zionist perspective, and the result of their work is rather curious. Although the material they furnish, and not infrequently even their own analyses, point to how Ostamark can be explained by the colonial model, this model changes when it is applied to Palestine. Indeed, it ceases to be colonial and mysteriously becomes something else, which is noncolonial, something that is either politically neutral and scientific or altogether national liberationist.

Two principles, which underlay Ruppin's colonizing approach, evinced the pure settlement vision. These in turn were congruous with the spatial concept of the German Colonization Commission. "One," Reichman and Hasson elaborate, "was to avoid penetration into areas densely inhabited by another national group, and the other was to form contiguous blocks of settlements."[45] Ruppin made this patently clear in a letter to the Zionist Executive, headed by Warburg: "For systematic colonization to work we need large contiguous areas, not too far from the harbors and railroads; such land can be found only among the large estate owners."[46] This strategy presumably explains a large transaction with the Sursuk family of absentee landowners in northern Palestine. Not mentioned is the fact that the indigenous tenants on the Sursuks' lands were then unceremoniously evicted. The other principle was the uncompromising insistence on white settler labor only, or, in this particular case, Jewish settler labor only. It is striking in this context how Reichman and Hasson cannot—or choose not to—see that Ruppin's imagination was actually guided by the colonial notion of the pure settlement colony.

Conclusion

The foregoing discussion adds an important dimension to studies on pre-1948 Palestine such as Shafir's and Lockman's. It shows that not only was the socioeconomic and political reality one of a settler colonial project forcing its way into a colony already inhabited by an indigenous community, but also that central figures in the settler community understood themselves, their circumstances, and the actions they took in terms of settler colonialism even if their language and values differed from those of the scholars mentioned here, including the author.

Arlosoroff, moreover, resorted to a *comparative method* to make sense of the question of joint organization, and to convince his audience that his analysis was correct not only intellectually but also, crucially, politically. It is not coincidental that all his examples, hypothetical or real, were settler colonial instances. Ruppin's explicit use of the German colonization project in the Ostmark as a model could not have evinced more clearly the pure settlement colony frame of mind. The purpose of the German project was to transform the Ostmark by dispossessing the Poles, that is, wresting the land away from them, and by creating communities that were purely German and in which there would be German labor only. In principle, the Zionist Israeli project in Palestine is similar, and it is ongoing with exponentially growing ferocity.

Notes

1. Here are some essential works: Caroline Elkins and Susan Pedersen, eds., *Settler Colonialism in the Twentieth Century* (New York: Routledge, 2005); Patrick Wolfe, "Land, Labor, and Difference: Elementary Structures of Race," *American Historical Review* 106, no. 3 (2001): 866–905; Gershon Shafir, *Land, Labor, and the Origins of the Israeli-Palestinian Conflict, 1882–1914*, updated ed. (Berkeley: University of California Press, 1996); "Israeli Society: A Counterview," *Israel Studies* 1, no. 2 (1996): 189–213; "Zionism and Colonialism: A Comparative Approach,"

in *Israel in Comparative Perspective: Challenging the Conventional Wisdom,* ed. Michael N. Barnett (Albany: SUNY Press, 1996), 227–245; David Prochaska, *Making Algeria French: Colonialism in Bône, 1870–1920* (Cambridge: Cambridge University Press, 1990); George M. Fredrickson, "Colonialism and Racism: The United States and South Africa in Comparative Perspective," in *The Arrogance of Race* (Middletown, CT: Wesleyan University Press, 1988), 216–235, and *White Supremacy: A Comparative Study in American and South African History* (Oxford: Oxford University Press, 1981); D. K. Fieldhouse, *The Colonial Empires: A Comparative Survey from the Eighteenth Century* (London: Weidenfeld and Nicolson, 1966).

2. Patrick Wolfe, *Settler Colonialism and the Transformation of Anthropology: The Politics and Poetics of an Ethnographic Event* (London: Cassell, 1999), 2. Wolfe's articulation of settler colonialism's distinctness is insightful. For a condensed expression of it, see his "Should the Subaltern Dream," in *Cultures of Scholarship,* ed. S. C. Humphreys (Ann Arbor: University of Michigan Press, 1997), 57–96.

3. For useful presentations of the hegemonic narrative, see Laurence J. Silberstein, *The Post-Zionism Debates* (New York: Routledge, 1999) and Uri Ram, *The Changing Agenda of Israeli Sociology: Theory, Ideology and Identity* (Albany: SUNY Press, 1995).

4. For Shafir, in addition to *Land, Labor, and the Origins of the Israeli-Palestinian Conflict,* see "Zionism and Colonialism: A Comparative Approach" and "Israeli Society: A Counterview"; Zachary Lockman, *Comrades and Enemies: Arab and Jewish Workers in Palestine, 1906–1948* (Berkeley: University of California Press, 1996); and "Exclusion and Solidarity: Labor Zionism and Arab Workers in Palestine, 1897–1929," in *After Colonialism,* ed. Gyan Prakash (Princeton, NJ: Princeton University Press, 1995), 211–241. They also offer succinct formulations—from a critical vantage point of course—of the hegemonic paradigm. See Shafir, *Land,* 1–7, and Lockman, *Comrades,* 3–8. For Perry Anderson, see "Agendas for Radical History," *Radical History Review* 36 (September 1986): 36.

5. Founded and led by V. Z. Jabotinsky, Zionist Revisionism was the right-wing alternative to Labor Zionism. It was the ancestor of Herut from 1948 to 1977; after 1977, several parties joined Herut to form Likud.

6. See Shabati Teveth, *Arlosoroff's Assassination* [in Hebrew] (Jerusalem: Schocken, 1982).

7. On Arlosoroff's life and oeuvre, see Zeev Sternhell, *The Founding Myths of Israel* (Princeton, NJ: Princeton University Press, 1999), by index; Shlomo Avineri, *Arlosoroff* (London: Peter Halban, 1989); and "Chaim Arlosoroff: A Social and Political Thinker" [in Hebrew], in *Haim Arlosoroff: Nation, State and Society; Selected Essays,* ed. Asher Maniv (Tel Aviv: Hakibbutz Hameuhad, 1984), 9–31. Sternhell's is the best study to date that does an ideological critique of labor Zionism in general, and A. D. Gordon and Hapoel Hatzair in particular. It is a thoroughly authoritative coup de grace to such lingering universalist socialist pretenses that labor Zionism may still have.

8. *Kitvey Hayyim Arlosoroff* [Chaim Arlosoroff's works], vol. 3 (Tel Aviv: Shtiebel, 1934), 135–171. The editor of *Kitvey* dates the essay to 1926, which seems to

me too early because in it Arlosoroff refers to a 1927 article by Lord Sidney Oliver (see page 161).

9. For more details see Shabtai Teveth, *Ben-Gurion and the Palestinian Arabs: From Peace to War* [in Hebrew] (Jerusalem: Schocken, 1985), 92–118; and Lockman, "Exclusion and Solidarity," 224–236.

10. Arlosoroff, "On the Question of Joint Organization," *Kitvey Hayyim Arlosoroff,* vol. 3, 138.

11. Sternhell, *The Founding Myths of Israel,* 3–47.

12. Arlosoroff, "On the Question," 146.

13. Arlosoroff, "On the Question," 147.

14. Arlosoroff, "On the Question," 147–153.

15. Arlosoroff, "On the Question," 157.

16. Arlosoroff, "On the Question," 157.

17. Arlosoroff, "On the Question," 158.

18. Arlosoroff, "On the Question," 160–161.

19. Arlosoroff, "On the Question," 161–162.

20. Arlosoroff, "On the Question," 162–168.

21. See Walter Laqueur, "The Arendt Cult," *Journal of Contemporary History* 33, no. 4 (October 1998): 495.

22. Shalom Reichman and Shlomo Hasson, "A Cross-cultural Diffusion of Colonization: From Posen to Palestine," *Annals of the Association of American Geographers* 74, no. 1 (March 1984): 57–70.

23. Reichman and Hasson, "A Cross-cultural Diffusion," 57–58.

24. Reichman and Hasson, "A Cross-cultural Diffusion," 63.

25. Reichman and Hasson, "A Cross-cultural Diffusion," 63–64.

26. Although the information that underpins this summary is contained in the Reichman and Hasson article, I prefer Shafir's interpretative register. See *Land, Labor, and the Origins of the Israeli-Palestinian Conflict,* 146–186.

27. Derek J. Penslar, *Zionism and Technocracy: The Engineering of Jewish Settlement in Palestine, 1870–1918* (Bloomington: Indiana University Press, 1991), 80–111.

28. Etan Blum, "On the German Origins of Hebrew Culture: The Repression of the Nationalist Role of Arthur Ruppin—'The Father of Jewish Settlement in the Land of Israel'" [in Hebrew], *Mitaam* 11 (2007): 71–93. Amos Morris-Reich's essay takes on the question of Ruppin's scientific racism and eugenics but clearly searches for mitigating circumstances. See his "Arther Ruppin's Concept of Race," *Israel Studies* 11, no. 3 (2006): 1–30.

29. It should be clarified that *weltanschauung,* an important concept in German philosophy, is a comprehensive and coherent set of ideas through which an adhering individual looks at the world and makes sense of it.

30. Blum, "On the German Origins," 75.

31. Blum, "On the German Origins," 76–77.

32. Blum, "On the German Origins," 76.

33. Blum, "On the German Origins," 77.

34. Blum, "On the German Origins," 78–79.

35. The translation, as Blum notes, is obfuscating, for Brenner used biblical language that masks the German-scientific register of the original. See page 81.

36. On the meeting with Günther see Morris-Reich, "Arther Ruppin's Concept of Race," 1–2, and Blum, "On the German Origins," 90.

37. Blum, "On the German Origins," 80–81.

38. Blum, "On the German Origins," 80–83.

39. Gabriel Piterberg, *The Returns of Zionism* (London: Verso, 2008).

40. Blum, "On the German Origins," 79.

41. Blum, "On the German Origins," 83.

42. Reichman and Hasson, "A Cross-cultural Diffusion," 64.

43. Reichman and Hasson, "A Cross-cultural Diffusion," 64.

44. Reichman and Hasson, "A Cross-cultural Diffusion," 64–68.

45. Reichman and Hasson, "A Cross-cultural Diffusion," 66.

46. Reichman and Hasson, "A Cross-cultural Diffusion," 66.

2. Colonial Occupation and Development in the West Bank and Gaza

Understanding the Palestinian Economy through the Work of Yusif Sayigh

LEILA FARSAKH

The Oslo peace process initiated in 1993 brought hopes for the emergence of a vibrant economy in the West Bank and Gaza Strip (WBGS), one that would provide a solid foundation for the establishment of a viable Palestinian state. Yet Palestinian economic growth since 1993 has been marked by major fluctuations and unsustainability. Palestinian real GDP per capita income in the West Bank and Gaza in 2007 was 30 percent lower than in 1999. Poverty touched 49 percent of Gaza and 25 percent of the West Bank in 2007.[1] The 2008–2009 Israeli war on Gaza destroyed whatever remained of Palestinian economic activity there, demolishing major social and economic infrastructure at a total estimated cost of $1.4 billion. The siege imposed on it since 2006 further severed its links to the West Bank, putting in jeopardy the unity of the Palestinian economy. Although real GDP grew by over 5 percent in the West Bank and by more than 9 percent in the Gaza Strip from 2009 to 2012, it was mainly fueled by international assistance, which amounted to over 20 percent of GDP.[2] Poverty rates still stood at 33.7 percent in the Gaza Strip in 2010, where over 71 percent of the population receives some form of aid.[3] The Israeli war on Gaza in November 2012 further proved the unsustainability of growth in the Occupied Territories.

This chapter analyzes Palestinian economic development over the past twenty years in light of the structural changes that have brought about the unstable and poor state of the Palestinian economy, drawing on the work of the Arab economist Yusif Sayigh. Sayigh was born in 1916 in Syria to a Syrian father and a Palestinian mother. He lived and worked in Palestine from 1925 until the Nakba in 1948. He studied and worked in Beirut and Iraq, received his PhD from Johns Hopkins University in the United States, and returned to the American University of Beirut, where he was professor of economics from 1958 to 1975. He was also a consultant for a number of economic organizations such as the Organization of Arab Petroleum Exporting Countries (OAPEC) and the Food and Agriculture Organization of the United Nations (FAO), and was a visiting scholar at Harvard, Princeton, and Oxford Universities. His writings focused on the challenges of development in Third World countries, the Arab world in particular. He wrote about the oil economies, the prospects for Arab economic integration, and the Lebanese business sector, among other topics. Among his most important contributions are *The Economies of the Arab World* (1978), *Arab Oil Policies in the 1970s* (1983), and *Elusive Development: From Dependence to Self-Reliance in the Arab Region* (1991), as well as over forty academic articles. His interest in the Palestinian economy came later in his life when he helped establish the 1992 PLO economic plan, which sought to define the sustainable economic bases for a viable Palestinian state that was supposed to emerge out of the Oslo peace process. He wrote a leading article in 1986 on what he termed the pauperization of the Palestinian economy, which he argued was the result of Israeli colonialism, a characterization few economists in the 1990s or early 2000s adopted.

This chapter argues that the economic record since the signing of the Oslo Accords in 1993 has not been development but, as Sayigh argued, pauperization. Sayigh's development thinking and approach to economic analysis is both helpful and necessary to understand the failure of the Palestinian economy. Sayigh's holistic view of what economic development should mean, his concern for sustainable growth, and his awareness of the political foundation and implications of economics provide us with insight into how we can, or he would say *should,* explain and measure Palestinian economic performance. Above all, Sayigh's insistence on the validity of situating the economics of the Israeli occupation of the West Bank and Gaza within a colonization framework of analysis can prove pertinent. Economists and international development agencies often shy away from using this framework when analyzing the pattern of economic growth in the Occupied Territories, either out of fear of sounding biased or because they want to focus solely on market mechanisms and their failure rather than explore the economic and political reasons underlying these mechanisms.

Yet the colonization framework of analysis can be helpful for understanding the peculiarity of the Palestinian economy. Such a perspective helps explain the unsustainability of Palestinian economic performance since 1967 and, more paradoxically, since 1993. It shows that the fluctuating performance of the Palestinian economy and its fragile structure is the outcome of Israeli territorial ambitions and Palestinian resistance to them, rather than the result of unmediated market forces or incomplete contracts.[4] Situating the economics of occupation within a colonization perspective also allows for a reconsideration of the role of the international community in indirectly perpetuating a colonial relation that the international legal system does not legitimize in principle. This reconsideration fosters a critical understanding of the ways in which a Palestinian state has been economically and politically compromised, despite the attempts by the Palestinian government since 2007 to lay the institutional and economic foundation of such a state and to seek full UN membership status in September 2011.[5]

The first section reviews the main elements in Sayigh's development thinking and his diagnosis of the Palestinian economy.[6] Parts 2 and 3 review the major characteristics of the economy of the West Bank and Gaza pre- and post-Oslo. Part 4 explains the determinants of Palestinian economic performance since Oslo and how they restructured the pattern of Israeli colonial domination, bringing to an end any viable project of Palestinian independence.

The Legacy of Yusif Sayigh's Development Thinking

Yusif Sayigh was a classical development economist, concerned with the specific challenges facing Third World countries as they seek to modernize and lift up from poverty. In 1961 he wrote that development is not only about wealth or growth, but about having a "better distribution of income and increased welfare for the masses." Only then, he continued, "can such a society be said to have achieved development in a full sense of involving both economic and social progress. . . . The content of development is social, political, and technological as well as economic."[7] Sayigh saw development as both an individual quest and a collective/national project of economic and social empowerment that is more comprehensive than what is meant today by the "trickle-down effect of growth."[8]

Sayigh was concerned with sustainable growth—called "balanced growth" at the time. In an era when development economists such as W. W. Rostow and others were stressing the importance of industrial growth in developing countries, Sayigh was emphasizing the importance of agriculture.[9] Like Arthur W. Lewis before him, he argued that agriculture plays a central role not just in providing food to the population but also in channeling savings and inputs to industry. Above all, he viewed agricultural growth as central to distributing wealth to the poor and thus creating a more equitable and just society. Sayigh had no qualms about advocating land reform and argued against relying solely on market forces to induce agricultural productivity and welfare.[10]

Sayigh also advocated for economic diversity in an oil-rich region. His writings on the Arab oil economies in *Arab Oil Policies in the 1970s* focused on the necessity of integrated development between the various sectors of the economy and on investing oil revenues in developing industrial and manpower sectors.[11] He lamented the failure of Arab oil-producing countries to diversify their economic production, to create a productive—rather than consumerist—labor force, and to invest in the economic complementarity of neighboring Arab countries. He predicted the ephemeral nature of growth in these countries due to their overreliance on oil revenues and their accumulation of financial capital mostly invested in the West rather than in the region.[12]

When it came to defining the means to achieve development, Sayigh was an advocate of state-led development.[13] Like most development thinkers in the 1950s and 1960s, he believed that the market cannot create sustainable equitable growth on its own. Like his contemporary Alexander Gerschenkron, Sayigh was conscious of the specific challenges that the Third World faces as late industrializers, such as dealing with stronger international competition than their predecessors had to.[14] Sayigh also argued that developing nations face more difficult domestic problems, ranging from the resistance of traditional leadership to change to fast population growth rates and strong popular demands (and mass demonstrations) for income redistribution. These conflicting demands are not easily reconcilable through the market. He argued that Third World countries need to pursue a different development strategy from the one followed by the Western or the Communist world. They need to rely on a nationalist interventionist approach in the economy and not simply on unregulated free market mechanisms. As he put it in 1961,

> If only by default, the underdeveloped countries have had to embark on their own [economic] systems. These systems will be elaborated and will continue to be distinctive for many years to come. The nature and dimension of the problems of underdevelopment necessitate this trend. The logic of underdevelopment itself forces a joint solution by the Visible Hand as well as the Invisible.[15]

Being a Third Worldist, Sayigh saw the potential for nationalism as an ideology and as a policy to bring about sustainable development. While aware that state-led development can go wrong since it can foster clientalism and inefficiency, he believed that a responsible and accountable national leadership would prevent corruption and ensure sustainable and equitable development. He also saw a key role for "the masses" in making this leadership accountable and representative.[16] He maintained that development could not be dissociated from democracy, for it necessitated the existence of a vibrant and responsible opposition force. Yet Sayigh's idealism and hopes of the 1960s were dashed by the 1970s. In his book *Arab Oil Policies* in 1983 and other articles, Sayigh lamented the failure of oil-producing states' leaders to be visionary and to avoid falling into the trap of becoming rentier economies, despite their nationalism. He also lamented the limits put on popular participation in decision making processes, which prevent citizens from holding their leaders accountable to their promises of development.

Being a nationalist, though, did not make Sayigh antimarket or antiglobalization. Sayigh was well aware of the importance of trade as a vehicle of growth. He simply wanted national leaders to gear trade toward inducing the structural changes necessary to transform a poor or rentier economy into a high-productivity economy. In his *Elusive Development: From Dependence to Self-Reliance in the Arab Region,* published in 1991, Sayigh wrote of the failure of Arab countries to become self-reliant due to their inability to capitalize on oil resources and international trade to diversify their sources of growth domestically by developing agriculture, industry, and human resources. He was also aware of the responsibility of oil-producing countries toward the world economy.[17] He called on oil-producing states to keep oil prices steady but not necessarily low, and advised them to invest their profits in their economy to create a vibrant industrial sector and a highly skilled labor force as well as to invest in regional and international markets. He also expected them to provide aid to poorer countries worldwide. Sayigh was a strong proponent of regional integration among Arab states along the EU model, in which he saw great economic opportunities for oil-producing countries to invest in labor-rich countries such as Yemen, Jordan, and Egypt.[18] He hoped that such economic integration would help the cause of Arab nationalism.

Sayigh thus had an integrated classical approach to understanding development and the means to achieve it. Development for him was a process of structural change that brings prosperity to the individual and to the nation, a process that is rooted in a social project that seeks to foster social justice in addition to growth. It is also a project that brings about the transformation of a poor economy into a self-reliant economy that is based on the interlinked growth of its agricultural and industrial sectors. Such an economy is globally integrated and uses international trade to foster sustainable linkages and growth among all its sectors. It remains reliant on a responsible national leadership that is determined to enhance the country's capabilities, especially its manpower, or what we today call human capital. Above all, Sayigh had a deep appreciation for the role of power and politics, both domestic and international, in shaping the pattern of growth, including who stands to gain or lose from it. He wrote extensively about superpower politics, whether vis-à-vis oil policies, the Arab-Israeli conflict, or the Iran-Iraq war, and their impact on the nature of economic growth in the Arab world.[19] For Sayigh, development takes place within a specific historical, social, and political context that must be well analyzed and capitalized upon. In developing countries, development cannot succeed without a strong state that is democratically accountable and works with and through market forces.

Sayigh and the Palestinian Economy, 1967–1993

Sayigh argued that the Palestinian economy did not and could not achieve development under occupation. In his 1986 article "The Palestinian Economy Under Occupation: Dependency and Pauperization," he asserted that the record of the then twenty years of occupation in the West Bank and Gaza Strip was pauperization, not growth. He maintained that reports of per capita incomes in the Occupied Territories were inflated, for Palestinian incomes did not grow as fast as Israel claimed and were lower than their levels in neighboring Arab countries.[20]

By pauperization, though, Sayigh did not simply mean personal or individual poverty. Revised studies and data have shown that between 1967 and 1990 per capita income in the West Bank and Gaza actually doubled. Moreover, if we look at issues of social justice, on which Sayigh was keen, we find that income distribution was not particularly unequal during the first twenty years of Israeli occupation. The wage gap between rich and poor, and especially between skilled and unskilled workers, actually narrowed during this period, largely because low-skilled workers had access to better-paying jobs in Israel as well as in the Gulf than in the domestic Palestinian labor market. What Sayigh meant by pauperization was the failure of the Palestinian economy to generate domestic sources of growth and eventually become self-reliant. As his work on Arab countries revealed, Sayigh considered an economy developed and "balanced" only when it has a sustainable agriculture capable of feeding a growing industrial sector, one that is led by a responsible accountable national leadership devoted to increasing the welfare of its population. This did not take place in the WBGS, the locus of what remained of Palestine and, since 1988, the areas considered the territorial foundation of a Palestinian state. On the national rather than the individual level, the Palestinian economy was neither productive nor "balanced." Rather, it witnessed a process of diminishing national productive capability. Sayigh's diagnosis was further substantiated and developed with the works of the United Nations Conference on Trade and Development, the World Bank, and Sara Roy, among others, even if they did not use the term "pauperization."[21]

However, what is significant about Sayigh's diagnosis is not simply how he termed it, but also how he explained it. As a classical development economist, he was particularly critical of dependency theory, which was popular in the 1970s and 1980s. The theory assumed a center-periphery relation in explaining stalled growth in developing countries, a relation of economic domination with ex-colonial powers keeping newly independent states dependent on their economic interests and priorities. Sayigh argued that such a center-periphery relation did not exist between Israel and the Palestinians. Instead, he maintained that Israel and the Palestinians constitute a single social formation and economy. Sayigh also asserted that dependency theory could not explain the Palestinian condition because the Palestinian economy under occupation underwent a process of "internal colonialism rooted in dispossession," not simply exploitation or extraction. As he put it in his 1986 article,

> The Palestinians have suffered external colonialism under the British, again at the hand of the pre-state Zionist movement, and now at the hands of the Israeli state as an occupier. In this last instance, the colonialism is of an internal nature, the effects of which go beyond the purely military or political aspects of the occupation. Internal colonialism is much more destructive than external colonialism because it combines the uprooting, dispossession, and displacement of the national population with the imposition of a stunting dependency on the inhabitants who remain. Thus, the Israeli occupation has not only usurped the decision making of the occupied by its very logic . . . but also increased its pressure on the West Bank and Gaza Strip by withholding such essential bases of economic growth as finance, capital goods, raw material, licenses, and vital infrastructural services.[22]

Sayigh used the term "colonialism" (rather than dependency or stalled development) to emphasize that Palestinian pauperization was not the result of external market forces but of a political Zionist project that disarticulated the Palestinian national economy, deprived the Palestinians of any sovereignty or economic authority, and created a structural economic dependency on Israel.[23] The elements of this dependent structure, which various studies further substantiate,[24] were:

Israel's control and expropriation of 38 percent of Palestinian land for the construction of Israeli settlements and Israel's management of the Palestinians through a military-controlled Israeli civilian administration.

Israel's restrictions on investment and financial flows into the West Bank and Gaza Strip through a restricted licensing system and by allowing only two banks to operate between 1970 and 1992.

Israel's restriction on industrial development and the failure of the Palestinian industrial sector to develop. Palestinian industry's GDP remained at less than 7 percent in the 1980s.

The failure of agriculture to become a source of growth. Agriculture faced increasing restrictions and competition from Israeli products, and agricultural laborers sought employment in Israel due to a lack of industrial jobs at home. Palestinian agriculture's share of the GDP and total employment was cut in half between 1967 and 1980. It represented less than 14 percent of GDP in 1993.

External financing of the economy through Palestinian labor commuting to Israel. Between 1970 and 1993, 25 to 40 percent of the Palestinian employed labor force worked in Israel, and their remittances represented 25 percent of the WBGS GDP. This employment was the main factor that explained the rise of per capita income in the pre-1993 era. Yet it also reflected Palestine's inability to generate enough domestic jobs to absorb its local labor force.[25]

Trade dependency on Israel, which became the source of 90 percent of Palestinian imports and the destination of 70 percent of its exports. The Palestinian economy was locked into what came to be known as a "one-sided" customs union with Israel that made the WBGS a captive market for Israeli exports. This "one-sided" union allowed Israeli products free access to the Palestinian markets but restricted the entry of Palestinian goods into Israel. It enabled Israel to collect and appropriate tariff revenues on goods destined for Palestinian areas, which were estimated to amount approximately to 12–21 percent of the WBGS GNP between 1970 and 1987.[26]

Although mainstream economists rarely used the colonization framework of analysis when discussing the economic conditions in the West Bank and Gaza, Sayigh considered it key to explaining why the Palestinian economy could not develop. He advocated political independence for the Palestinians as the means to end colonial domination and eradicate pauperization. The establishment of a sovereign Palestinian state would, in his view, provide the first prerequisite for growth, since it would ensure national sovereignty over land and economic resources. In the PLO Development Plan that he led in 1992, Sayigh set out his development strategy for viable growth in Palestine, growth that emphasized responsible state planning, investment in human capital, and reliance on trade.[27] He highlighted the need to plan for the development of weak sectors, particularly agriculture and industry. He also emphasized the importance of planning for large-scale public works that would provide employment for the poor in rural areas and refugee camps to decrease their reliance on the Israeli labor market. He pushed for Arab and Palestinian diaspora capital to be invested in the West Bank and Gaza Strip and stressed the importance of trade with Arab countries and the world at large as a vehicle for Palestinian prosperity. For Sayigh, these were the means to eliminate, or at least reduce, Palestinian dependency on Israel. They were also in line with his nationalist stand, with his view on the importance of aid and Arab investment in fostering development, and with his emphasis on the economic benefits of regional Arab integration more generally.

The Economics of the West Bank and Gaza Strip Since Oslo

The Oslo peace process promised to reduce Palestinian dependence on Israel and lay the foundation for a vibrant economy. The preamble to the Economic Protocol of the Interim Agreement on the West Bank and Gaza Strip (also known as Oslo II, 1995) clearly stated that its aim was to "lay the groundwork for strengthening the economic base of the Palestinian side and for exercising its right of economic decision-making in accordance with its own development plans and priorities." It sought to do so by allowing the establishment of a Palestinian Authority (PA) that had the mandate to define and manage Palestinian development as it saw fit. In contrast to the pre-Oslo period, when the Israeli civil administration managed and restricted economic growth in the WBGS, after 1993 Palestinians had the autonomy to plan their economy and were in a position to develop their industry, establish a monetary fund, open banks, and make investment decision in various sectors. Sayigh would have welcomed this economic autonomy but would have considered it far from optimal, as he believed that political sovereignty is indispensible for sustainable economic growth.

The Oslo Agreement redefined the nature of trade relations with Israel, rather than severing relations as Sayigh would have advised. A special customs union agreement that allowed the PA to trade with a number of countries other than Israel on a series of agreed-upon items was one such change.[28] The new customs union also allowed Palestine to receive customs revenues collected by Israel on goods destined for the Palestinian economy, something that had never occurred before 1993. This union, though, did not guarantee free movement of Palestinian labor into Israel, as it kept the regulation of these flows under Israeli jurisdiction. It was hoped that the trade of goods would replace the movement of labor from the less-developed Palestinian economy to the advanced Israeli economy.

The Oslo Agreement also sought to lay the foundation for a sound Palestinian economy by allowing injections of international aid in sectors that most needed it. Prior to 1993, aid was severely restricted and was not geared toward national development. Whatever aid entered the Occupied Territories was limited and channeled through Jordan or small aid agencies and did not amount to more than $200 million for the period 1987–1992.[29] After Oslo, Arab and foreign aid was allowed in, following Sayigh's recommendation about the importance of external finance to jump-start Palestinian development on a sound and sustainable basis. However, aid under Oslo was managed by the World Bank and the IMF rather than by the PA.

Economic Fluctuation and Pauperization

Contrary to all expectations, the net result of the Oslo peace process was not growth, let alone development. Economic growth since 1993 has fluctuated and on average has been negative. Real GDP per capita income in 1999, the year in which economic activity was at its highest in the twenty-year period 1993–2013, was at $1,683. This was nearly 30 percent higher than its level in 1993, that is, pre-Oslo, when it stood at $1,342. Yet real GDP per capita income in 2007 was at $1,217, over 32 percent lower than its level in 1999 and 7 percent lower than its level in 1993.[30] Between 2008 and 2011 real GDP grew again, recording a high of 10.5 percent in 2011, but it dropped again to 5.1 percent in 2012. The growth came after a war on Gaza and was fueled largely by aid. It remained unsustainable and conditional on Israeli checkpoint policies.[31] GDP per capita for the Occupied Territories hovers today at $1,619, still lower than its level in 1999.

Palestinian economic performance since Oslo has been characterized by four main features. First, growth remained erratic. Economists and international agencies working on the Palestinian economy tend to distinguish the Oslo years, 1993–2000, from the post-Oslo years, 2000–2012, which were marked by the second Intifada, the Israeli disengagement from the Gaza Strip in 2005, and the political and territorial severance between Gaza and the West Bank after 2007. This distinction is useful insofar as the first period is characterized by fluctuating economic growth rates and sporadic sectoral expansion. Revised figures today reveal that the Palestinian GDP grew by 8 percent per annum on average between 1994 and 1999, with 1996 being a negative year of growth and 1999 being one in which the GDP grew by 12 percent; this was fueled by growth in the public sector as well as growth in the financial and construction sectors. Poverty rates dropped from 19 percent to 11.4 percent in the West Bank and from 32 percent to 21 percent in the Gaza Strip between 1996 and 1999. Unemployment also fell to less than 15 percent in Gaza and to 9.2 percent in the West Bank by 1999.[32] Yet this growth was not sustainable, and its structural weaknesses were revealed and accentuated with the economic downturn that followed the second Intifada.

The period between 2000 and 2012 was characterized by a clear case of Sayigh's pauperization, but at a much larger scale than what he reported in 1986. Poverty in 2007 touched 49.7 percent of the population in Gaza and 19 percent of the population in the West Bank. Although in 2010 it dropped to less than 34 percent and 16 percent, respectively, it remains higher than its level in the 1980s or 1990s. It remains at 22 percent of the population in the WBGS. After 2000, unemployment was over 20 percent in the West Bank and between 33 and 45 percent in Gaza. The territorial and political split between the West Bank and Gaza after Israel's siege on Gaza in 2006 only aggravated the Palestinian economy's downturn despite all attempts by Salam Fayyad's government since 2007 to lay the economic and institutional foundation of a sustainable Palestinian state. Although the GDP grew in the West Bank and Gaza by over 5 percent per annum after 2008, as mentioned this growth was fueled by international aid and was unable to raise real per capita income in 2012 to above its level in 1999.[33] The economy of the Gaza Strip since 2006 has been functioning under the duress of war and siege, and thereby in an underperforming autarkic capacity that has not been able to alleviate the growing poverty of its population. In sum, the economic record of nearly twenty years of the Oslo peace process has been one of fluctuating declining income, not sustainable growth.

The second major characteristic of the Oslo years was the change in the structure of economic growth in the Occupied Territories. Growth started to rely on finance rather than industrial production or trade. The banking sector expanded for the first time since 1967, as over ninety-six bank branches and a stock market opened. Financial instruments such as mortgages and options were also introduced, and the service and construction sectors expanded. Yet industry—contrary to Sayigh's recommendations—did not take a lead in development, even though some high-tech sectors did, particularly in telecommunications and computer services. These industries remained dependent on access to material in Israel or through it, and as such could not become self-reliant.[34] Moreover, the industrial link to agriculture remained weak. Agricultural production fluctuated and, far from becoming food sufficient as Sayigh would have recommended, it saw its share in GDP drop from 13 percent to 5 percent in 2009.[35] Despite the customs union agreement and the fact that after 1993 the Palestinians were allowed to trade with some European and Arab countries, trade fluctuated and foreign investment failed to materialize. The private sector expanded, mainly in the financial and service realms, but it also began to face the problem of domestic monopolies that limited its scope of competition and efficiency. Growth was fueled by aid and PA investment, but in ways in which Sayigh would have disapproved of, since it made the Palestinian economy dependent on outside help. After 2001 the Palestinian economy received between $1.1 to $1.5 billion per year in aid, the equivalent of over 20 percent of its GDP, covering over 70 percent of the PA budget.[36]

The third economic feature of the Oslo period was rising inequalities, a development Sayigh warned against. Income inequality in the West Bank and Gaza pre-1993 was relatively low, thanks in large part to Palestinian employment in Israel. By contrast, it increased in the post-Oslo years, as work for unskilled labor in Israel was restricted and demand for skilled labor in public jobs in the WBGS increased. The influx of international aid contributed significantly to this problem, as it enhanced the demand for highly paid international staff. International aid also expanded the Palestinian NGO sector, whose members are paid more than those employed in the domestic private or public sector.[37] Just as important, inequality spread regionally. Average wages are between twenty-five and thirty-five percentage points lower south of the West Bank and in the Gaza Strip than in Ramallah, where most of the international staff and their conspicuous consumption tend to concentrate.[38] Meanwhile, the gap in per capita income between the West Bank and Gaza grew to staggering levels. In 2012 nominal per capita income in the West Bank was nearly double that in the Gaza Strip ($1,924 versus $875). Poverty levels in Gaza remained twice as high as in the West Bank.[39]

The fourth important economic characteristic of the Oslo years was growing economic fragmentation via the steady separation of the West Bank from the Gaza Strip and the economies of the Occupied Territories from Palestinians inside Israel. Sayigh could not have imagined such a development, and its institutionalization confirmed the destruction of any possibility of viable Palestinian economic development. Prior to 1990, trade between the West Bank and the Gaza Strip was regular and the movement of people was free. Between 1993 and 1999, however, trade between the two regions diminished by at least 30 percent, and the movement of people between them ceased. Particularly since 2001, business relations between Palestinians inside Israel and those in Gaza have decreased, largely as a result of Israeli closures and permit policies.

The separation of the economies of the West Bank and Gaza Strip was created through the Interim Agreement's sanctioned permit and checkpoint policies. It was further institutionalized with Israel's sieges on the Strip in 2006, 2008–2009, and again in November 2012. The separation was most alarming not only for its being commercial and physical but also for its having become structural, as each area developed its own sources of growth. The Gaza economy became dependent on public investment and increasingly on the informal sector, while the West Bank was able to rely more significantly on the private sector and international aid. Public employment in the Gaza Strip absorbs up to 35 percent of total employment, while in the West Bank it represents less than 15 percent. Beginning in the mid-1990s Gaza was also made to separate more clearly from Israel and the international world market, whereas the West Bank was allowed to continue to rely on the Israeli labor market and international goods market. This separation has been solidified with the Israeli sieges on Gaza in the 2000s that left the Strip deprived of any access to international markets, except through illegal tunnels via Egypt. The contrast between the two Palestinian areas was best revealed by their ability to rely on the Israeli labor market to absorb the growing Palestinian labor force. The West Bank continued to export 10–15 percent of its employed labor force to the Israeli labor market through the 1990s and 2000s, while Gaza had less than 2 percent of its employed labor in Israel after 1996.[40] In 2012 84,000 Palestinians from the West Bank still worked in Israel and the settlements, compared with zero from Gaza.[41] After 2006, Gaza developed and relied mainly on an informal tunnel economy linked to Egypt, while the West Bank continued to import Israeli and foreign products, albeit regulated by a myriad of permit and checkpoint policies.

Determinants of Palestinian Economic Performance Since Oslo

The economic outcome of the Oslo years is the result of the West Bank and Gaza's changing relation to Israel and the structural constraints imposed on the PA in its management of the economy. The Palestinian economy after 1993 could not access international markets as Sayigh and others recommended. It continued to need the Israeli market, and its access to it became politically and militarily conditioned. The Palestinian economy's growth was conditioned by unilaterally declared Israeli security concerns, which the Oslo Agreement institutionalized.

What is colonial about the economic structure in place since 1993 is the way it has enabled Israel to continue to expropriate Palestinian land while depriving the PA of control over Palestinian economic resources. Though the Oslo Agreement promised to lessen Israeli control of the Occupied Territories, it sanctioned Israel's continued expropriation of Palestinian lands. As is well known, the Interim Agreement in 1995 maintained Israeli control of 59 percent of the West Bank, which came under Area C. It also legally endorsed Israel's claim over the land, since the PA accepted the legal rights of Israelis in areas under its control as well as Israel's sole jurisdiction over its settlements.[42] Between 1993 and 2010 Israel built over one hundred new settlement outposts and expanded existing settlements such as Maale Adumim and Ariel. Settlement housing grew by nearly 4 percent per annum after 2000, and the number of settlers in the West Bank (including East Jerusalem) more than doubled, increasing from 242,000 in 1993 to over 54,000 in 2012.[43] What is new about Israeli colonialism after 1993 are the forms of boundary and spatial control that were institutionalized via Oslo and the al-Aqsa Intifada, and that led to the pauperization of the population and compromised Palestinian independence.

Restructuring Access to Israel

Israeli policies of permits, closure, and checkpoints, introduced after 1990 and institutionalized with the Oslo Agreement, are key in explaining the fluctuation of economic growth and the segmentation of Palestinian economic activity.[44] Between 1994 and 1999, Israel imposed over 484 days of closure in the West Bank and Gaza Strip. Since 2000, the Gaza Strip has been under continuous closure, which explains why its poverty rates increased and its economic performance has been weak. Economic performance improved during the absence of closures and fell sharply after the intensification and institutionalization of checkpoints after the al-Aqsa Intifada. Between 2002 and 2008 Israel installed over 604 checkpoints, compared with 230 temporary or floating checkpoints for the period 1993–1999. By 2006, Israel had divided the WBGS into largely eight segmented areas that are cut off from one another through permanently built checkpoints rather than temporary military patrol. In 2012, there were still 99 fixed checkpoints in the West Bank and an average of 310 flying checkpoints. In the meantime, Israel's construction of the separation barrier that commenced in 2002 is further eroding Palestinians' access to their land and to employment opportunities. The 708-kilometer wall, 62.1 percent of which was built by 2012, is preventing over 250,000 Palestinians, or 11 percent of the West Bank Palestinian population, from reaching their land. Upon completion, the wall will enable Israel to incorporate 11.8 percent of West Bank land into its unilaterally defined border, well into the 1967 Green Line.[45]

These territorial measures, combined with Israel's control over Area C, have led to economic and geographic fragmentation of the West Bank and Gaza. These measures induced not only poverty but also inefficient autarkic development, as Palestinian cities could not trade with each other. West Bank exports shrank by over 70 percent between 2000 and 2006, and trade between West Bank towns shrank by over 50 percent.[46] Since 2007 and Salam Fayyad's government, economic performance has improved in the West Bank, not thanks to international trade, but as a result of aid and development of credit lending. Domestic and international trade cannot act as an engine of growth as called for by Sayigh. The sieges imposed on Gaza since 2006 provide poignant proof of the deterioration of economic and social life in the absence of trade. Poverty defined the lives of 71 percent of the Strip's population by 2008. Israel's declared territorial and security measures are colonial insofar as they facilitate the exploitation and appropriation of Palestinian land by Israel while tying Palestinian survival, not to mention growth, to Israeli military and territorial considerations.

Thus, Israel has economically reshaped rather than ended Palestinian dependence. Initially dependent on labor access to Israel in the pre-Oslo period, the Palestinian economy has become increasingly constrained by Israel's unilaterally declared security measures. The World Bank now calls these restrictions *economically,* not simply security, driven. They impose restrictions on economies of scale, on access to resources, and on investment prospects and potentials.[47] The West Bank remains heavily dependent on customs revenues transferred from Israel to the PA and on the reduction of Israeli checkpoints in order to continue to grow. The Gaza Strip has had no access to Israel after 2006 as a result of Israel's sanctions against it, but this situation has not made Gaza more autonomous or prosperous. Since the disengagement from Gaza in 2005, Israel has pursued a policy of economic strangulation and sieges, which have killed over 1,500 Palestinians and cost $2 to $3 billion in destroyed infrastructure and homes. Such policies have led Gaza to form new, largely illegal and informal economic links with Egypt. Gaza is deprived of customs revenues as well as basic goods for construction and industry. There are over one thousand tunnels built under Gaza to link it to Egypt, and they are largely under the control of an oligarchy of clan leaders dictating the flow and price of goods entering the Strip. This situation is not economically optimal since it fosters rent-seeking activities, inequality, and inefficient allocation of limited resources. The siege limits the ability of the government to reduce unemployment and poverty, let alone create sustainable growth, given the lack of access to capital and outside markets.

The Public Sector

Economic growth since Oslo has become dependent on the performance of the PA, which, as Sayigh predicted in his thoughts on responsible state planning, had a mandate to promote local and foreign investment, help the growth of the private sector, and establish a basis for fiscal discipline and rigor. Its ability to fulfill this role was constrained not only by the limited territorial jurisdiction it was given, which spans Area A (20 percent of the West Bank), but also by the nature of the trade relations established with Israel, as discussed above. Since 2007 the PA government under Salam Fayyad has pushed for a series of institutional and economic measures intended to prove the ability of the Palestinians to generate employment and domestic growth and to form a solid foundation of an independent state.[48] Despite international support for this effort, the PA failed to become economically independent from Israel or from international aid. Customs clearance from Israel continued to represent 70 percent of the PA's fiscal revenues despite PA attempts to increase revenue from local taxes. Israel often withheld its clearance payment for political reasons, increasing the fiscal crisis of the PA and limiting its scope of action. This situation only aggravated the PA's dependence on the donor community, which has injected over $1.1 billion in budget support since 2005 to keep the PA solvent.

Moreover, despite the PA's effort to create the institutional and economic environment that would encourage private sector development and lay the basis of an independent state, the private sector remained weak and unable to promote sustainable growth. Although the private sector had generated over one hundred thousand new jobs in the late 1990s, it was not able to absorb the labor force at its growth rate of 3 percent per annum. Most of the private sector growth and employment generation has been in the construction and financial sectors. The industrial sector in particular failed to generate enough jobs, as its growth was curtailed by restrictions on trade and market access. Agricultural employment during this period fell from absorbing 13 percent of the labor force in 1999 to less than 6 percent in 2010, and it continued to hold disguised unemployment, that is, laborers working only seasonally and not at full capacity.

As a result of this situation, since 1994 the public sector has become the employer of first resort. Employment with the PA ministries and security forces absorbed 32 percent of the employed labor force in Gaza and up to 18 percent of the employed labor force in the West Bank.[49] Public employment absorbed all those who no longer were allowed to work in Israel. Security forces dominated public sector employment; 60,000 to 80,000 employees out of a total of 153,000 public wage earners were employed in security.[50] Their wages represented a significant drain on the PA's finances, constituting over 53 percent of PA expenditures. This major factor in the PA's budget deficit was often remedied by international aid (which ironically opposed public employment). Since 2007 the Hamas-led government in Gaza has increased taxes on the population and has tried to bring tunnel economies under its control to augment its fiscal revenues, but these actions have further burdened the impoverished population.

Meanwhile the PA failed to be transparent or accountable, as Sayigh would have recommended. Its reform policies since 2007 advance what some consider a neoliberal agenda that not only hastens economic inequality but also risks compromising the Palestinian national project of liberation.[51] It is an agenda that has not reduced the reality of monopolies or enhanced competition. The Oslo economic and security structure facilitated the creation of monopolies, particularly because they were more successful than individual companies in claiming and centralizing customs clearance from Israel. These monopolies included PA and private sector actors closely tied to the procurement of security services and other goods. They were firmly linked to Israeli military companies or parastatal Israeli monopolies, such as cement and tobacco. The development of rent-seeking activities of this sort, which are costly for private sector development and indicate a restructuring of economic dependency on Israel rather than its elimination—and which Sayigh warned against—was unavoidable in the absence of free and open access to international markets. Israel remained the main source of imports and exports as well as the gateway to the outside world, while contacts between Israeli and Palestinian businessmen became mediated through a few monopolies with close ties to the security establishments.

International Aid

Another major structural change brought about by the Oslo Agreement was the central, new role given to the international donor community in helping the Palestinian economy. Before Oslo, Israel restricted the transfer of aid or other financial flows into the WBGS. With Oslo, the international community saw an opportunity to help lay the foundation of a viable Palestinian state, which the Road Map for Peace endorsed in 2003 and which the PA sought in the form of full UN membership in September 2011. Between 1994 and 2000 the donor community disbursed $3.2 billion, the equivalent of the annual WBGS GDP. This money went toward setting up Palestinian ministries, generating employment projects, and building infrastructure, as well as paying the salaries of PA employees and sustaining the PA's budget. After 2000 the donor community is reported to have disbursed an average annual sum of $1.1 billion to the Palestinian economy. The donors' PA budget support stood at $1.8 billion in 2009, the equivalent of 32 percent of the WBGS GDP.[52] It dropped in 2012 to $1.1 billion, which is considered insufficient for the ailing economy of the West Bank and the besieged economy of Gaza. Aid directed to the PA went mainly to the West Bank until 2012, when Qatar promised $400 million in aid to Gaza. If delivered, this aid would cover over a third of the Strip's GDP.[53]

Moreover, the World Bank, the IMF, and the Ad Hoc Liaison Committee (AHLC) become advisors of the PA, helping it formulate and manage its economic policy.[54] They sought to lay the foundation for a Palestinian economy that would be characterized by a vibrant private sector, free markets, and a responsible, small, and fiscally rigorous public sector. However, the World Bank and IMF soon found themselves defending economic policies long considered inefficient—ones they had been busy dismantling elsewhere. Thus, while concerned with PA overspending, especially in regard to public employment in mainly security-related and inefficient administration, they could not stop it. They actually financed such employment, which they deemed necessary to prevent a total collapse of Palestinian income. This was in view of Israel's restriction on Palestinian labor across the Green Line, the imposition of closures by Israel, and the rise of poverty.

International donor agencies often found themselves in the central, though contradictory, position of bailing out the PA and increasing its dependence while having to intervene with Israel. The donor agencies had power over the PA insofar as they could determine the amount and direction of the aid they gave. At the same time Israel's unwillingness to cooperate with the international community to end the occupation constrained their ability to make the PA economically viable. The contradictions in the international institutions' interventions highlight the power asymmetries of the Oslo peace process, as well as the way in which the international community has become indirectly implicated in a relation of domination it was supposed to help dismantle. This contradiction also shows the limits of international aid in stopping Palestinian pauperization, as best revealed in the case of Gaza since the Hamas election of 2006.

This strong international financial intervention raises the question of the extent to which the international community is financing the occupation—an occupation it has always refused to legitimize. This situation becomes all the more problematic if the international community leans toward accepting it as a given, rather than challenging it. The World Bank report on the disengagement from Gaza, entitled *Stagnation or Survival? Israeli Disengagement and Palestinian Economic Recovery* (2005), does not mention the occupation as the source of Palestinian economic demise; rather, it focuses on the issue of closure. It does not call for abolishing the closures but for finding ways to accommodate them.[55]

This is a significant development that reflects the international community's willingness to accept, at least indirectly, a colonial relation based on land expropriation and the oppressive mechanism of separation and control in the name of security.

Conclusion

After over forty-five years of occupation, the Palestinian economy is fragmented and pauperized, both at the individual and at the national level. Yusif Sayigh's development paradigm shows us that the reason for this catastrophic result is Israeli colonialism. What his works could not have predicted is how the structure of Israeli colonialism changed after Oslo as a result of Israel's ability to convince the world to accept the preeminence of its security over the illegality of its occupation. As Israel retreated from being the manager of the Palestinian economy to being the gatekeeper of Palestinian finances, trade, and mobility, it has been able to continue to expropriate Palestinian land, pauperize the Palestinian population, and fragment the Palestinian economy. It has thereby succeeded in destroying the Palestinian state project, despite the international endorsement of this right.

Sayigh's work remains relevant today insofar as it reminds us that individual prosperity cannot be separated from national growth. It also shows that politics remains foundational to economics. He might have been surprised at the level of pauperization that the Palestinian economy reached by 2012, but he had warned that economic development cannot be achieved without political independence. His work shows that the PA could not create the basis for a viable economy given its limited territorial control and lack of sovereignty, not to mention its lack of accountability. His work on aid remains insightful in reaffirming how aid can be wasted and politically compromising when the international community becomes lender of first and last resort without holding Israel accountable to international law. His use of colonialism as an analytical paradigm to explain Palestinian economic performance demonstrates a need to incorporate power and law, not security, into any discussion of the present and future of Palestinian and Israeli economic prospects.

As Gaza is strangled and made to trade with Egypt as it did before 1967 and the West Bank is fragmented and increasingly tied to Jordan, we are at a crossroads in terms of how we analyze the Palestinian economy and its prospects. We can either witness war and prison economies develop further, bringing more despair and waste, or we can rethink peace economics in radical terms. Rethinking will call for a need to incorporate Israeli colonialism into any economic analysis, acknowledge the Palestinian political and economic struggle for freedom and equality, and find a way to hold the international community accountable to its responsibility to uphold international law—otherwise, it will waste more of its money as well as its moral obligation. Such a shift would uphold Sayigh's legacy.

Notes

1. World Bank, *Palestinian Economic Prospects: Aid, Access and Reform,* Economic Monitoring Report to the Ad Hoc Liaison Committee (Washington, DC: World Bank, 22 September 2008), 10–21. Poverty is defined as a family income of NIS 2,300 per month or less (approximately six hundred dollars per a household of six people).

2. World Bank, *Stagnation or Revival? Palestinian Economic Prospects,* Economic Monitoring Report to the Ad Hoc Liaison Committee (Washington, DC: World Bank, 21 March 2012), 4–5; Palestine Economic Policy Research Institute (hereafter MAS), *Palestine Social and Economic Indicators,* no. 31 (Ramallah: MAS, January 2013), 1 (figures are calculated from Table 1).

3. World Bank, *Coping with Conflict: Poverty and Inclusion in the West Bank and Gaza* (Ramallah: World Bank, October 2011), 16–17.

4. See, for example, Jimmy Weinblatt and Arie Arnon, "Sovereignty and Economic Development: The Case of Israel and Palestine," *Economic Journal* 111, no. 472 (2001): 291–308.

5. See Palestinian Authority, *Homestretch to Freedom* (Ramallah: Palestinian Authority, 2010) and *Palestinian Reform and Development Plan* (Ramallah: Palestinian Authority, 2008).

6. It is important to note here that the term "Palestine" should include all Palestinians, whether they are living in the West Bank and Gaza, inside Israel, or in the diaspora. However, data on the latter are difficult to find, and most literature refers to the Palestinian economy as the one existing in the West Bank and Gaza Strip. I will adhere to this definition here.

7. Yusif Sayigh, "Development: The Visible or the Invisible Hand," *World Politics* 13, no. 4 (July 1961): 566.

8. "Trickle-down effect of growth" is a term often used by neoclassical economists to describe the ability of unmediated market forces to benefit the poor by enabling everyone to work and gain income by the sheer forces of supply and demand for jobs and goods.

9. Yusif Sayigh, "The Place of Agriculture in Economic Development," *Land Economics* 35, no. 4 (1959): 301.

10. Sayigh, "The Place of Agriculture in Economic Development," 301. For Rostow, see *The Stage of Economic Growth: A Non-Communist Manifesto* (Cambridge: Cambridge University Press, 1964). For Lewis, see "Economic Development with Unlimited Supply of Labor," *Journal of the Manchester School of Economics and Social Studies* 22, no. 2 (1954): 139–191.

11. Yusif Sayigh, "Problems and Prospects of Development in the Arabian Peninsula," *International Journal of Middle Eastern Studies* 2 (1971): 40–58.

12. Yusif Sayigh, *Elusive Development: From Dependence to Self-Reliance in the Arab Region* (New York: Routledge, 1991); *Arab Oil Policies in the 1970s* (Baltimore: John Hopkins University Press, 1983); *The Economies of the Arab World* (London: Palgrave Macmillan, 1978).

13. Sayigh, *Arab Oil Policies in the 1970s;* "Problems and Prospects of Development in the Arabian Peninsula"; and "Development: The Visible or the Invisible Hand."

14. Alexander Gerschenkron, *Economic Backwardness in Historical Perspective: A Book of Essays* (Cambridge, MA: Harvard University Press, 1962).

15. Sayigh, "Development: The Visible or the Invisible Hand," 583.

16. Sayigh, "The Place of Agriculture in Economic Development," 303–304.

17. Yusif Sayigh, "Arab Oil Policies: Self-Interest Versus International Responsibility," *Journal of Palestine Studies* 4, no. 3 (Spring 1975): 59–73.

18. Sayigh, *Elusive Development;* and Yusif Sayigh, *The Arab Economy: Past Performances and Future Prospects* (Oxford: Oxford University Press, 1982).

19. Sayigh, *Elusive Development.*

20. Yusif Sayigh, "The Palestinian Economy Under Occupation: Dependency and Pauperization," *Journal of Palestine Studies* 15, no. 4 (Summer 1986): 46–67, especially 60–62.

21. See Sara Roy, *The Political Economy of De-Development* (Washington, DC: Institute for Palestine Studies, 1995); World Bank, *Investment in Peace: Developing the Occupied Territories,* 6 vols. (Washington, DC: World Bank, 1993); UNCTAD, *Prospects for Sustained Development in the Palestinian Economy of the West Bank and Gaza Strip* (Geneva: UNCTAD, 1992). The World Bank and UNCTAD tended to use the terms "stalled growth" and "stalled development," whereas Roy coined the term "de-development."

22. Sayigh, "The Palestinian Economy Under Occupation: Dependency and Pauperization," 52.

23. The difference between internal and external colonialism might appear superfluous, but what Sayigh wanted to stress with the term "internal colonialism" was Israel's expropriation of Palestinian self-government and control over resources and economic management, as opposed to a sole interest in cheap raw materials or the use of the Occupied Territories as a captive market, as was the case with Britain's occupation of Palestine.

24. See Leila Farsakh, *Labor Migration to Israel: Labor, Land and Occupation* (London: Routlege, 2005) as well as Sayigh, *Elusive Development.*

25. See Farsakh, *Labor Migration to Israel,* chap. 5.

26. See, among others, Ussama Hamid and Radwan Shaban, "One-Sided Customs and Monetary Union: The Case of the West Bank and Gaza Strip under Israeli Occupation," in *The Economics of Middle East Peace,* eds. Stanley Fischer, Dani Rodrik, and Elias Tuma (Cambridge, MA: MIT Press, 1993), 142.

27. PLO, *The Palestine Economic Development Plan* (Tunis: PLO, 1992).

28. Noman Kanafani, "Trade-A Catalyst for Peace?" *The Economic Journal* 111 (2001): 276–290.

29. Farsakh, *Labor Migration to Israel,* 40–44.

30. World Bank, *Palestinian Economic Prospects,* 7; MAS, *Palestine Economic Monitor 1994–2000* (Ramallah: MAS, 2001), 163; MAS, *Economic and Social Monitor* (Ramallah: MAS, 2013), 1.

31. World Bank, *Stagnation or Revival?,* 16.

32. MAS, *Palestine Economic Monitor,* 51–56, 164–169.

33. World Bank, *Stagnation or Revival?,* 16.

34. Helga Tawil-Souri, "Digital Occupation: Gaza's High-Tech Enclosure," *Journal of Palestine Studies* 41, no. 2 (Winter 2012): 27–43.

35. MAS, *Overview of the Palestinian Economy* (Ramallah: MAS, 2010), 5–6.

36. Raja Khalidi and Sobhi Samour, "Neoliberalism as Liberation: The Statehood Program and the Remaking of the Palestinian National Movement," *Journal of Palestine Studies* 40, no. 2 (Winter 2011): 8.

37. Anne Le More, *International Assistance to the Palestinian People: Political Guilt, Wasted Money* (London: Routledge, 2008); Anne Le More, Michael Keating, and Robert Lowe, eds., *Aid, Diplomacy, and Facts on the Ground: The Case of Palestine* (London: Chatham House, 2005).

38. This figure is based on average wage data provided by the Palestinian Central Bureau of Statistics, June 2011.

39. World Bank, *Stagnation or Revival?,* 17; MAS, *The Palestinian Economy,* 2012, unpublished data.

40. Leila Farsakh, "The Political Economy of Israeli Occupation," *Electronic Journal of Middle Eastern Studies* 8 (Spring 2008): 41–58.

41. Calculated from MAS, *Economic and Social Monitor,* 7.

42. Articles 12, 16, 22, and 27 from Annex III, Protocol Concerning Civil Affairs, Oslo II Agreement. See Farsakh, *Labor Migration to Israel,* for further details.

43. Foundation for Middle East Peace, *Report on Israeli Settlements in the Occupied Territories,* various issues from 1996, 2000, and 2013. http://www.fmep.org /settlement_info/settlement_database.html.

44. See Farsakh, *Labor Migration to Israel,* chap. 7, for further discussion of the Oslo Agreement and how it institutionalized Israeli security measures.

45. B'tselem, accessed 28 February 2013, http://www.btselem.org/statistics.

46. World Bank, *Palestinian Economic Prospects,* 42–45.

47. World Bank, *Palestinian Economic Prospects,* 39–49. The term "economies of scale" refers to the increase in efficiency of production as the number of goods being produced increases. This happens as a result of open markets and free trade and investment.

48. See Palestinian Authority, *Homestretch to Freedom* and *Palestinian Reform and Development Plan.* See also World Bank, *The Underpinnings of the Future Palestinian State: Sustainable Growth and Institutions,* Economic Monitoring Report to the Ad Hoc Liaison Committee (Washington, DC: World Bank, 13 April 2010).

49. MAS, *Palestine Economic Monitor,* 2002 and 2007.

50. Stanley Fischer, Alice Alonso-Gamo, and Uli E. Von Allman, "Economic Developments in the West Bank and Gaza Strip Since Oslo," *Economic Journal* 111, no. 472 (2001): 254–275; MAS, *Economic and Social Monitor,* 12.

51. Raja Khalidi and Sobhi Samour, "Neoliberalism as Liberation," 16–18.

52. World Bank, *The Underpinnings of the Future Palestinian State*, 8.

53. "Qatari Emir Visits Gaza," *New York Times*, 23 October 2012.

54. The IMF has effectively overseen the Palestinian Finance Ministry, helping it plan the Palestinian taxation and fiscal system and supervising its internal accounts. It has also become the interlocutor with the Israeli Finance Ministry, ensuring that customs revenues are transferred to the Palestinian Authority. The World Bank is the manager of donor funds, deciding their allocation by sector as well as by ministry.

55. World Bank, *Stagnation or Survival?*, 15–17.

3. War, Peace, Civil War

A Pattern?

TAMIM AL-BARGHOUTI

Since 1974, there has been a pattern of war, peace or appeasement, and then civil war or dissent in the ranks of the Palestinian national movement. After the wars of 1971 in Jordan and 1973 between the Arabs and Israel, the PLO adopted the Step-by-Step Program, which opened the door for a two-state solution. This was followed by the establishment of the Rejection Front within the PLO.[1] After the 1982 Israeli invasion of Lebanon, the Fatah leadership of the PLO accepted the Saudi-sponsored Arab Peace Initiative, which was followed by the first Palestinian civil war in Tripoli, Lebanon. After the 1987 Intifada and the 1990–1991 regional war in which the PLO sided with Iraq, the Palestinian leadership openly accepted the two-state solution. This was followed by the creation and the consolidation of the Islamic Resistance Movement—Hamas—as an alternative manifestation of the Palestinian struggle against Israel. The Israeli reoccupation of the West Bank in 2002 was followed by the election of a moderate Palestinian leadership, one that was openly endorsed by both Israel and the United States. This move toward appeasing Israel triggered a chain of events that included a Hamas electoral victory in 2006 and a short military confrontation with Fatah forces in Gaza that left Hamas in control of the Strip.

This pattern is a result of the structural contradictions in the Palestinian national movement; though the movement is antisystemic, it is born out of and dependent on the very system it seeks to change. The Palestinian national movement is in constant need of international recognition and domestic legitimacy, and recognition and legitimacy are at once interdependent and mutually exclusive. To gain recognition, the Palestinian movement must have some support among the Palestinians, but it also must accept some aspects of the system it was created to fight; this causes it to lose its legitimacy and, consequently, its recognition. Every move toward a deal with the colonizer causes the national movement to lose legitimacy, and every loss of legitimacy prevents the national movement from living up to its commitments under any deal with the colonizer, hence rendering such a deal worthless. This contradiction between legitimacy and recognition, and the Palestinian national movement's desperate need for both, might allow it to reach a peace settlement—but it makes such a settlement unlikely to last.

This situation is not unique to Palestine, but rather is characteristic of the colonially created states in the Middle East and the Arab national liberation movements therein. As such, the failure of the peace process is part of the larger failure of the colonially created state system in the region as a whole. Nonstate actors performing the functions of the state—sometimes even more efficiently than the state—present themselves as the heir apparent to that system.[2]

The Pattern: War, Peace, Civil War

In 2005 Helga Baumgarten published a comparative study discussing the rise and fall of three incarnations of the Palestinian national movement.[3] The first was the Movement of Arab Nationalists (MAN);[4] the second, the Fatah-led Palestine Liberation Organization (PLO); and the third, the Islamic Resistance Movement (Hamas). The first two dominated the Palestinian political arena successively for almost twenty years before each started to lose its legitimacy among Palestinians and eventually its recognition by the international community as the main representative of the Palestinian people. Baumgarten argues that Hamas is on the same route as its two predecessors.

The move from Arab nationalism, the main doctrine of MAN, to Palestinian nationalism, to Islamism, according to Baumgarten, results from the military and political failures of the first two ideologies in achieving their declared goal of liberating Palestine. It remains to be seen what the fate of the third movement will be. Baumgarten argues that all three movements began with the uncompromising demand for the liberation of all of Palestine from the Mediterranean Sea to the River Jordan, and eventually they had to accept the existence of the state of Israel and modify their goal to be the establishment of a Palestinian entity in the West Bank and Gaza. This pattern predicts that Hamas will eventually come to terms with Israel's existence as well.

According to Baumgarten, the Palestinian national movement seems to be stuck in a vicious circle of denial: when the national leadership recognizes the impossibility of achieving the liberation of all of historical Palestine, it is replaced by another leadership that insists the task is achievable, only to come to terms with the same harsh reality and lose its legitimacy to the subsequent generation of more radical leaders. One gets the impression that a significant portion of the Palestinian public cannot be convinced that "Israel is here to stay," and it is that portion of the Palestinian public that allows the more radical version of Palestinian nationalism to succeed the less radical versions.

While Baumgarten's work provides very useful insight into the existence of a pattern in recent Palestinian history, in this essay I take issue with assumptions about the cyclical nature of this pattern. In fact, one can argue that there is a linear aspect to it. At first glance it might be difficult to ascertain a move toward either radicalization or moderation in the succession of the three incarnations of Palestinian nationalism. MAN did not recognize Israel's right to exist, nor did it formally embrace the two-state solution. Fatah, on the other hand, accepted, de facto, the two-state solution quite early in its history, in 1974, only five years after it had come to lead the PLO. Hamas's acceptance of a truce with Israel if the latter withdraws from lands occupied in 1967 can hardly count as acceptance of Israel's existence. The line seems to break: a radical form of Palestinian Arab nationalism in the 1950s is followed by a relatively moderate Palestinian nationalism in the 1970s and 1980s, which is then followed by a radical Islamic movement.

A closer look, however, presents us with a different picture. The three movements consistently move away from the colonially created state system. MAN was completely dependent on the mobilization of colonially created Arab states for the liberation of Palestine. The PLO was a semistate actor that agreed to the establishment of a semistate entity inside and outside Palestine. Hamas, on the other hand, began as a nonstate actor with no immediate ambition to establish a Palestinian state in the Occupied Territories. It follows that the need for outside recognition has decreased as the Palestinian movements have become increasingly radical with regard to the means by which to liberate Palestine.

This discussion will focus mainly on the PLO and Hamas, their emergence, their moves toward peace or appeasement with Israel, and the implications of those moves vis-à-vis the cohesion of the Palestinian national movement. MAN emphasized that the liberation of Palestine should take place through the coordinated efforts of Arab armies, or through the establishment of a united Arab state that would then move to liberate Palestine. MAN even hesitated to support attacks conducted by Palestinian guerrillas against Israel in the late 1950s, stating that the real fight should be left to the Arab armies—mainly to the rising might of Nasserite Egypt and the United Arab Republic (UAR).[5] When such attacks gained popularity, they were excused by MAN as a prelude to the involvement of Arab armies in what it hoped was a forthcoming War of Liberation.[6]

In the early 1960s, with the failure of the union between Egypt and Syria, the involvement of Egypt in the civil war in Yemen, where it was fighting a proxy war against Saudi Arabia, and as Egypt became more dependent on its Soviet allies, it became clear to Palestinians that Egypt might not be up to the task of an all-out war against Israel. This was also clear because neither the Soviet Union nor the United States seemed enthusiastic about an Arab nationalist union led by Egypt. The Soviet Union opposed the union with Syria, making it clear that it would only support Arab nationalism inasmuch as it blocked American influence in the region. Similarly, the United States, during a short period of improved relations with Nasser in his confrontation with Abdul Karim Qasim's communist regime in Iraq, made it clear that it would only support Arab nationalists inasmuch as they stopped communist influence in the region. Neither of the two superpowers, who recognized Israel, wanted the Jewish State to suffer a crippling defeat that might jeopardize its very existence and pave the way for an all-powerful Egypt in the region.

Essentially, the state system established in the interwar period by Britain and France and consolidated by the United States and the USSR after World War II did not allow for MAN's objective of liberating Palestine and uniting the Arabs. Nonetheless, MAN's strategy was to depend on that very system—on states like Egypt and Syria—to change it. As a result, the movement's position was weakened and had to give way to the more radical guerilla groups who argued for a Palestinian nationalist movement that would directly assault Israel without waiting for an all-out, state-led Arab war.

In 1964, the Arab League established the PLO under Nasser's auspices with the declared goal of liberating Palestine. The Palestinian National Covenant, the PLO's constitution, explains that "this Organization is responsible for the movement of the Palestinian people in its struggle for the liberation of its homeland, in all arenas whether liberational, organizational, political, financial and all that the Palestinian cause needs on the Arab and international fronts."[7] By creating the PLO under the patronage of Egypt and the rest of the Arab state system, the responsibility for the liberation of Palestine fell from state actors to a nonstate actor. This was due to the realization on the part of the Arab states that they could not achieve their two main goals—the liberation of Palestine and the achievement of Arab unity. This inability was not only the product of the uneven balance of power between the Arab states and the United States and the USSR., but also the fact that both the political systems of the Arab states and Israel were born from the same womb. The international law that guaranteed the existence and independence of Arab states was the same law that guaranteed the existence and independence of Israel. If an Arab government were to liberate Palestine, it would gain tremendous legitimacy and support from its population, but it would lose all recognition internationally. In the eyes of international law, the UN Security Council, and, most importantly, the two superpowers at the time, it would be an occupier of Israeli lands and an aggressor. Delegating the task to a nonstate actor relieved the Arab states from such difficulties, but it also meant that true change would not occur. While the international system had room for national liberation movements and guerrilla warfare that fought proxy wars in regions where superpower competition was high, these movements were not powerful enough to change the colonial entities upon which the existence of the international system depended. That system—vital to both superpowers since the end of World War II—was thus kept intact. Furthermore, delegating the task of liberating Palestine to the PLO did not make the PLO immune to the weaknesses of the state system. After all, the PLO was born out of that system, and its very existence depended on the recognition of the Arab states that created it.

The 1967 war made Arab states even keener to assign the PLO the task of war against Israel. The victory at the Battle of Karameh in March 1968, to which both Fatah forces and the Jordanian army contributed, was mainly attributed to the former.[8] The symbolism of a small Palestinian guerilla force able to halt the advance of the Israeli army into Arab territories, immediately following the sweeping defeat of the combined forces of Egypt, Jordan, and Syria, was vital in building Fatah's reputation as the alternative means by which Palestine's liberation was to be achieved. Being more radical than most Arab regimes and having the will to engage Israel militarily with no regard for the conventional military balances of power were two pillars of Fatah's appeal as a national liberation movement. Yet these two pillars by which Fatah and the PLO gained legitimacy jeopardized the states that hosted the PLO. The more the PLO engaged Israel from, say, southern Lebanon, the more Lebanon came under the threat of Israeli attack. The more powerful the PLO became in Jordan, the more danger it posed to the Jordanian monarchy. Instead of jeopardizing their existence as states at war with Israel—as states fighting against the post–World War II system that maintained their existence—they were now in jeopardy as states hosting an organization fighting that system. The PLO fought the state system, thus breaching the sovereignty of host countries as it used their territory to wage war against Israel, and it also struggled to keep these countries' recognition and support.

In 1969, the PLO formulated its secular democratic state agenda, which sought the establishment of a secular democratic state in Palestine where Muslims, Christians, and Jews enjoyed equal rights. This made the PLO's ultimate goal look more like a regime change within one country than a drastic change in the entire map of the region. It also meant a departure from the previous Arab nationalist agendas that involved uniting Palestine with the rest of the Arab world.

This move toward compromise was coupled with a move to regulate the PLO's military presence in Lebanon, confining it to the southern parts of the country. Egypt sponsored the PLO's agreement with Lebanon. The following year, tensions in Jordan resulted in civil war. Again, Egypt came to the PLO's rescue, summoning both Yasser Arafat and King Hussein of Jordan to an Arab League Summit in Cairo, where an agreement similar to the one reached with Lebanon the previous year was signed. Palestinian fighters were to be confined to the areas of Jerash and Ajlun in the north, and they were to respect Jordanian sovereignty. It is worth noting that the burst of hostilities in Jordan was partly triggered by a disagreement between Nasser and the PLO, as the former had accepted an American peace initiative whereby Israel was to withdraw from the lands it occupied in the 1967 war in return for Arab recognition of the right of all states in the region (including Israel) to live in peace within secure borders. This was incongruent with the PLO's 1969 program, and several factions voiced their opposition to the Egyptian acceptance of the American plan. The war in Jordan shortly followed, making this a prelude to the pattern described above: a move toward peace with Israel, followed by civil war on the Arab front. However, at this early stage the split occurred within the Palestinian-Egyptian-Jordanian entente/alliance, rather than within the ranks of the Palestinian liberation movement proper.

The 1973 War, the Step-by-Step Program, and the Rejection Front

After the 1973 war, during which Egypt and Syria had regained some of their territories in Sinai and the Golan, the political atmosphere changed in the region. An international peace conference was to take place and the question of representing the Palestinians came to the forefront. It was clear from the results of the war that negotiations would only take place regarding the land Israel had occupied in 1967, and that the Palestinian program of 1969 was incompatible with regional and international agendas. Continuing with that program would have caused international recognition to go to Jordan instead of the PLO. In 1967, the land in question was officially Jordanian, and was recognized as such by the international community. When the Security Council, in its famous Resolution 242 of November 1967, emphasized the inadmissibility of the acquisition of land by force, it was referring to the lands owned by recognized member states, not lands claimed by national liberation movements with little or no international recognition. Henry Kissinger, American secretary of state at the time, wrote,

> I predict that if the Israelis don't make some sort of arrangement with Hussein on the West Bank in six months Arafat will become internationally recognized and the world will be in chaos. . . . If I were an advisor to the Israeli Government, I would tell the Prime Minister: "For God's sake do something with Hussein while he is still one of the players."[9]

Under the threat of being replaced by Jordan, the PLO had to change its strategy. The regional and, therefore, the international recognition of the PLO as a representative of the Palestinian people, on which the very existence of the PLO depended, was now in question. To keep that recognition, the PLO had to move a few steps closer toward recognizing Israel. In July/August 1974, the Palestinian National Council approved the Ten Points Program, otherwise known as the Step-by-Step Program. This program, which specified the PLO's future liberation strategy, argued obliquely for the establishment of a Palestinian national authority in any part of Palestine that got liberated.[10] This was made to look like a step toward the liberation of the rest of Palestine. Article 2 of the resolution read,

> The PLO will struggle by every means, the foremost of which is armed struggle, to liberate the Palestinian land and to establish the people's national, independent and fighting sovereignty *on every part of Palestinian land to be liberated.* This requires the creation of further changes in the balance of power in the favor of our people and their struggle. (emphasis added)[11]

Yet, in the context of the peace settlements anticipated after the 1973 war, the establishment of a Palestinian national authority in any part of liberated Palestine seemed to only be possible with Israel's consent. The price of such consent would be the recognition by Palestinians of Israel's right to exist in a large part of historic Palestine. The first step on the road to the liberation of Palestine would therefore be the last.

The change in tactics was in fact a change in strategy. Nonetheless, it was necessary for the PLO to keep the recognition of the regional and international state system on which its very existence depended. Just after the Palestinian National Council passed the Step-by-Step Program, the Arab League recognized the PLO as the sole legitimate representative of the Palestinian people. Before the end of 1974, the PLO was given a seat as an observer at the UN General Assembly, and Yasser Arafat addressed the organization in November of that year. In his famous speech about the olive branch and the rebel's gun, Arafat pointed to the double nature of the PLO, but also to its fatal contradiction. The gun was the source of the PLO's legitimacy among the Palestinians and the olive branch was the source of international recognition; together, however, the branch and the gun would eventually cause the PLO to lose both.

Immediately following the acceptance of the Step-by-Step Program in 1974, and specifically because of its implicit concession toward the recognition of Israel, a Rejection Front formed. This Front, consisting of a coalition of Palestinian factions that did not accept the new PLO strategy, was led by the second-largest faction of the PLO, the Popular Front for the Liberation of Palestine (PFLP). This constituted the first political split in the ranks of the PLO, yet it did not result in an all-out interfactional war. The move toward the recognition of Israel was, after all, implicit, and the authors of the Step-by-Step Program still insisted that the Palestinian national authority established in any part of Palestine would be a fighting authority whose main goal was to liberate the rest of Palestine. Moreover, the position of Palestinian refugees in Lebanon and the PLO forces centered there was becoming increasingly difficult, as the Lebanese civil war which began in 1975 was to reveal. Due to these factors, the disagreement over the Step-by-Step Program did not erupt into armed confrontations among Palestinians.

The 1982 Invasion of Lebanon, the Arab Peace Proposal, and the Palestinian Civil War in Tripoli

In 1981, the war between Iraq and Iran began. The Syrian-Iranian axis against the Iraqi-Saudi axis emerged, with serious implications for the Palestinians in Lebanon. Tensions between pro-Syrian and anti-Syrian factions of the PLO erupted. Saudi Arabia proposed its first pan-Arab peace initiative, whereby Israel was to withdraw from the lands it occupied in 1967 in return for Security Council guarantees for all states in the region to live in peace. The PLO, still entangled in the Lebanese civil war, needed to keep its military forces united and could not risk accepting that proposal—the same reason that prevented it from accepting Egypt's invitation to join the peace talks with Israel in the previous decade. The rest of the Arab world, including the Iraqi wing of the anti-Syrian alliance, did not want to look soft on Israel, as two years prior, Egypt's membership in the Arab League was suspended after it signed a peace treaty with the "Zionist enemy."

A year later, the tables had turned. After the Israeli invasion of Lebanon and the expulsion of PLO forces from Beirut in the summer of 1982, the same proposal was presented at the Arab summit in Morocco and was accepted. The PLO had moved decisively toward the Iraqi-Saudi axis. It was now totally dependent on Arab financial and diplomatic support for its existence, as it no longer had bases bordering Israel and had no significant military leverage. The PLO accepted the Saudi proposal with the hope that Arab recognition would lead to American recognition, which would eventually lead to Israeli recognition and the establishment of some form of Palestinian authority in the Occupied Territories.

As argued above, the pursuit of recognition led to the partial loss of legitimacy, as a number of Palestinian factions in Lebanon shifted their alliances to Syria and refused to accept the Saudi peace initiative. They claimed to be the true representatives of the Palestinian people, and an inter-Palestinian civil war ensued in Tripoli. Palestinian camps loyal to Yasser Arafat were brutally bombarded by Palestinian factions allied with Syria, as well as by

Lebanese civil war factions, especially the pro-Syrian Amal movement. As the PLO joined the Iraqi-Saudi axis, which by the end of the 1980s included Egypt and Jordan, it moved slowly toward the United States and the recognition of Israel. The split caused after the 1982 Arab summit continues to this day.

The Intifada, the Peace Process, and Hamas

In December 1987, Palestinians began what was to become the first Intifada, which provided the PLO with both opportunities and risks. On the positive side, the Intifada demonstrated to the world that the PLO was influential in the areas that mattered most: the Palestinian Occupied Territories. On the other hand, the PLO had to make sure that Israel would not find alternative representatives for the rebellious population of the Occupied Territories with whom to negotiate. The threat of the emergence of Palestinian organizations influential in the West Bank and Gaza that were not PLO factions was real, as was the classic threat of the Israelis negotiating with the Jordanians, from whom they had wrested the West Bank in the first place. Reluctant to engage in a fight with a clearly radicalized Palestinian population, Jordan severed all legal and administrative connections with the West Bank.

Almost at the same time, the PLO declared the independence of the state of Palestine. In the declaration of independence, carefully phrased, the PLO referenced UN Resolutions 242 and 338. Hence, the de facto recognition of Israel was incorporated into the very declaration of the Palestinian state's independence.[12] As such, the recognition of the state that Palestine was supposed to replace was the condition for the existence of Palestine herself. And, while the map of mandatory Palestine was defined by Britain's military campaign in 1917, the map of the Palestinian state declared in 1988 was defined by the Israeli campaigns of 1948 and 1967. The recognition of the colonial definition of the colonized self was the condition for that self's independence. As in other Arab countries, independence involved the internalization of colonialism.

The pattern was again repeated as the first Intifada developed. The Islamic Resistance Movement (Hamas) entered Palestinian politics. Hamas morphed out of the Gaza branch of the Egyptian Muslim Brotherhood, and was not part of the PLO. It did not accept the idea of creating a secular state in Palestine, nor did it accept the idea of creating a Palestinian state only in the West Bank and Gaza Strip. Hamas's position stood in contrast to the

PLO's inclination toward recognizing Israel and reaching a peaceful settlement on the basis of UN Resolutions 242 and 338.

The split in Palestinian politics, though nonviolent during most of the first Intifada, was the most serious since the civil war of 1983 in Tripoli mentioned above. For the first time since its establishment, the PLO faced a well-organized competitor for the representation of the Palestinian people from within Palestine. Hamas's very existence challenged the PLO's claim to be the sole legitimate representative of the Palestinian people, as established in the 1974 summit. It should be emphasized that the very same concession that caused the PLO to gain that recognition from the Arab League and the world, that is, the Step-by-Step Program, was the reason why Hamas could challenge the PLO. In other words, what a certain concession gave the PLO in terms of international recognition it took away in terms of domestic legitimacy. Ironically that loss of legitimacy eventually leads to the erosion of international recognition.

The Gulf War of 1990 found the PLO siding with Iraq, again in fear that an unpopular pro-American position might result in the emergence of an alternative leadership in the territories. Yet this pursuit of legitimacy almost cost the PLO its international recognition, and Saudi Arabia and Kuwait discontinued their funding of the organization and deported thousands of Palestinians. When American president George H. W. Bush brought the Arabs and the Israelis to the negotiating table in Madrid in 1991, the PLO was not present; rather, a mixture of independent figures of prominence from the Occupied Territories under the auspices of the Jordanian delegation were invited. To reverse this loss of international recognition, the PLO engaged Israel in secret negotiations that resulted in the Oslo Accord of 1993 (known officially as the Declaration of Principles on Interim Self-Government Arrangements).

The military campaign led by Ariel Sharon against the Palestinian territories in 2002, which was followed closely by the death of Yasser Arafat, was then followed by a Palestinian presidential election won by a "moderate," Mahmoud Abbas. Abbas was the Palestinian politician endorsed by both the United States and Israel. Both countries had put pressure on Arafat to appoint him as his prime minister. Abbas' selection by Fatah was clearly a move toward appeasing Israel after the military campaign in the West Bank. Following the pattern, appeasing Israel inevitably triggered a chain of events that heightened tensions between Fatah and Hamas. In the next parliamentary elections in 2006 (see Ghanem, this volume), Hamas won the majority of both the popular and electoral vote. The power struggle that followed ended in the expulsion of Fatah forces from Gaza and the establishment of two separate Palestinian authorities.

From Fatah's point of view, it could be argued that Hamas's electoral victory was not the result of the peace process itself, but rather the result of Israel's delay in fulfilling its commitments and the subsequent failure of peace as manifested in the events that led to the second Palestinian Intifada in 2000. From an Israeli point of view, the very existence of Hamas and the reluctance of the Palestinian Authority to crack down on it was one of the main reasons why the peace process failed. Regardless of this debate, it remains sound to argue that the PLO's choice to engage in the peace process allowed Hamas to appear as a clearly distinct political alternative. And regardless of the success or failure of the peace process, Hamas could still attract those Palestinians who claimed all of Palestine as their homeland and who were unwilling to accept even the best anticipated outcome of the negotiations, namely the two-state solution. It is also sound to argue that this percentage of Palestinians was high enough to challenge the PLO's claim to the exclusive representation of the Palestinian population and to frustrate the negotiations or jeopardize their outcome.

Today Fatah and some of the other factions ruling the West Bank as the Palestinian Authority (PA) recognize Israel, although the PA's territories are suffocated by more than six hundred roadblocks and checkpoints, a separation wall, and hundreds of settlements. Hamas does not recognize Israel, but maintains Gaza, a piece of land free of settlements and checkpoints, which survived an all-out Israeli war in late 2008–2009 and another major attack in 2012. The severe loss of legitimacy by the PLO leadership caused the international community to contemplate direct and indirect negotiations with Hamas. Much of the Middle East, whether from the Syria-Iran axis or the axis of Jordan, Saudi Arabia, and pre-revolution Egypt, recognized Hamas's potency as an alternative leadership.

The Causes of the Pattern: The Process of Colonial Nation Redefinition

What causes the above pattern? Is it unique to Palestine, or does it have precedents with other national liberation movements in the region? It was mentioned above that recognition and legitimacy are both crucial for a national liberation movement because these movements adopt the colonial definition of the nation. The fruition of the national struggle must result in a nation state, one recognized by the international community, and most importantly by the colonial power itself. It is one of the main arguments of postcolonial theory, from Fanon (1961) to Said (1978 and 1993) to Negri (2000 and 2008), that the process of colonialism involves the redefinition of the colonized by the colonizer. Robinson Crusoe gives Friday his name. But in doing so, Crusoe also makes Friday his slave. When Columbus named an island, he also claimed ownership of it.

The establishment of nation states is therefore part of colonial name giving. People of a certain piece of land are trapped into political institutions, including borders, not necessarily of their choosing. Such institutions are designed to serve the concerns and interests of the colonial powers that create them. For this process to take place, however, "native" cooperation is crucial. Native cooperation helps reduce the costs of running the colony via native classes whose economic and social interests are congruent with those of the colonial powers. This guarantees the continuation of the colonial relationship even after the end of actual occupation. Dependence becomes the precondition for independence, and independence becomes a form of native self-colonization.

Colonial powers recognize a cooperative group of natives as representatives of the whole population. Yet, for this group to be of any use to the colonial power, its members require support from the population they represent. As such, this group falls into what I have termed the paradox of representation:[13] they are recognized as representatives of the people precisely because they misrepresent them, yet that very misrepresentation, that is, cooperation with the occupiers, requires them to be legitimate, true representatives of the people—at least to some extent. Essentially, they need to be heroes for their treason to work.

This process is complicated by the fact that groups vying for the recognition of the colonial power as representatives of the people are not homogenous or unanimous. Because power in a colony is granted by the occupying force, different groups compete to prove to the colonial power that they are the real representatives, both by showing the extent to which they can cooperate and sell a deal to their constituencies, and by showing how influential they are among the population by sabotaging any deal that is pursued by their competitors.

The paradox of representation inevitably leads to the paradox of replacement, whereby the national liberation movement makes two contradictory promises in order to secure both recognition and legitimacy: to the population it makes the promise of independence and an end to military occupation, and to the colonial power it makes a promise to use that independence to preserve colonial interests. Indeed, structural constraints that guarantee the use of independence in a way congruent with colonial interests are carved into the very treaties that grant that independence and into the very structure of the newly independent institutions, from the borders to the economy.

When the French and the British occupied what remained of the Ottoman Caliphate, they created the current state system in the Middle East. Despite the fact that Iraq and Egypt received their nominal independence in the interwar period, it can be argued that the de facto independence of most Arab states was actually granted and consolidated after World War II. The very same international law that brought about and guaranteed the existence of these states constrained them and ensured that they could not curtail colonial interests, such as the British policy of establishing a national home for the Jews in Palestine.

If we apply this pattern to the Palestinian national movement, it fits quite neatly. The map of Palestine made into golden necklaces hanging around the necks of many Palestinian women is a British product, part of the redefinition of the people of the Levant—the majority of whom are Muslim Arabs—into territorial states in need of British and French mandatory supervision. Once these states were given the name Friday, they were forced to accept the Crusoe mandate. Yet, with the creation of Israel, the people of Palestine had to undergo another redefinition of the nation. Palestine became the West Bank and Gaza, and the Palestinians became dwellers of these two parts of historical Palestine, to the exclusion of Palestinian refugees in the diaspora as well as Palestinians who remained in the land occupied in 1948.

An independent Palestinian state in these territories would be designed to serve the interest of the Crusoe that created it, namely the state of Israel. Securing the state of Israel would be the precondition for creating the state of Palestine. The logic of the peace process is to replace the Israeli occupation with a Palestinian independence that more or less performs the very same functions of that occupation. As early as the first decade of the twentieth century, this logic was evident. Evelyn Baring, Earl of Cromer and the British colonial proconsul in Cairo, wrote in 1908,

> What Europeans mean when they talk of Egyptian self government is that the Egyptians, far from being allowed to follow the bent of their own unreformed propensities, should only be permitted to govern themselves after the fashion in which Europeans think they aught to be governed.[14]

In another passage he envisioned independent Egypt as a "skillfully constructed automaton" that would do what it was designed to do by its European makers:

> Once explain to an Egyptian what he is to do, and he will assimilate the idea rapidly. He is a good imitator, and will make a faithful, even sometimes a too servile copy of the work of his European caretaker. His civilization may be a veneer, yet he will readily adopt the letter, the catchwords and jargon, if not the spirit of European administrative systems. His movements will, it is true, be not un-frequently those of an automaton, but a skillfully constructed automaton may do a great deal of useful work. This feature in the Egyptian character is of great importance in connection with the administration of the country.[15]

In Palestine, a group of natives also willing to cooperate with a similar plan had to be found, and because they had to act as middlemen between Israel and the Palestinians, they had to exhibit both the qualities of legitimacy and leniency. Due to the genuine contradiction between the demands of the Palestinians and the Israelis, every inch gained toward Israeli recognition is an inch lost from Palestinian legitimacy. Once a leadership loses legitimacy, it becomes useless to the colonial power. Without the strength to fulfill its promise of securing colonial interests with native hands, the cycle closes.

The Results of the Pattern: The Failure of the Peace Process and the Failure of the Regional State System

It is not difficult to show how such a pattern can frustrate the possibilities of a lasting peace agreement between the Palestinians and Israel, and by extension between the Arabs and Israel. The colonial state system that created and protected both modern Arab political regimes and Zionism has not been able to reconcile its internal contradictions so far. Any attempt at peace with Israel will find enough Palestinians to denounce it, and those Palestinians will find enough regional supporters, states and nonstates, with whom they can form a rejection front blocking the peace process.

On the other hand, the weakening of the state system is a global phenomenon that accelerated after the end of the Cold War. During the Cold War, both superpowers saw centralized states as a means by which to control lands and resources: each superpower strengthened certain colonially created states to block its adversary from expanding its influence, ideology, markets, and military bases. By the end of the Cold War, however, the United States expanded to the areas from which the Soviet Union withdrew, the European Union and NATO expanded eastward, and the United States had military bases in central Asia.

The Middle East, a zone where there had been an unwritten agreement that no large superpower military deployment would take place, and where wars were fought by proxy, was finally penetrated by American forces in 1990 and 1991. The states in the Middle East, as in other parts of the world, were now obstacles to globalization—that is, the economic, political, and ideological expansion of the United States in the world. This trend of weakening the state system has resulted in the emergence of nonstate actors working against globalization. Indeed, in the Middle East, Islamic nonstate actors were the immediate answer to American expansion.[16]

Palestinians realized that after Iraq's defeat in 1991, no regional war with regular armies was to be waged against Israel in the near future. After 2002, it was also clear that the semistate established by the Oslo Agreement in the West Bank would not be able to protect itself either, while the nonstate actor Hamas could. Similar messages have been coming out of Iraq since 2003 and Afghanistan since 2001.[17] They were also in evidence in Lebanon in 2000 and 2006. In all these cases, nonstate actors were able to frustrate the military endeavors of the United States and Israel, while conventional colonially created states could not. In sum, the situation in Palestine is part of a regional situation in which colonially created nation states lose ground to nonstate actors because they have failed to perform the basic tasks for which any state is to be held accountable, namely defense against foreign military intervention.

Israel is no exception to this post–Cold War trend in which the importance of states diminishes; with the advent of American troops in the region, Israel's geostrategic importance to the United States as an advanced allied military base in an otherwise impenetrable region decreased. Moreover, not unlike many Arab regimes, Israel has to come to terms with its own contradictions. While the main contradiction of Arab states has been that they are simultaneously colonial and anticolonial, Israel's main contradiction is that it is Jewish and non-Jewish. It is a state for Jews in a land densely populated by non-Jews. Furthermore Israel is supposedly a safe haven, yet it has been constantly unsafe since its establishment. Sixty years after Israel's establishment, the formal Israeli narrative defines the state as a home for the survivors of the Holocaust. Yet a Jew is safer in Berlin than he is in Haifa, the reason being that in Haifa there are non-Jews denied the same rights the Jews enjoy.

While Jews outside Israel can become citizens of Israel according to the Israeli law of return, Palestinians who were driven out of their lands in 1948 are denied that right. If the millions of Palestinian refugees were to become Jewish tomorrow, they would be allowed to return. However, they are in exile because they adhere to the wrong religion. This can hardly solve Israel's security problem. Because Israel is meant to be a safe haven for the Jews alone, that is, to the exclusion of the non-Jewish population of the land, it cannot be safe. It follows that it is as much a dilemma for Israel to entrust a Palestinian state with its security as it is for the Palestinians to accept a state of their own whose main function is to secure Israel rather than the Palestinians.

The prospects for a solution are grim. There is nothing to motivate Israel to make peace with the PLO while it does not control Gaza, and there is no reason to reach a deal with Hamas as long as the West Bank remains effectively in Israel's hands. On the Palestinian side, there is nothing to motivate Hamas to make concessions to the PLO, whose leadership lost almost all the support it might have had in Gaza when it let Israel pound the strip for three weeks in 2008–2009, while blaming Hamas for the war. And nothing motivates the PLO to relinquish its dominance over the West Bank, as Hamas has flexed much less muscle there than it has in Gaza.

Some, like Khaled Hroub, see in Hamas's pragmatic language and gestures before and after the 2008 war a gradual move toward reconciliation, not only with Fatah but also with Israel.[18] There does appear to be a de facto consensus in Palestine about the broad lines of the political solution with Israel. It involves the recognition that the issues of the right of return and

Jerusalem might be too hard to tackle in the near future, but until they are, a Palestinian entity, preferably a state, should be established in the rest of the West Bank and Gaza. Fatah calls this the Step-by-Step Program, while Hamas calls it a long-term truce.

The pattern described in this paper suggests that if Hamas follows Fatah's trajectory, a significant portion of the Palestinian population will dissent, causing Hamas to lose some of its representative capacity. It is noteworthy that Hamas's sister organization, the Islamic Jihad, has not accepted the principle of the long-term truce, nor has it participated in the Palestinian political process under Oslo. As argued, the competition over representation of the colonized population is characteristic of colonial politics. But it is also true that none of the factions competing to represent the colonized people succeed in keeping their legitimacy once they have made the concessions necessary to gain the occupying power's recognition.

Even if all of the above difficulties were overcome and a two-state solution were reached, it is clear that it would not involve the actual return of Palestinian refugees to Israel. Allowing them to return would amount to relinquishing the Jewish identity of Israel and establishing the single secular democratic state advocated by the PLO in 1969. Not allowing the refugees to return would mean that the nascent state of Palestine would have to deal with the fact that refugees from 1948 form up to 50 percent of its population.[19] The prospect of such a state to be both democratic and friendly to Israel would be slim. And because financial monitoring is the most important task of democratic parliaments, an undemocratic state is likely to be corrupt. The refugees will gain neither the economic nor the political fruits of the deal. Either their rebellion will be directed at Israel, causing it to retaliate against the Palestinian state, since it will have failed to live up to its commitment toward Israel's security, or the refugees might challenge the Palestinian government. Both patterns have occurred since 1993.[20] Hamas and other movements directed their attacks against Israel for most of the 1990s and attacked the Fatah-dominated Palestinian Authority forces in Gaza in 2007. The two-state solution is thus likely to create an unstable Palestinian dictatorship.

In Israel, the demographic trends show that the Arab population will pose a serious threat to the Jewishness of the state in only a few decades. The political mobilization and organization of the Arab citizens of Israel and their open rejection of Israelization have also been singled out by forces in Israeli politics as a serious threat to Israel. Measures suggested have included forcing Arab citizens to take an oath of allegiance to Israel as a democratic and Jewish state in order to keep their citizenship rights. The rights of citizenship held by Arab citizens of Israel are not equal to the rights of citizenship enjoyed by Jewish citizens of Israel, mainly because of the issue of the right of return, through which a Muslim or Christian citizen of Israel cannot bring back a relative from a refugee camp in Lebanon, while a Jewish citizen can bring a Jewish friend from anywhere in the world and make him or her a co-citizen. The two-state solution is therefore likely to produce a discriminatory, apartheid-like political system in Israel, which will also be unstable.

If security and stability are the two goals of the peace process, they are unlikely to be realized. On the other hand, the general trend in the region calls for a serious revision of the colonial contradictions that plague the system of colonially created nation states. The very existence of Israel as a nation state fortified against the Palestinians should be revised, as should the legitimacy and efficiency of the system of Arab nation states confined in their colonially created boundaries and institutions. Such states are unable to defend themselves or relieve their populations from having to wage the wars their rulers promised to wage decades ago. A political system in Palestine and the region in which people have equal rights to choose where and how to live might be a utopia, but the failure of other "realistic" solutions might cause us to consider the practicality of a utopia.

Notes

1. The Rejection Front was an alliance of Palestinian factions opposing the Step-by-Step Program. The Front included the left-leaning Popular Front for the Liberation of Palestine, the pro-Syrian Saʿiqa, and the pro-Iraqi Arab Liberation Front.

2. This paper is an attempt to apply to the Palestinian case a model of the behavior of national liberation movements and colonially created states that I presented in my 2008 work, *The Umma and the Dawla: The Nation State and the Arab Middle East* (London: Pluto Press, 2008). I previously applied this model to the Egyptian national liberation movement and the pan-Arab nationalist movements of the early years of the twentieth century.

3. Helga Baumgarten, "The Three Faces/Phases of Palestinian Nationalism, 1948–2005," *Journal of Palestine Studies* 34, no. 4 (Summer 2005): 25–48.

4. Also known as the Arab Nationalists Movement (Harakat al-Qawmiyyin al-ʿArab).

5. In 1958, a union was declared between Egypt and Syria to form the United Arab Republic. The strategic threat this union posed to Israel's existence raised hopes among Palestinians and other Arabs, but the union disintegrated three years later.

6. Baumgarten, "The Three Faces/Phases of Palestinian Nationalism."

7. *Malaf Watha'iq Falastin* [The File of Palestine documents], 2 vols. (Cairo: Wizarat al-Irshad al-Qawmi, 1969), 1275.

8. In March 1968, the Israeli army crossed into Jordan and attacked the town of Karameh, in the Jordan Valley. The ensuing battle, called the Battle of Karameh, resulted in the Palestinian fighters and Jordanian army repulsing the Israeli army and claiming victory, one that the two nations celebrated after the losses of 1948 and 1967.

9. Helena Cobban, *The Palestinian Liberation Organization: People, Power and Politics* (New York: Cambridge University Press, 1984), 60.

10. Article 4 states, "Any step taken towards liberation is a step towards the realization of the Liberation Organization's strategy of establishing the democratic Palestinian State specified in the resolutions of the previous Palestinian National Councils."

11. Cobban, *The Palestinian Liberation Organization*, 62.

12. UNSC Resolution 242 adopted on 22 November 1967 called for "the termination of all claims or states of belligerency [in the Middle East] and for the respect for and acknowledgement of the sovereignty, territorial integrity and political independence of every State in the area and their right to live in Peace within secure and recognized boundaries free from threats of acts of force." UNSC Resolution 338 of 22 October 1973 called for an immediate ceasefire and the implementation of Resolution 242.

13. Tamim al-Barghouti, *The Umma and The Dawla: The Nation State and the Arab Middle East* (London: Pluto Press, 2008), 91–97.

14. Evelyn Baring, Earl of Cromer, *Modern Egypt* (London: Macmillan, 1908 [1962]), 874.

15. Baring, *Modern Egypt*, 579.

16. The establishment of Al-Qaᶜida, according to its own leaders, came in reaction to the American deployment in Saudi Arabia.

17. It is important to note the variations in nonstate actors. For example, in their 2005 article Strindberg and Wärn present a convincing argument regarding the differences between Hamas and Hizbullah on the one hand and al-Qaᶜida on the other. Anders Strindberg and Mats Wärn, "Realities of Resistance: Hizballah, the Palestinian Rejectionists, and al-Qaᶜida Compared," *Journal of Palestine Studies* 34, no. 3 (Spring 2005): 23–41. It is also noteworthy that the military campaigns of the United States or Israel in Palestine, Lebanon, Iraq, and Afghanistan have not yet achieved their declared goals.

18. Khaled Hroub, "A New Hamas Through its New Documents," *Journal of Palestine Studies* 35, no. 4 (Summer 2006): 25–27.

19. See Emile Sahliyeh's work on the demographics of the West Bank and how the refugees and urban university students played a crucial role in the first Intifada.

Emile Sahliyeh, *In Search of Leadership: West Bank Politics Since 1967* (Washington, DC: Brookings Institution, 1988).

20. On the support Hamas enjoys among deprived Palestinians and especially those living in refugee camps, see Are Knudsen's article, "The Hamas Enigma," *Third World Quarterly* 26, no. 8 (2005): 1373–1388.

PART 2

Politics, Law, and Society:
Twenty-First-Century
Developments and Paradigms

4. Palestinians Following the 2006 Legislative Election

A Critical Election?

AS'AD GHANEM

Elections and change of government are part of the democratic process. Following every democratic election, a government continues its performance as the executive branch or is changed. Such a change is a reflection of the changing preferences of the people, the collective of citizens. The change can be reflected in two ways. The first, in which the new government continues the policies of the previous one, is common and can be considered regular or gradual change, with minor alterations that reflect the guiding principles of the new ruling party or parties or the personal preferences of the newly elected leaders. These elections can be classified as "regular elections."

The second mode of change, in which a deep and fundamental change occurs in the agenda or the political, economic, or social situation of the state or in its international status, is "critical elections."[1] Such critical elections occurred in the United States in 1860, after which the Civil War started around the question of the future of the union. Such elections also occurred in Germany in 1933, when the National Party and Hitler took power democratically and promoted a revolutionary change in German internal and external policies. Another example is the South African elections of 1989, which signaled the end of the apartheid regime. Smooha and Peretz consider the 1992 Israeli elections as critical elections, in that following those elections Israel entered a new phase in its relationship with the PLO.[2]

The second Palestinian legislative elections in 2006 were also critical elections, in that the Islamic Resistance Movement (Hamas) won with a vast majority.[3] The PLO and the Palestinian Liberation Movement (Fatah) did not accept this victory or the transfer of power to Hamas. Israel and the United States declared the Hamas government a "terrorist entity." Above all, the Palestinian national movement collapsed and lost its status as a unified voice representing the Palestinian demand for self-determination. This collapse coincided with the establishment of two competing Palestinian entities, one in the West Bank and one in the Gaza Strip, that followed the election. As such, the effort to establish a Palestinian state and to resolve the conflict reached a dead end because of this deep internal schism and the inability to confront the Israeli occupation.

The Palestinian Legislative Elections: A General Framework

For a few months before the 2006 Palestinian legislative elections, several Palestinian political parties and organizations contributed to a campaign for the amendment of the previous electoral law, on the basis of which the first Palestinian legislative and presidential elections had been held in 1996.[4] The previous law was criticized for being too traditional, for upholding clan leadership, and for facilitating the monopoly of power by the larger parties. According to this law, the West Bank and the Strip were divided into sixteen election districts, and local coalitions were able to affect the election results with little intention of addressing real political needs and aspirations. Public demands for the amendment of the law mounted, and the National Campaign for Amending the Electoral Law was established.

The new electoral law aimed at encouraging all factions and parties to participate in Palestinian political life and leadership, especially in the Palestinian Legislative Council (PLC) and vis-à-vis the formation of governments. It established a mixed electoral system, combining the proportional and the constituency systems in equal measure, with 50 percent of the representatives elected according to the old sixteen election districts and 50 percent elected via the proportional system, with the whole territory under the Palestinian Authority (PA) considered one district for the sake of the election. The proportional system allowed for the participation of all parties that reached the minimum ballot tally, and the constituency system encouraged independent candidates to run in one of the sixteen constituencies in the West Bank and Gaza Strip.

In order to implement this system efficiently and to encourage greater participation, the number of PLC seats was increased from 88 seats to 132 seats. The new law divided the seats into 66 for the proportional system and 66 for the constituency system. In addition to proportional representation, the new law also encouraged wider participation through the following revisions:

The minimum age of nomination was reduced to twenty-eight years from thirty years, so as to facilitate the participation of young leaders.

The minimum percentage of votes required for the candidate lists to be eligible to participate was set at 2 percent, in order to encourage the participation of smaller parties. (According to the old system the winning candidates were those who received the largest number of votes in the polls.)

A quota was introduced for the representation of women in the PLC, according to which every list should include a woman candidate among the first three names, as well as an additional seat for a woman among the next four names, and another among every successive five names on the list. In the old system there was no quota for women.

It is noteworthy that consultations between Fatah and Hamas took place in 2005 regarding the introduction of a further amendment to the electoral law. The aim of this amendment was to adopt a full proportional system for the parties and lists participating in the elections and to abolish the constituency system, with the whole country considered a single electoral area. The motivation of both powers in holding these consultations was their respective problems in forming electoral lists.

Fatah faced serious problems in carrying out primary elections within its ranks due to the large number of the movement's members who wished to run for office. A number of Fatah's well-known leaders and cadres expressed criticism in the media regarding the conflict among various streams within the movement.

The Hamas movement faced difficulties from as early as October 2005, when many of its leaders who had been expected to run in the elections in the West Bank were arrested by Israel. As a consequence, proportional representation would have reduced the personal influence of individual candidates and encouraged elections on the basis of political affiliation.

The 2006 Legislative Elections

The number of registered voters for the January 2006 elections was 1,340,673—811,198 in the West Bank and 529,475 in the Gaza Strip. Four hundred and fourteen candidates competed in the elections in 16 constituencies, and 314 candidates representing 11 candidate lists competed at the national lists level.

The constituencies for the elections were Bethlehem, Dayr al-Balah, Gaza, Hebron, Jenin, Jericho, Jerusalem, Khan Yunis, Nablus, Northern Gaza, Qalqilya, Rafah, Ramallah and al-Bireh, Salfit, Tubas, and Tulkarm. The lists that participated in the elections were the Alternative Alliance Bloc (an alliance of the Democratic Front for the Liberation of Palestine [DFLP], the People's Party, and Fida); Independent Palestine, led by Mustafa Barghouti; Martyr Abu Ali Mustafa (the Popular Front for the Liberation of Palestine [PFLP]); Change and Reform (Hamas); Fatah; and the Third Way, led by Salam Fayyad and Hanan Ashrawi. The following five lists of smaller blocs failed to reach the minimum vote: the list of Martyr Abu Mazen, Palestinian Justice, the National Coalition for Justice and Democracy, Freedom and Social Justice, and the Freedom and Independence list.

The elections were conducted under the supervision of approximately seventeen thousand individuals under the direction of some five hundred international observers, headed by former U.S. president Jimmy Carter, as well as approximately twelve thousand local observers representing the candidates and lists, and various institutions and NGOs. Approximately thirteen thousand policemen were deployed throughout the West Bank and Gaza Strip to protect over one thousand polling stations.

The first phase of the elections was held on Saturday, 21 January 2006, in what was known as the advance vote of security forces, in which security forces in all constituencies cast their votes at polling stations three days ahead of the main elections. In a statement by the Palestinian Central Elections Committee, the number of security officers registered to vote amounted to 58,708, of whom 53,227 cast votes, which equaled 90.7 percent of the total number registered. The number of security officers registered to vote in the Gaza Strip was 36,091, and the remainder were registered in the

West Bank. In the Gaza Strip, 32,853 voted, equaling 91 percent of the total, and 20,374 voted in the West Bank, or 90.1 percent of the total. The security personnel voted in seventeen centers, six in the Gaza Strip and eleven in the West Bank. The Central Elections Commission indicated that the aim of holding a special election for the security forces prior to the main elections was to allow the police to ensure the smooth running of the elections for civilians on election day.

The Central Elections Commission, local and international observers, and official and private bodies stressed that the elections were conducted in an atmosphere of democracy, integrity, and transparency, and that no violations were recorded. In this context, observers and political analysts agree that the holding of elections in such a manner constituted an impressive achievement on the part of the Palestinian people at all levels, including the PA and the various other factions. This was especially true given the skepticism expressed by many regarding the Palestinian people's ability to manage their own affairs.

Participation in the Elections

The Central Elections Commission announced the final results of the elections. The most important are as follows:

The total voter turnout was 77.69 percent.

The number of voters in the West Bank was 585,003, which equaled 74.18 percent of the eligible electorate. The number of voters in the Gaza Strip was 396,079, or 81.65 percent of the total electorate, bringing the total number of voters to 981,082. This figure constituted 77.69 percent of the total number of eligible voters: 1,340,673.

The highest voter turnout was recorded in the Rafah constituency in the Gaza Strip, where it reached 89 percent. The lowest turnout was in Jerusalem, where 22,661 of the 47,742 registered voters, or 47.5 percent, cast votes.

The Results of the Election and Their Statistical Significance

The Hamas "Change and Reform" list won seventy-four seats, which accounted for 56 percent of the total number of council seats. This figure included forty-five seats in the constituencies and twenty-nine from the candidate lists under the proportional system. Hamas supported four independent candidates via the Change and Reform list who were successful. This brought the number of Hamas-loyal PLC seats to seventy-eight, equaling 59 percent of the total seats in the PLC. The Fatah movement won forty-five seats, or 34 percent of the total, including seventeen seats in the constituencies and twenty-eight seats from the proportional candidate lists.

The results for the other lists are as follows: the Popular Front won three seats and the Alternative, Independent Palestine, and Third Way each won two seats. However, these lists failed to win any seats at the constituency level.

The results clearly indicate that Hamas's Change and Reform list beat the Fatah list at the constituency level by a twenty-eight-seat landslide of forty-five to seventeen. However, the difference between the two movements at the proportional level was very small—one seat—as Hamas won twenty-nine seats and Fatah twenty-eight seats. In addition to the four independents supported by the Hamas movement, no other list won any seat at the constituency level. This result can be explained by the fact that the behavior of Palestinian voters at the district level was based more on individual than party-based considerations. Furthermore, Hamas's candidates were not known for suspected involvement in financial or political corruption, whereas the Fatah candidates, especially former members of the PLC, had been harshly criticized regarding financial and administrative malpractice and their failure to achieve tangible gains during their term in the outgoing council.

The results recorded for the Hamas and Fatah proportional candidate lists were close (44 percent and 42.5 percent, respectively). This fact has led some analysts to conclude that at the district level, the amendment to the electoral law that established a mixed proportional and constituency system served Hamas rather than Fatah, and that, had the elections been held on a constituencies-only basis, centered on individual candidates instead of partisan affiliation, the difference in seats would have been even more favorable to Hamas.

Votes and Voting

The total number of votes obtained by electoral lists varied slightly compared to the number of seats obtained by each list. For example, while each of the Alternative, Independent Palestine, and Third Way lists won two seats,

Table 4.1. Distribution of PLC seats won by the electoral lists and their percentages of the total of 132 seats

List	Percentage	Seats obtained
Change and Reform (Hamas)	56	74
Fatah	34	45
Independent (Backed by Hamas)	3	4
Abu Ali Mustafa (Popular Front)	2.5	3
Alternative (Democratic Front, People's Party, and Fida)	1.5	2
Independent Palestine (Mustafa Barghouti and independents)	1.5	2
Third Way (Salam Fayyad and Hanan Ashrawi)	1.5	2
Total	100	132

Table 4.2. Distribution of seats won by the electoral lists under the proportional system and their percentages of the total of 66 seats

List	Seats obtained	Percentage
Change and Reform (Hamas)	29	44
Fatah	28	42.5
Third Way (Salam Fayyad and Hanan Ashrawi)	2	4.5
Abu Ali Mustafa (Popular Front)	3	3
Alternative (Democratic Front, People's Party, and Fida)	2	3
Independent Palestine (Mustafa Barghouti and independents)	2	3
Total	66	100

Table 4.3. Number of seats won by the electoral lists under the constituency system and their percentages of the total of 66 seats

List	Seats obtained	Percentage
Change and Reform (Hamas)	45	68
Fatah	17	26
Independents	4	6
Total	66	100

Table 4.4. The number of votes obtained by electoral lists and their percentages of the total number of voters

List	Votes	Percentage
Third Way (Salam Fayyad and Hanan Ashrawi)	23,513	2.5
Independent Palestine (Mustafa Barghouti and independents)	26,554	2.8
Alternative (Democratic Front, People's Party, and Fida)	28,779	3.0
Abu Ali Mustafa (Popular Front)	41,671	4.3
Fatah	403,458	42.1
Change and Reform (Hamas)	434,917	45.4
Total	958,892	100.0

the number of votes recorded for each list differed by thousands of votes. Likewise, the number of votes received by Hamas was over thirty thousand higher than the number received by Fatah.

The Nomination Policy

Table 4.5 indicates that Fatah followed a nomination policy according to which the number of candidates was equal to the number of seats allocated to each constituency, while Hamas nominated fewer candidates than the number of seats allocated to certain constituencies. Hamas announced that it adopted this policy in order to encourage coordination with the other lists and independents, and perhaps because a few quota seats were reserved for Christians in some constituencies. While Fatah nominated candidates for 100 percent of the allocated seats and won only 24.2 percent of them, Hamas nominated candidates for only 85 percent of the allocated seats and won as many as 82 percent of them.

At the proportional level, Hamas nominated a list of fifty-nine candidates, of which twenty-nine were elected, and Fatah nominated a list of forty-five candidates, of which twenty-eight were elected, as illustrated in Table 4.6.

Factors Affecting the Election Results

Most analyses of the 2006 Palestinian elections attribute the decline of Fatah and the victory of Hamas to three factors, the first pertaining to the Fatah movement, the second to Hamas, and the third to the surrounding circumstances at the Palestinian, Arab, and international levels.

Table 4.5. A comparison between the number of nominated and elected candidates for Hamas and Fatah at the constituency level

		Hamas		Fatah	
Constituency	Allocated seats	Nominated candidates	Elected candidates	Nominated candidates	Elected candidates
Bethlehem	4	2	2	4	2
Dayr al-Balah	3	3	2	3	1
Gaza	8	5	5	8	0
Hebron	9	9	9	9	0
Jenin	4	4	2	4	2
Jericho	1	1	0	1	1
Jerusalem	6	4	4	6	2
Khan Yunis	5	5	4	5	1
Nablus	6	5	5	6	1
Northern Gaza	5	5	5	5	0
Qalqilya	2	2	0	2	2
Rafah	3	3	0	3	3
Ramallah and al-Bireh	5	4	4	5	1
Salfit	1	1	1	1	0
Tubas	1	1	1	1	0
Tulkarm	3	2	2	3	0
Total	66	56	46	66	16

Table 4.6. A comparison between the number of nominated and elected candidates for Fatah and Hamas at the proportional level

Party	Number of nominated candidates	Number of elected candidates
Hamas	59	29
Fatah	45	28

Analyses of factors related to the failure of Fatah discuss its loose organization and lack of homogeneity in the absence of a charismatic personality capable of attracting the public after the death of Yasser Arafat. Other factors that led to the decline in Fatah's popularity include open conflicts between the different wings within the movement, the absence of democracy and the automatic renewal of the leadership, the existence of a gap between the leadership and the cadres, the endemic corruption within the movement, and the failure of the Fatah-led peace process.

The factors that helped Hamas garner wide support include its resistance to Israel; the extensive social and educational services provided by the movement to Palestinian society, especially the working and middle classes; the clear discipline among the Hamas ranks; and the party's adaptation to the transformations taking place within the movement. In addition, Hamas was able to establish balanced relations with the various Palestinian and Arab parties, thereby avoiding an Arab-Palestinian conflict, despite its designation as a terrorist organization.

The surrounding circumstances that affected the results included the integrity of the elections, which reflected the choice of the people, and the Palestinian people's wish to defy the American and Israeli positions toward Hamas, which aimed to either prevent Hamas from participating in the elections or cut off financial aid to the Palestinian people if Hamas ran and won.

HAMAS'S UNITY VERSUS DISCORD WITHIN FATAH

The Palestinian elections revealed sharp differences within Fatah's ranks, which were characterized by the following features:

Two separate Fatah candidate lists were nominated, one headed by Marwan Barghouti and the other by Ahmed Qurie^c (Abu ^{c}Alaa). The two lists reflected the depth of the conflict between the younger generation, represented by the Fatah Supreme Committee and headed by Barghouti, and the old guard, represented by Fatah's Central Committee and led by Mahmoud Abbas (Abu Mazen) and Abu ^{c}Alaa.

Deep differences within Fatah emerged in the primary elections, which were marred by violence and fraud, including attacks on Fatah elections centers, the burning of ballot boxes, bombings, and shootings. Ultimately the results were rejected by most Fatah members, which resulted in a decision to cancel these elections and form a committee to survey the opinions of Fatah members in different districts, with the goal of forming a single list headed by Marwan Barghouti—which, of course, never came to pass. Many of Fatah's members filed their nominations as independent candidates at the level of the constituencies, which reduced the chances of the movement's official candidates, against whom the independent candidates competed.

By contrast, Hamas gave a strong impression of internal unity by forming a single list and avoiding conflicts. Furthermore, candidates were nominated at the constituency level without creating competition among the movement's members, which had a positive influence on Palestinian public opinion.

A SUCCESSFUL VERSUS A DISORGANIZED ELECTORAL CAMPAIGN

Hamas's electoral campaign was modern and well-organized, and it received extensive media coverage. The campaign had many strengths, including its use of the internet, media and legal advisors, unified campaigning for the candidates, scheduled field visits, and various team activities. Additionally, Hamas's members participated en masse in well-run electoral campaigning activities with a religious element, an advantage Fatah lacked.

By contrast, Fatah's electoral campaign lacked unified activities in which the candidates could participate; indeed, Fatah's candidates often had separate campaigning offices. Similarly, Fatah's candidates presented individual electoral programs and had their own aides and supporters, with the result that competition sometimes developed between them, mainly due to personal differences. Additionally, Fatah, unlike Hamas, did not exploit modern means of communication, such as the internet.

PROTEST VOTES

Corruption in various forms—including political, financial, and administrative corruption, bribery, nepotism, the squandering of public money, and financial misappropriations—had been a prominent feature in Fatah's management of the PA, and doubtlessly played a role in shifting the support of the Palestinian electorate in the direction of Hamas. This shift was to some extent a protest against Fatah's performance over the previous decade. However, Hamas supporters downplayed the significance of this factor, arguing that a protest vote against Fatah did not necessarily result in a vote for Hamas, given that there were nine other electoral lists besides those of Hamas and Fatah.

VOTES OF DEFIANCE

Some believe that foreign interference in the Palestinian elections had a negative impact on the outcome of the elections for Fatah. Indeed, reports that the United States was providing funds to some of Fatah's candidates dealt a blow to the movement, especially in light of its inability to refute the reports unequivocally. In addition, Israel's incitement against Hamas and its calls for the movement to be banned from participating in the elections, together with threats from the United States and the European Union to cut off aid to the Palestinian people in case of a Hamas victory, served to bolster support for the movement in defiance of foreign intervention.

HAMAS'S SACRIFICES VERSUS FATAH'S POLITICAL LINE

The election results arguably reflected the reality of the Palestinian situation, which had undergone a profound change due in large part to the al-Aqsa Intifada. Indeed, the great sacrifices made by Hamas, which played an active and strong role in the Intifada, may have transformed it into a viable alternative to the PA and the PLO.

Fatah's policy during the Intifada, however, was unclear. Some members of Fatah supported negotiations and accepted political initiatives, while others, represented by the al-Aqsa Martyrs' Brigade, called for a return to armed resistance. This divergence further highlighted the continuing disunity within Fatah, which stood in contrast to the unified positions adopted by Hamas on all political issues.

THE MARTYRDOM OF HAMAS'S LEADERS VERSUS THE MYSTERIOUS DEATH OF YASSER ARAFAT

There is no doubt that the Israeli assassination of most of Hamas's leaders, including Shaykh Ahmad Yassin and Dr. ʿAbd al-ʿAziz Rantisi, resulted in a magnification of the movement's popularity. In contrast, Fatah's inability to provide an explanation for the death of President Arafat and the mystery that shrouded this event adversely affected the movement, despite the popular sympathy for Arafat.

THE LOCAL ELECTIONS (MUNICIPAL AND VILLAGE COUNCILS)

The success of Hamas in the 2005 local elections[5] influenced the party's subsequent success in the 2006 legislative elections. Hamas's victory in the 2005 metropolitan municipalities, compared to Fatah's poor showing and its failure to form consolidated candidate lists, contributed to Hamas's success by lifting the morale of its supporters and strengthening their resolve to record a further victory in the elections to the Legislative Council. In contrast, Fatah's supporters lost confidence during the municipal elections.

The election results were significant in a number of additional ways. The broad participation of the political parties represented a change in that none of the Palestinian factions boycotted the elections, with the exception of the Islamic Jihad movement. On the contrary, as many as eleven candidate lists representing different political factions participated, on top of hundreds of independent candidates at the constituency level. Moreover, the relatively high level of popular participation and voter turnout (77.69 percent) indicated a high degree of political awareness among Palestinians and their ability to make choices independently. These positive developments should be considered against the backdrop of the failure of foreign interventions, principally on the part of Israel, the European Union, and the United States. Their various interventions, as outlined above, as well as Israel's arrests of Hamas operatives starting on 25 September 2005, did not have the desired effect on the outcome of the elections. In fact, these interventions not only failed but likely had the reverse effect on some voters by encouraging them to vote for Hamas.

On the domestic front, the election results indicate the failure of the Palestinian left to form an electoral alliance, despite the common principles held by its parties and factions. The leftist factions even traded accusations of blame over the failure to form such a coalition. The only leftist alliance formed was the Alternative Alliance Bloc, which included the Democratic Front for the Liberation of Palestine (DFLP), the People's Party, and Fida, but it left out the PFLP, Independent Palestine, and the other five small leftist lists, which politically weakened the Bloc.

In addition, various personalities failed to provide a third competitor to challenge Hamas and Fatah. Many popular national and independent figures made efforts, together with numerous factions and parties, to form a united national list as a third political current in the Palestinian arena. However, the differences between the parties, particularly disagreements over the senior position on the candidate list, precluded the formation of such a list.

Five of the smaller lists that participated in the elections failed to achieve the minimum of 2 percent of the votes, even with their votes combined; together they received as little as 1.8 percent of the votes. Thus these factions had almost no support among the Palestinian public, despite the fact that they are members of the PLO, are represented within its bodies, and have been longtime recipients of PLO subsidies. The election results therefore require that these factions reconsider their political and organizational choices.

The opinion polls by and large failed to predict the results of the elections, which indicates a low level of credibility for opinion polling centers among Palestinian citizens. These centers predicted that Fatah would win close to sixty seats, Hamas around fifty seats, and the Independent Palestine list (i.e., Mustafa Barghouti and the independents) eight seats. The actual results, however, were seventy-four seats for Hamas, forty-five seats for Fatah, and only two seats for Independent Palestine. The opinion polling centers attribute the large discrepancy between the predicted and the actual results to reluctance among voters to reveal their opinions for security reasons. In other words, Hamas's supporters were averse to disclosing their voting preferences out of fear of persecution, whether from the occupation authorities or the Palestinian security services.

The Central Elections Commission, however, performed strongly and transparently, protecting voters from blackmail or pressure and abiding by the election law and associated regulations. These qualities had been in evidence in the period prior to the elections, when the Commission insisted on the prior receipt of voter registration forms and that polling be conducted at sites it specified, rather than at the security services' headquarters.

The Transfer of Power to Hamas

Before election day on 14 January 2006, Palestinian president Mahmoud Abbas (Abu Mazen) stressed that he would respect the results of the upcoming elections, but he conditioned his participation in the government on its adherence to the Oslo Agreement. Abu Mazen declared in an interview with Al Jazeera that "in 1994, we returned to Palestine on the basis of the Oslo Agreement, which established the Legislative Council and all subsequent agreements with Israel. Anyone who wishes to participate in the government should do so on this basis. If Hamas wants to participate, it must respect this on the principle of a single authority."[6]

When the election results were declared, Ismail Haniya, the Hamas leader in Gaza, stated that Hamas would deal with the existing situation without recognizing the signed agreements. Haniya further pointed out that "we must not give in . . . and adapt our people to the reality of the occupation."[7]

The differences between the two parties and their political platforms were apparent in the designation letter issued to Haniya by President Abbas on

21 February 2006, in which he asked Haniya to ensure that his government adhere to the Declaration of Independence, the resolutions of the National Council, the Basic Law of the PA, and the resolutions of the Arab summits.[8] In a statement delivered to the PLC on 27 March 2006, to seek its confidence in his government, Haniya avoided directly addressing recognizing Israel and stressed the need to tackle basic issues.[9]

The PLC granted confidence to the Hamas government on 28 March 2006, based on the support by the Hamas majority and the Popular Front. Fatah and the other factions voted against granting confidence to the government on the grounds that its political program was unrealistic.

After the formation of the government, President Abbas tried to advance his political agenda without having reached an agreement with Hamas. He thus relayed to the Israelis his readiness to engage in instant peace negotiations on the basis of the Road Map for Peace. On 6 February 2006, *Haaretz* reported that Abu Mazen had conveyed messages through various channels that he was still in charge of overseeing political communications, even after the election of Hamas. The Palestinian delegates to the negotiations with Israel demanded the continuation of the established political dialogue as well. Israeli prime minister Ehud Olmert heeded these messages and said that he would continue contacts with Abu Mazen.[10]

The head of Hamas's political bureau, Khaled Mishʿal, declared in an interview with a Russian newspaper, *Nejvetsi Gazette,*[11] that his movement would put an end to its armed struggle against Israel should the latter withdraw from all of the Occupied Territories. Mishʿal had previously made a statement that Hamas "would agree to a long-term truce with Israel if the Jewish state withdrew to the 1967 borders and recognized all the rights of the Palestinian people."[12] Likewise, Ismail Haniya acknowledged that Hamas was ready for a long-term truce with Israel as a prelude to achieving regional stability.[13]

Fundamental Disagreements between Hamas and Fatah and the Crisis of the Palestinian National Movement

Since the 2006 elections, the rivalry and tension between the two organizations have degenerated into street battles between their militias, the burning down of party headquarters and government ministries, and the use of live fire to disperse Fatah demonstrators. Waves of anarchy have taken the form of mutual recriminations and violent confrontations between Hamas and Fatah members.

In early February 2007 the two groups waged street battles in several Palestinian cities. Saudi Arabia's King Abdullah invited them to a conference in Mecca to try to reach an agreement.[14] On the ground, however, the confrontations escalated and continued to claim lives among militants as well as civilians and bystanders.[15] King Abdullah's intervention and other calls for a ceasefire and reconciliation have related chiefly to the procedural dimensions of a compromise between Hamas and Fatah and their respective leaderships, including proposals for a national unity government. However, these calls have disregarded the depth of the schism within the Palestinian national movement and Palestinian society in the West Bank and Gaza Strip.

The crisis among the Palestinians is so severe that the street fighting and confrontations chronicled by the media scarcely scratch the surface. The problem runs so deep that the Palestinians have actually lost the ability to function efficiently, internally or externally, as a single national group. This problem can be traced back to the fundamental processes within the Palestinian national movement that emerged in the 1970s and 1980s and subsequently intensified, particularly after the signing of the Oslo Accords and the establishment of the Palestinian Authority.[16]

These processes that fully ripened following the 2006 legislative election play out on several levels.

Ideology

Fatah, established in 1957, later affiliated itself with the PLO and eventually gained control of it. In 1988 it passed resolutions to accept the notion of two states for two peoples; later, in 1993, it recognized Israel and signed the Oslo Accords. The PLO agreed to the establishment of a Palestinian state on the land occupied in 1967. Unlike Fatah, Hamas, established in 1988, sees all of Mandatory Palestine as an Islamic *waqf* (property). Consequently it does not recognize Israel and is not willing to accept it as a fact on Muslim ground.

Policy

Fatah and the PLO believe that it is in the Palestinian interest to deal with Israel and establish an alliance with it (and with its main ally, the United

States). Hamas, by contrast, prefers to establish alliances with countries that are opposed to American hegemony, such as Syria and Iran. Politically, Hamas refuses to implement the three conditions set by Israel and the international community at large: recognition of Israel, recognition of the PLO and the agreements signed by it, and condemnation and abandonment of terrorism. Hamas's refusal to accept these conditions is the main reason for Israel and the international community's boycott of its government, and for the economic blockade of the PA and its citizens.

Military Action

Fatah and the PLO favor negotiations and are opposed to military operations by Palestinians inside pre-1967 Israel. Hamas, by contrast, supports the armed struggle everywhere, including against Israeli citizens within Israel proper.

Legitimacy and Representation

Fatah and the PLO, including its various member organizations, consider the PLO to be the sole national representative of the Palestinian people and invite Hamas to join it. Hamas, however, considers itself to represent all the Palestinians.

The Power Struggle within the Palestinian Authority

This conflict goes back to 2003 and the rivalry between Abu Mazen, then Palestinian prime minister, and then-president Yasser Arafat. Until March 2003, the PA had no prime minister, but rather a presidential system under Arafat, whose position was established in accordance with the Oslo Accords in 1993. All decision-making power, both executive and managerial, was held by Arafat. In March 2003, in response to pressure exerted by the Quartet and the United States, which maintained that he was dysfunctional and not making any effort to prevent terrorism, Arafat agreed to appoint a prime minister, and accepted Abu Mazen's candidacy. This concession contrasted with his previous vigorous opposition to such a step before the definitive establishment of a Palestinian state. The Legislative Council amended the 1996 Basic Law and instituted the position of prime minister, conferring its holder with executive powers previously reserved for the president. The creation of this position generated serious power struggles within the PA and Fatah. Arafat was careful to retain full decision-making powers and did not allow Abu Mazen to compete with him, in particular because the latter enjoyed the support of the United States and Israel.

The law that created the post of prime minister also created confusion with regard to the respective powers of the president and prime minister. For example, Article 39 of the original Basic Law stipulated that the president was the supreme commander of the Palestinian forces, but in the amended law the prime minister, through the minister of the interior, was made responsible for the Palestinian police, the preventive security force, and the civil defense forces, while the other military arms, such as the presidential guard, remained under the president's command. This confusion has caused power struggles between the presidency and the government, as well as tensions between factions.

Conclusion

The existential crisis that currently affects the Palestinians and their national movement is no accident. It is, in fact, a direct result of historical processes that intensified after the establishment of the Palestinian Authority in 1994 and erupted into the public sphere in the post-Arafat age following the legislative elections of January 2006. The critical elections results and the internal crisis following the elections led to a real and almost equal splitting of the national movement into two parts.

Despite continuous efforts from 2007 to today to overcome the deep split between the two wings of the Palestinian national movement[17] (efforts that intensified following the acceptance of Palestine as an observer state by the UN General Assembly in October 2012), a political reconciliation initiated by Abu Mazen and supported by Hamas and its leader Mish'al has not been implemented. To the Palestinians themselves and to the outside world, the Palestinians still maintain two separate entities of political and diplomatic relations, each of which broadcasts its own message. In such a situation the Palestinians are incapable of responding to any initiative to settle the problem of the occupation or the Palestinian problem as a whole. There is no doubt that, since late 2006, the Palestinians have been deeply split, which has permitted Israel to recycle its old refrain that "there is no Palestinian partner" and to claim that it cannot reach an agreement with representatives of only one-half of the national movement. This crisis has prevented and will continue to prevent a Palestinian consensus that would permit progress in the political process. Unquestionably, any discussions aimed at putting an end to the conflict will have to wait for fundamentally different conditions than those that prevail today.

Notes

1. V. O. Key, "A Theory of Critical Elections," *Journal of Politics* 17, no. 1 (February 1995): 3–18; David Brady, *Critical Elections and Congressional Policy Making* (Stanford, CA: Stanford University Press, 1988); Walter Deana Burnham, *Critical Elections and the Mainsprings of American Politics* (New York: Norton, 1970).

2. Sammy Smooha and Don Peretz, "Israeli's 1993 Knesset Elections: Are They Critical?," *Middle East Journal* 47, no. 3 (1993): 445–463.

3. As'ad Ghanem, "Founding Elections in a Transitional Period: The First Palestinian General Elections," *Middle East Journal* 50 (1997): 513–528.

4. Ghanem, "Founding Elections in a Transitional Period."

5. The local elections were held in four stages. The first stage was for 26 local councils in the West Bank on 23 December 2004 and for 10 local councils in the Gaza Strip on 27 January 2005. The second stage was held on 5 May 2005 for 84 local councils—76 in the West Bank and eight in the Gaza Strip. The third stage was held on 29 September 2005 for 104 local councils in the West Bank. Elections scheduled for the Jenin district and the Gaza Strip were postponed due to the Israeli evacuation of settlements in these areas at that time. The fourth and final stage was held on 15 December 2005 and included 44 local entities' councils, including the metropolitan municipalities of Hebron, Nablus, Ramallah, al-Bireh, and Jenin.

6. Abbas's statement was made in an interview with Walid Omari on Al Jazeera on 14 January 2006.

7. "Haniya: Hamas Must Deal with the Reality of the Occupation Without Accepting the Signed Agreements,"*al-Ayyam* (Palestine), 27 January 2006.

8. The letter was reproduced in *al-Ayyam* (Palestine) on 5 February 2006.

9. The speech delivered by Ismail Haniya before the PLC in the confidence session was held on 27 March 2006. It appeared on the front page of *al-Ayyam* (Palestine) on 28 March 2006.

10. Olmert's statements were published on the front page of *al-Quds* (Palestine) on 7 February 2006.

11. This article was republished by *al-Ayyam* (Palestine) on 14 February 2006 under the title "Mashaal: Hamas Will Stop Its Military Struggle if Israel Withdraws to the 1967 Borders."

12. "Mashaal: Hamas Will Stop Its Military Struggle."

13. *Al-Ayyam* (Palestine) published Haniya's acknowledgment on its front page on 31 May 2005.

14. See, for instance, the Palestinian newspapers *al-Ayyam, al-Hayyat al-Jadeeda,* and *al-Quds* on 29 January 2007, as well as the Arab and Israeli press on the same day.

15. See the Palestinian, Israeli, and world press on 30 January 2007.

16. As'ad Ghanem, *The Palestinian Regime: A Partial Democracy* (London: Sussex Academic, 2001).

17. Such efforts include the signing of the reconciliation agreement between Fatah and Hamas in Cairo on 4 May 2011.

5. Before Gaza, After Gaza

*Examining the New Reality
in Israel/Palestine*

SARA ROY

In the nineteen years since the Oslo process began, Palestinians have suffered losses not seen since the beginning of Israeli occupation and arguably since the Nakba, the losses of 1948. The scholar Joseph Massad has compellingly argued that it is wrong to think of the Nakba as "a history of the past"; rather, it is "a history of the present," a historical epoch that remains a living, ongoing reality without end.[1] Yet, what has changed is the conceptualization of loss itself, which has assumed altogether new dimensions. For now it is less a matter of defining losses that demand redress than of living in an altered, indistinguishable, and indeterminate reality in which those losses have no place, no history, and no context, where reclamation is, in effect, meaningless, without purpose or justification. This altered reality has been shaped and defined over the last few years by certain critical paradigmatic shifts in the way the Palestinian-Israeli conflict is conceptualized, understood, and addressed. I will touch upon some of these shifts, ending with a brief reflection on the changing socioeconomic reality in Gaza.

Key Paradigm Shifts: Reconfiguring the Defining Conceptual Framework

Since the beginning of Israeli occupation there has always been an implicit and often explicit belief among Palestinians, many Israelis, and members of the international community that the occupation can and will end, and that Israel's expansion into Palestine will be stopped. This was how many understood the Oslo process. The belief that occupation is reversible and should be reversed was largely unquestioned and uncontested and was the catalyzing force behind many social, economic, and political initiatives. This belief has itself been reversed and is powerfully illustrated in the formalization, institutionalization, and acceptance by Israel and the international community of Palestinian territorial and demographic fragmentation and cantonization. This represents a key paradigmatic shift in the way the conflict is understood and approached.

The changes imposed on Palestinians over the last two decades have shown that the occupation cannot be stopped, at least not in the short- or medium-term. If occupation has changed over time it is in the sheer nature of its expansion and force, not in its mitigation, contraction, or inversion. The etiology and imperative of expansion remains unchallenged, and it is doubtful that it could be stopped even if the Israeli leadership wanted to stop it, which they do not. Perhaps the most powerful illustration of occupation's power lies in the continued expansion of Israeli settlements and their infrastructure and in the building of the separation barrier or wall.

The effect on Palestinians has been extremely damaging. Not only have lands and the use of those lands been lost—at least 38 percent of the West Bank is under Israeli control and inaccessible to Palestinians[2]—but Arab lands are being incorporated and consolidated into a new spatial and political order that aims to eliminate any physical separation between Israel and certain (and increasing) areas of the West Bank, diminishing the presence of Palestinians and precluding the emergence of any viable entity that could be called a Palestinian state (even on the eastern side of the barrier).

The denial of territorial contiguity and the reality of territorial and demographic fragmentation were facilitated by the physical isolation of the West Bank and Gaza, which was largely complete by 1998, illustrating that their separation had long been an Israeli policy goal. According to the Israeli journalist Amira Hass,

> The total separation of the Gaza Strip from the West Bank is one of the greatest achievements of Israeli politics, whose overarching objective is to prevent a solution based on international decisions and understandings and instead dictate an arrangement based on Israel's military superiority.... Since January 1991, Israel has bureaucratically and logistically merely perfected the split and the separation: not only between Palestinians in the occupied territories and their brothers in Israel, but also

between the Palestinian residents of Jerusalem and those in the rest of the territories and between Gazans and West Bankers/Jerusalemites.[3]

Indeed, the Israeli economist Shir Hever revealed that on 20 April 2007, in a lecture delivered at the Van Leer Institute, Brigadier General Yair Golan, then commander of Israeli forces in the West Bank, stated that "separation and not security is the main reason for building the Wall of Separation and that security could have been achieved more effectively and more cheaply through other means."[4]

This points to another important paradigm shift. Prior to Oslo there was a belief among Israelis and within the international community that peace and occupation were incompatible. The former could not be achieved in the presence of the latter. This, too, has changed. In recent years, more and more Israelis are benefiting from the occupation. Their lives have been made easier by the vast settlement road network built in the West Bank and by an improved economy resulting from a perceived containment of the conflict. Settlements are now regarded as natural outgrowth, a needed constituency providing protection and security, with important familial links to Israel proper. Thus, the integration of the settlement blocs and their infrastructure into Israel—that is, the argument that the West Bank is part of Israel—is no longer extraordinary or contentious; on the contrary, it is necessary and normal.

For many Israelis and several key international donors it is no longer a question of normalizing the occupation but of removing the term altogether since it no longer applies, especially in light of a strong and expanding Israeli economy and the virtual cessation of suicide attacks inside Israel.[5] In fact, silence about the occupation has become the key condition for continued international funding of the Palestinian Authority (PA). Hence, Palestine's effective dismemberment and the permanence of territorial fragmentation (as well as the policies of collective punishment that often accompany them) are accepted by the international community as legitimate and benign and totally manageable, especially with the virtual absence, until recently, of any criticism from Palestinian officialdom. Separating from the Palestinians and doing what is necessary politically, militarily, and economically to ensure and maintain that separation have also become increasingly routine.

In point of fact, many, if not most, Israelis are untouched by the everyday exigencies of the occupation, having little if any exposure to them. The occupation has been transformed from a political and legal issue with international legitimacy into a simple dispute over borders where the rules of war apply, rather than those of occupation. In this regard, Israel has successfully recast its relationship with Gaza from one of occupation to one of two actors at war, a recasting the international community has also come to accept. Indeed, some international actors now deny the existence of occupation altogether. In this regard George Bisharat observes, "Israeli military lawyers have pushed to re-classify military operations in the West Bank and Gaza Strip from the law enforcement model mandated by the law of occupation to one of armed conflict. Today most observers—including Amnesty International—tacitly accept Israel's framing of the conflict in Gaza as an armed conflict, as their criticism of Israel's actions in terms of the duties of distinction and the principle of proportionality betrays."[6]

This no doubt accounts, in part, for the overwhelming popular support among Israelis for the devastating war on Gaza. Hence, many Israelis and members of the international community no longer feel uncomfortable with the occupation at a time when the occupation has grown more repressive and perverse.

The inapplicability of occupation as an analytical (and legal) framework leads to another important paradigm shift regarding Israel's intentions toward the Palestinians and their territories. This shift is from one of ongoing occupation to one of annexation and imposed sovereignty (i.e., claiming that the West Bank or parts of it are de facto sovereign Israeli territory).

This shift is illustrated in part by the following policies: the building of the separation wall; massive Israeli settlement expansion; the continued confiscation of Palestinian lands; the building of the massive settlement road network from which Palestinians are effectively barred; limited access to the Jordan Valley by nonresident Palestinians; the isolation of Gaza and its physical, economic, and demographic separation from the West Bank; and the subsequent reshaping of the Palestinian-Israeli conflict to center on Gaza alone and on Israel's hostile relationship with Hamas. A critical feature of this reshaping has been the transformation of Palestinians into a humanitarian problem, which I discuss below, and the identification of Gaza solely with Hamas and therefore as alien.

Hence, any resistance by Palestinians to Israel's repressive occupation, including attempts at economic empowerment, is now considered illegitimate and unlawful. Indeed, Palestinians have been severely punished for trying to defend themselves against policies that oppress them.[7] Rather, they and the governments elected to represent them are expected—indeed required—by

Israel, the United States, the European Union, and some Arab states, to submit to Israeli actions—in effect, to collaborate with Israeli policy—and oppose any form of popular resistance to those actions.[8] Within this new paradigm Palestinians become aliens and intruders in their own land, living in submission and dependence. Any notion of a human community among Palestinians, let alone a national or economic one, ceases to exist. Nowhere is this more evident than in Gaza.

The paradigmatic shift from occupation to annexation also has been accepted by key members of the international community, especially after Hamas's electoral victory and seizure of Gaza. Not only have major donors participated in the draconian sanction regime imposed on Gaza, but they have privileged the West Bank over Gaza in their programmatic work. Donor strategies now support and strengthen the fragmentation and isolation of the West Bank and Gaza Strip and divide Palestinians into two distinct entities, offering exclusivity to one side—economically, politically, and diplomatically—and criminalizing the other. The West Bank is deserving of sustenance and Gaza, deprivation.

What emerges are, in effect, two political-economic models. The West Bank model is characterized by restricted levels of institution-building, isolated pockets of business and commercial development themselves shaped by a cantonized geographical entity, and the professionalization of security forces. This model is devoid of political content and does nothing to confront the occupation; to the contrary, it advocates silence and represses criticism. There is also the Gaza Strip model, characterized by siege, isolation, collective punishment, and economic subjection with a leadership strengthened by the occupation but unable to do anything to address it.[9] Both models have failed, and their failure underlines the fact that the Palestinian state has long been an Israel-U.S. project, not a Palestinian one.

Increasingly, economic activities are evolving as a response to decline and breakdown and to the unwillingness of the donor governments to meaningfully, that is, politically, challenge the status quo. This unwillingness represents nothing less than collusion with maintaining Israel's occupation.

Transforming Palestinians into perpetrators, without claim, has assumed different dimensions since the election of Hamas, particularly with regard to the changing nature of physical destruction in the West Bank, which represents another critical change. The Israeli journalist Amira Hass has described to me a steady process of destroying many vestiges of Palestinian life in the West Bank as they have historically existed. Old roads long used by

Palestinians traveling between major towns and surrounding villages are being eliminated, as are traditional intersections, buildings, and certain commercial areas. What is happening is no less than the erasure of a Palestinian presence in the West Bank.

Another new and related feature is the increasing bureaucratization of Israel's system of control, or what the Israeli scholar Neve Gordon calls the privatization of Zionism. Gordon argues that while the state was long responsible for urban planning and development inside Israel and the West Bank, incrementally the task has been subcontracted to the corporate sector.[10] In the West Bank, this shift (in tactics as opposed to strategy) is illustrated by the fact that some military checkpoints are no longer manned by soldiers but are administered by private Israeli security companies. This is also true for the Erez crossing point from Israel into Gaza.

Hence, in addition to the political imperatives underlying checkpoints, terminals, and other physical barriers, there is now an entrenched bureaucratic imperative that has its own interests, needs, and priorities. Bureaucratizing this structure depoliticizes it by making it a necessary and permanent part of everyday life. One must add to this Israel's intense, almost complete bureaucratic control of everyday life in the West Bank and Gaza.

Key Paradigm Shifts: Sectoral Level Changes

The Economy

"We started with food aid and we have returned to food aid." This was the conclusion of a Palestinian economist in Ramallah in 2007. Her words powerfully capture what is perhaps the most dramatic paradigm shift in the way Palestinians are perceived and addressed: from a society (worthy of) pursuing developmental change to an impoverished community seeking relief, what the analyst Sami Abdel Shafi refers to as "engineering Palestinians into perpetual beggars."[11]

The resulting "humanitarianization" and immiseration of Palestinians—turning Palestinians into charity cases and paupers—has many illustrations. In 2007, for example, 30 percent of income earned by Palestinians between 1972 and 2006 was being brought into the economy as emergency aid resulting in large part from Israel's severing of economic and commercial ties after four decades of integration and forced dependence.[12] In 2008, external aid to the PA equaled almost 30 percent of GDP, which means that without such donor aid, there would be fiscal collapse.[13] By 2008, approximately 80 percent of families in Gaza relied on humanitarian aid to survive, compared to 63 percent in 2006; currently that figure remains largely unchanged. Between 1999 and early 2008, the number of families receiving food aid from UNRWA increased from 16,174 to 182,400, or 860,000 people (although other estimates place this number at 750,000).[14] Furthermore, the World Food Programme was feeding an additional 302,000 Gazans, meaning that over 1.1 million out of 1.4 million people in Gaza were receiving food aid in 2008.

The shift from political to humanitarian priorities derives from several factors:

The total fragmentation of the geographical base of the Palestinian economy, with the complete separation of Gaza and the West Bank and the division of the West Bank into at least eleven cantons and subcantons on no more than 62 percent of the land.

The use of aid as a form of punishment inflicted by Israel (in the form of closure and then blockade) and, critically, by the international community.[15]

The growing ineffectiveness of international aid, particularly after 2006, as assistance—composed in large part of humanitarian relief and services—was being provided outside any economic framework, having little if any bearing on sustainable development.

Hence, the steady imposition of Israeli imperatives unchallenged, and then actively supported by, the international community, coupled with the use of aid as a punitive weapon, gave rise to a clear shift in the way some foreign governments, aid agencies, and other international organizations approached Israeli-Palestinian relations. This shift, acutely clear after the January 2006 elections, moved strongly away from any commitment to Palestinian self-determination toward one that emphasized relief and charity[16]—helping people survive while they are being contained and punished and their economy disabled.

Indeed, the precipitous decline of the private sector, the driver of economic growth whose impact on the sustained health of the economy is enormous, provides a powerful illustration of economic disablement and the impoverishment it produces. Prior to the horrendous attack on Gaza, for example, the private sector was on the verge of collapse due to Israeli closure and blockade preventing the import of raw materials and the export of finished products. Before Hamas's June 2007 takeover of the Strip, 54 percent of Gaza's employment was generated by the private sector. Gaza's manufacturers imported 95 percent of their inputs and exported their finished products primarily to Israel and the West Bank. Between June 2005 and September 2008, the number of operating factories in Gaza had declined from 3,750–3,900 to 23.[17] Approximately 100,000 people, virtually the entire private sector, lost their jobs.[18]

Perhaps more ominous was the growing informalization of the economy. Prior to the December 2008 invasion of Gaza, the World Bank observed a "redistribution of wealth from the formal private sector towards black market operators."[19] Indeed, Gaza's growing tunnel trade with Egypt has turned the once-impoverished town of Rafah into a busy market where a variety of goods, including weapons, can now be purchased. Rafah's growing economy is yet another illustration of fragmentation and the distortion it produces, of creating economic islands—be they in Gaza or the West Bank—that the World Bank correctly termed "development dead-ends."[20] Furthermore, said the Bank, the "near absence of private sector activities" combined with a financial crisis deriving from the inability of people to pay for services such as water, garbage collection, and sewage treatment, and the inability to import spare parts and supplies, also resulted in the collapse of the municipal sector.[21] This represented no less than the change in Gaza's already fragile economy from one driven in large part by private-sector productivity to one dependent on public-sector salaries and humanitarian assistance, a condition that obtains to varying degrees in the West Bank as well.[22]

Yet this transformation or paradigm shift that reduces Palestinians from a political to a humanitarian issue has been accompanied by another equally dangerous paradigm shift. Since the Hamas victory in January 2006, Israel's policy goal is no longer just the isolation of Gaza but its disablement, as seen in a policy shift from one that addresses the economy in some manner (whether positively or negatively) to one that dispenses with the concept of an economy altogether. That is, rather than weaken Gaza's economy through punishing closures and other restrictions as it has long done, the Israeli government has, since June 2006, imposed a form of indefinite blockade—

replacing closure—that treats the economy as totally irrelevant, a dispos-
able luxury.[23]

This was underlined by the Israeli Supreme Court's decision approving
fuel cuts to Gaza in October 2007 (permissible since it would not harm "essential humanitarian needs" of the population),[24] followed in January 2008
by electricity cuts and in May 2008 by a lowering of acceptable levels for fuel
and electricity. The court stated, "We do not accept the petitioners' argument
that 'market forces' should be allowed to play their role in Gaza with regard
to fuel consumption."[25] Thus, according to the Supreme Court, it is acceptable to harm Palestinians and create a humanitarian crisis for political reasons. Or as the analyst Darryl Li put it, "In place of any legal framework, the
state has proposed—and the court has now endorsed—a seemingly simple
standard for policy: once 'essential humanitarian needs' are met, all other
deprivation is permissible."[26]

It is no longer—and in fact has not been for quite some time—a question of economic growth, change or reform, freedom or sovereignty, but of
essential humanitarian needs, of reducing the needs and rights of 1.65 million people in Gaza to an "exercise in counting calories"[27] and truckloads of
food. In this way, Israeli policy blurs and, in fact, justifies the destruction
of Gaza's economic capacities, which was largely completed with the 2008–
2009 war. Within such a scenario aid can, at best, be no more than a pallia-
tive "slowing down socioeconomic decline [rather] than a catalyst for sustainable economic development."[28] Writing about the West Bank, the World
Bank similarly observed, "Large amounts of donor aid have produced insig-
nificant growth and an increase in economic dependency despite the consistent improvement in [PA] governance and security performance."[29]

The Social Sector

Summarizing the approach of the donor community toward Palestinians
post-Hamas, Dr. Thomas Neu, a development specialist with over thirty
years of experience in the West Bank and Gaza, lamented, "You don't de-
stroy a society in order to build it up again."[30] While it is certainly premature
to argue the demise of Palestinian society, it is absolutely essential to argue
its decline. This decline has a long history and is marked by many factors af-
fecting the West Bank and Gaza. Perhaps the most important concerns the
family unit, which despite the continuous pressures imposed on it has re-

mained remarkably resilient and adaptable but is now increasingly less so. The pressures resulting from territorial fragmentation and economic blockade have been onerous.

The family unit has been weakened by an expanding humanitarian crisis, resource dispossession, internal violence and disorder, and heightened insecurity. Traditional buffers in times of economic distress such as remittances, investments, loans, and solidarity payments have markedly decreased due in large part to Israel's long-standing regime of economic restrictions and to the international economic and financial boycott. The family also has suffered greatly as a result of factors tied to or resulting from two decades of political violence and economic regression. To name just a few: early marriage; the oppression of women; the traumatization of children with violence the defining feature in their lives, which became even more extreme with the war on Gaza; the loss of childhood and growing incivility among children; the diminished authoritative role of the father resulting from his inability to provide for and protect his family; the receding of traditional forms of authority; the weakening of socializing institutions such as the school and the political faction; the decline of the community; and declining health care and educational access. These are old problems, but what is new—and long argued to me with a palpable urgency—is their level of acuity, another critical paradigm shift.

If there is a powerful and consistent theme among the many people interviewed over the last few years—Palestinians, Israelis, and internationals (especially members of the donor community)—it is this: that the situation in Gaza and the West Bank is rapidly approaching a watershed in terms of the damage inflicted on the individual, the family, and the community. The fear of unabated and irreversible decline is deep and unprecedented and directed to the fact that Palestinians are approaching a degree of damage and loss that will take billions of dollars and generations of Palestinians to reverse. This reality has many illustrations that include a population in which, conservatively, 75 percent of its members now suffer from severe depression; in which nearly 75 percent of all those injured between September 2000 and September 2008 were between ten and twenty-nine years old; and in which 62 percent of those killed between September 2000 and June 2008 were between fifteen and twenty-nine years of age.[31] Economically, socially, and demographically, it is impossible to outrun the reality of Gaza and the West Bank.

Against their growing deprivation, brutalization, and isolation, people are, by lack of choice and force of circumstance, turning inward. Hence, the dislocating impact of territorial fragmentation and isolation on Palestinian life is seen in another important paradigmatic shift—the localization or at-omization of life and the reconceptualization of community. Since 2000, ac-cess restrictions have created an even greater sense of place, in very practi-cal ways. The time disappeared when a Gazan and a Nabulsi might meet at Birzeit University and eventually get married; by 2004 they were unable to even meet each other and would encounter objections from their families, who did not want their son or daughter to be unavailable to them even for visits. The same became true for business transactions; gone were the days when a foreign NGO might hire a Hebron-based construction firm to carry out a project in Nablus. The result has been a lack of intermixing. There have been fewer interactions and friendships as people enter into increasingly different political and structural situations (which, of course, the Israelis encourage as part of a divide-and-rule system of selectively applied carrot-and-stick inducements).

Israel has forced Palestinians to internalize the reality imposed on them; people choose to remain in or near their localities because it is often too dif-ficult to move beyond them and in Gaza it is impossible to do so. Conse-quently, human, economic, and social activities increasingly devolve to the locality, the neighborhood, and even the street (as was the case in Gaza prior to Hamas's June 2007 takeover), becoming more atomized and insular. The result is clear: the emergence of particularism over universalism, the lat-ter being far more evident as a value and a goal during the first Intifada. By 2004, people were already estranged from each other, their localities sepa-rated. Because of this the concept of community has been redefined in terms that are particular and near: *we* are worse off because *they* have one more gate, one more road, one more clinic.

In this regard there also has emerged a growing religiosity among people that is not fundamentalist in character but rather an attempt to find comfort in religion. This has been accompanied by an increasing emphasis on fami-lies and children and celebrations and festivals[32] in an attempt, perhaps, to restore a sense of normalcy and empowerment within a political and struc-tural situation that is decidedly abnormal and disempowering, to make, as Lisa Taraki has written, "the very pursuit of happiness a manifestation of resilience and resistance at the same time"[33]—in effect, to redefine the community within the boundaries of the enclave and to redefine solidarity as the ability to live within it.[34] In this regard, the second Intifada represented a dramatic deterioration from the first, which aimed to create a consciousness of a people and a national collective, something that became increasingly difficult, if not impossible, after 2000.

The redefinition of community in this narrowed and confined sense has other consequences. By robbing people of time and space, this fragmented reality militates against positive risk-taking and change (especially in so diminished an economic environment). This is because a great deal of creative and productive human energy is being used to survive in a malformed system, one that is made more extreme by the hostility and violence between Fatah and Hamas. The result is no less than the de-development of the human being.

The reconceptualization of community as enclave further speaks to the way in which spatial dislocation may impact political identity. For example, the word "Palestine" is used in two ways—to describe a geographical and historical region, and to describe a Palestinian state. Yet, perhaps for the first time in the history of the Palestinian national movement—itself virtually destroyed—the two have little if any connection to each other. The connection between identity—social, economic, and political—and territory is being destroyed by institutionalized fragmentation and the mitigation of society. In a very real sense, Palestinians can no longer walk or traverse the land in order to claim it as they have for so long; only the Jewish people can.[35] Palestinians are less and less part of the natural landscape, which supports Amira Hass's claim with regard to the physical destruction of the Palestinian presence in the West Bank.

After the War on Gaza

After Israel's December 2008 invasion, Gaza's already compromised conditions became virtually unlivable. Livelihoods, homes, and public infrastructure were damaged or destroyed on a scale that the Israel Defense Forces itself admitted was indefensible.[36] Among the ruins lie 1,500 factories and workshops; nearly half of 122 health facilities, including 15 hospitals; 280 schools and kindergartens; and 58,000 homes.[37]

These data are part of an overall picture of infrastructural damage and destruction that will cost at least $2 billion to address. Observers report destruction on a tremendous scale. In Gaza today, there is a profoundly diminished private sector and virtually no industry. The 2008 assault also destroyed 5,000 acres of agricultural land, including over 300,000 fruit-bearing trees and 305 agricultural wells. Most productive activity has been extinguished. One powerful expression of Gaza's economic demise—and the Gazans' indomitable will to provide for their families—is its burgeoning tunnel economy that emerged long ago in response to the siege and the absence of alternatives that it created. Thousands of Palestinians have been employed digging tunnels into Egypt—around one thousand tunnels are reported to exist although not all are operational. According to local economists, by 2009 between 66 and 90 percent of economic activity in Gaza—once considered a lower middle-income economy (along with the West Bank)—was devoted to smuggling.[38]

According to the World Food Programme, the Gaza Strip requires a minimum of 400 trucks of food every day just to meet the basic nutritional needs of the population. Yet despite a 22 March 2009 decision by the Israeli cabinet to lift all restrictions on foodstuffs entering Gaza, only 653 trucks of food and other supplies were allowed entry during the week of 10 May 2009, at best meeting 23 percent of required need.[39]

Indeed, according to Amira Hass, by May 2009 Israel allowed only thirty to forty commercial items to enter Gaza, compared to four thousand approved products prior to June 2006 when the Israeli soldier Gilad Shalit was abducted.[40] Although restrictions on the entry of food were in practice lifted during the summer of 2010 in response to international pressure after the Gaza flotilla killings, critically needed materials for economic reconstruction and private sector rehabilitation are still banned, as is freedom of movement. Without an immediate end to Israel's blockade and the resumption of trade especially, as well as the movement of people outside the prison that Gaza has long been, the current crisis will grow more acute.

Adding to Gaza's misery is the huge rehabilitative burden of the five thousand injured and the social burden of families left without breadwinners. Following the 2008 assault one hundred thousand Gazans were left homeless, internally displaced, and temporarily residing in fifty-eight UNRWA shelters or with private families (who themselves lost breadwinners).[41] This too will strain the economy. However, the greatest problem facing Palestinians, especially children, is psychological trauma, which long preceded the December assault but which has been made more acute because of it. Children remember that the first attack on Gaza occurred while they were in school. Approximately 161 of UNRWA's 221 schools now have psychosocial support programs but many more are needed.[42]

Furthermore, the long-term impact of the enormous damage incurred by the educational system, already seriously eroded before the hostilities began, is another critical and inestimable constraint, with 80 percent of sixth-grade pupils in Gaza failing math, science, English, and Arabic in 2008. Children returned to schools that were badly damaged or destroyed, with potentially unexploded ordnance lurking on the premises. Those that are functioning report shortages of drinking water, textbooks, and other supplies such as desks, which were used as firewood during the fighting.

Given these restrictions, among many others including the internal disarray of the Palestinian leadership, one wonders how the reconstruction to which President Obama has referred will be possible. There is no question that Palestinians in Gaza must be helped immediately. Programs aimed at alleviating suffering and reinstating some semblance of normalcy are ongoing but at a scale shaped entirely by the extreme limitations on the availability of goods. In this context of repressive occupation and heightened restrictions, what does it mean to reconstruct Gaza? How is it possible under such conditions to empower people and build sustainable and resilient institutions able to withstand expected external shocks? And what exactly are Palestinians being asked to sustain: an economy that the World Bank says has been "hollowed out" by Israel's security regime?[43] This, too, points to the critical need to shift the political discourse away from the notion of state building, which has proven empty, to one of ending the occupation, or what Palestinians now term "liberation." Planning for long-term sustainable change, let alone development, in the presence of the stranglehold of Israeli occupation is a futile and meaningless exercise, as the last few decades have made painfully clear. The occupation must end; then one can discuss about what arrangement should follow.

A few months after the war ended, I spoke with some friends in Gaza, and the conversations were profoundly disturbing. My friends spoke of the deeply felt absence of any source of protection, be it personal, communal, or institutional. There is little in society that possesses legitimacy, and there is a fading consensus on rules and an eroding understanding of what they are for. Trauma and grief overwhelm the landscape despite expressions of resilience. "We have lost all sense of the ordinary—what it is like to live an ordinary day—and perhaps more importantly we fear we will never be able to retrieve it, no matter how desperately we try." The feeling of abandonment among people appears profound, understood perhaps in their growing inability to identify with any sense of possibility. But what struck me most of all was this comment: "It is no longer the occupation or even the war that consumes us but the realization of our own irrelevance."

Toward what possible good can the infliction of such mass suffering contribute? The situation in Gaza continues to deteriorate despite the astounding resilience of its people. What is happening there is nothing less than the slow but steady destruction of an economy, a society, and a way of life in which any sense of a future resides.

Ultimately Gaza's fate, like that of all Palestinians, does not lie in food convoys or enhanced levels of foreign assistance but in the rule of law and its just enforcement. Absent this, we shall all bear responsibility for Gaza's demise.

Notes

Earlier versions of this chapter were first presented as lectures in various academic forums in Australia in 2008 and in the West Bank. Some passages appear in Sara Roy, "Reconceptualizing the Israeli-Palestinian Conflict: Key Paradigm Shifts," *Journal of Palestine Studies* 41, no. 3 (Spring 2012): 71–91. Reprinted with permission.

1. Joseph Massad, "Resisting the Nakba," *Al-Ahram Weekly* 897 (May 2008): 15–21.

2. United Nations Office for the Coordination of Humanitarian Affairs, "The Humanitarian Impact on Palestinians of Israeli Settlements and Other Infrastructure in the West Bank," July 2007. This figure has gone as high as 50+ percent but the more conservative one is used here. See, for example, World Bank, "Movement and Access Restrictions in the West Bank: Uncertainty and Inefficiency in the Palestinian Economy," 9 May 2007, 1–2 and 5–6.

3. Amira Hass, "An Israeli Achievement," 20 April 2009, http://www.Bitterlemons.org.

4. Shir Hever, *The Political Economy of Israel's Occupation: Beyond Mere Exploitation* (London: Pluto Press, 2010).

5. By 2008, the Israeli shekel was one of the fifteen strongest currencies in the world. See Jeff Halper, "Rethinking Israel after 60 Years," Israel Committee Against Home Demolitions (ICAHD), 2008.

6. George Bisharat, "Changing Rules of War," *San Francisco Chronicle,* 1 April 2009, http://www.sfgate.com/cgi-bin/article.cgi?f=/c/a/2009/03/31/EDKP16PF6S.DTL.

7. John Whitbeck, correspondence with the author.

8. John Whitbeck, correspondence with the author. Also see Bashir Abu-Manneh, "In Palestine, A Dream Deferred," *The Nation*, 18 December 2006, http://www.thenation.com/doc/20061218/abumanneh; and Virginia Tilley, "A Beacon of Hope: Apartheid Israel," *Counterpunch*, 5 December 2006.

9. Mouin Rabbani, "Political Consequences of Israel's Gaza War" (paper presented at symposium on "Palestine and the Palestinians Today," Center for Contemporary Arab Studies, Georgetown University, 2 April 2009).

10. Daniel Levy, "A More Private Occupation," *Haaretz*, 11 April 2008, http://www.haaretz.com/hasen/pages/ShArt.jhtml?itemNo=973974; and Neve Gordon and Erez Tzfadia, "Privatising Zionism," *Guardian* (London), 14 December 2007, http://www.guardian.co.uk/commentisfree/2007/dec/14/privatisingzionism.

11. Sami Abdel Shafi (presentation via phone at Gaza symposium, Harvard Law School, 31 March 2009). See also Ilana Feldman, "Gaza's Humanitarianism Problem," *Journal of Palestine Studies* 38, no. 3 (Spring 2009): 22–37.

12. See Atif Kubursi and Fadle Naqib, "The Palestinian Economy Under Occupation: The Economics of Subjugation and Dynamics of Dependency" (paper presented at the University of London School of Oriental and African Studies, January 2007), 27–28.

13. World Bank, "Palestinian Economic Prospects: Gaza Recovery and West Bank Revival—Economic Monitoring Report to the Ad Hoc Liaison Committee," 8 June 2009, 6.

14. CARE International, Catholic Agency for Overseas Development, Amnesty International, Christian Aid, Medecins du Monde UK, Oxfam, Save the Children UK, and Trocaire, "The Gaza Strip: A Humanitarian Implosion," 2008, 4n6. See also Ian Black, "Sanctions Cause Gaza to Implode, Says Rights Group," *Guardian* (London), 6 March 2008, www.guardian.co.uk/world/2008/mar/06/israelandthepalestinians.humanrights.

15. For example, USAID policy changes after Hamas's legislative (and municipal) election victories.

16. The Palestinian Grassroots Anti-Apartheid Wall Campaign, "The Occupation's 'Convergence Plan': Legitimizing Palestinian Bantustans," 28 May 2006, http://www.stopthewall.org/occupations-convergence-plan-legitimizing-palestinian-bantustans.

17. Sara Roy, "Treading on Shards," *The Nation*, 17 February 2010; World Bank, "Palestinian Economic Prospects: Aid, Access and Reform," 22 September 2008, 7 and 22.

18. World Bank, "Palestinian Economic Prospects: Aid, Access and Reform," 22.

19. World Bank, "Palestinian Economic Prospects: Aid, Access and Reform," 22.

20. World Bank, "Palestinian Economic Prospects: Gaza Recovery and West Bank Revival," 6.

21. World Bank, "Palestinian Economic Prospects: Aid, Access and Reform," 22.

22. For an examination of the economic costs of the occupation on Israel, see Shlomo Swirski, *The Cost of Occupation: The Burden of the Israeli-Palestinian Con-*

flict 2008 Report, Information of Equality and Social Justice in Israel (ADVA), June 2008.

23. Darryl Li, "From Prison to Zoo: Israel's 'Humanitarian' Control of Gaza," *Adalah Newsletter* 44 (January 2008), 2. Also see HCJ 9132/07, Jaber al-Basyouni Ahmed v. The Prime Minister, http://mfa.gov.il/NR/rdonlyres/938CCD2E-89C7 -4E77-B071-56772DFF79CC/0/HCJGazaelectricity.pdf.

24. Li, "From Prison to Zoo," 1.

25. Li, "From Prison to Zoo," 2; See also Darryl Li, "Disengagement and the Frontiers of Zionism," *Middle East Report,* 16 February 2008.

26. Li, "From Prison to Zoo," 2.

27. Li, "From Prison to Zoo," 3.

28. World Bank Group, "Palestinian Economic Prospects: Gaza Recovery and West Bank Revival," 6.

29. World Bank Group, "Palestinian Economic Prospects: Gaza Recovery and West Bank Revival," 6.

30. Dr. Thomas Neu, interview with the author, Fall 2007, Washington, DC.

31. World Bank, "Palestinian Economic Prospects: Aid, Access and Reform," 21; Palestinian Central Bureau of Statistics (PCBS), "Youth in Palestinian Territory, Statistical Indicators," 12 August 2008.

32. Paul Beran (lecture at the Center for Middle Eastern Studies, Harvard University, 18 July 2008).

33. Lisa Taraki, "Enclave Micropolis: The Paradoxical Case of Ramallah/Al Bireh," *Journal of Palestine Studies* 37, no. 4 (Summer 2008): 17.

34. Sara Roy, *Hamas and Civil Society in Gaza: Engaging the Islamist Social Sector* (Princeton, NJ: Princeton University Press, 2011), 224–225.

35. In this regard see Raja Shehadah, *Palestinian Walks: Forays into a Vanishing Landscape* (New York: Scribner, 2008).

36. Norman G. Finkelstein, *This Time We Went Too Far: Truth and Consequences of the Gaza Invasion* (New York: OR Books, 2011), 66; Amos Harel, "IDF Probe: Cannot Defend Destruction of Gaza Homes," *Haaretz,* 15 February 2009.

37. Finkelstein, *This Time We Went Too Far,* 62 and 74; and Harel, "IDF Probe." There are by now many sources documenting the damage and statistics vary. See United Nations, "Report of the United Nations Fact Finding Mission on the Gaza Conflict," 25 September 2009 (The Goldstone Report); Oxfam International, "Situation Report," 10–16 May 2009 (internal document); Israeli Committee Against Home Demolitions, "Statistics on House Demolitions During Operation Cast Lead," April 2009; Physicians for Human Rights-Israel and Dan Magen, "'Ill Morals': Grave Violations of the Right to Health During the Israeli Assault on Gaza," March 2009; Human Rights Watch, "Rain of Fire: Israel's Unlawful Use of White Phosphorus in Gaza," March 2009; Palestinian Authority-Ramallah, "The Palestinian National Early Recovery and Reconstruction Plan for Gaza 2009–2010," International Conference in Support of the Palestinian Economy for the Reconstruction of Gaza, Sharm al-Sheikh, 2 March 2009; National Lawyers Guild, "Onslaught: Israel's Attack on Gaza and the Rule of Law," February 2009; Amnesty

International, "Fueling Conflict: Foreign Arms Supplies to Israel/Gaza," 23 February 2009; Defense for Children International, 7 February 2009, http://www.dci-pal.org/english/display.cfm?DocId=1056&CategoryID=1; Jan McGirk, "Gaza's Health and Humanitarian Situation Remains Fragile," *Lancet,* 4 February 2009; and various reports by the United Nations Office for the Coordination of Humanitarian Affairs. For an excellent analysis of the 2008 offensive and its impact see Finkelstein, *This Time We Went Too Far.*

38. Sara Flounders, "An Underground Economy and Resistance Symbol: The Tunnels of Gaza," *Workers World,* http://www.workers.org/2009/world/gaza_0212, 8 February 2009.

39. Internal documents from donor NGOs and other aid agencies make this clear. See also Ma'an News Agency, "Israel Opens Gaza Crossings for Aid, Fuel, Grain," 11 May 2009, http://www.maannews.net/en/index.php?opr=3DShowDetails@ID=3D37723; Dion Nissenbaum, "Israeli Ban on Sending Pasta to Gaza Illustrates Frictions," McClatchy Washington Bureau, 25 February 2009; and UN Office for the Coordination of Humanitarian Affairs (IRIN), "Israel-OPT: Gaza Children 'Afraid to Return to School,'" http://www.irinnews.org/Report.aspx?ReportID=83088, 23 February 2009.

40. Amira Hass, "Israel Bans Books, Music and Clothes from Entering Gaza," *Haaretz,* 17 May 2009, http://www.haaretz.com/hasen/objects/pages/PrintArticleEn.jhtml?itemNo=1086045. Shalit was subsequently released in October 2011 in a prisoner exchange between Israel and Hamas.

41. United Nations Population Fund, Programme of Assistance to the Palestinian People, "Gaza Crisis—Impact on Reproductive Health, Especially Maternal and Newborn Health and Obstetric Care" (draft report), 10 February 2009, 1.

42. UN Office for the Coordination of Humanitarian Affairs, "Israel-OPT: Gaza Children 'Afraid to Return to School.'"

43. World Bank, "Palestinian Economic Prospects: Gaza Recovery and West Bank Revival," 6.

6. The Legal Trajectory of the Palestinian Refugee Issue

From Exclusion to Ambiguity

SUSAN MUSARRAT AKRAM

At the end of 2011, out of a total Palestinian population of about 11.2 million persons, some 7.4 million were refugees or internally displaced.[1] The Palestinian people constitute one of the largest and longest-standing unresolved situations of displacement in the world; about one in three refugees worldwide is Palestinian.[2] Given the size and protracted nature of this refugee flow, one would imagine that a great deal of energy would be expended on adapting international legal principles to craft a durable solution for this problem. Instead, it is often said that the Palestinian refugee problem is unique, that existing principles are inapplicable, that existing legal instruments do not cover Palestinian refugees, and hence that the problem is intractable.[3]

Since the drafting of the Universal Declaration of Human Rights in 1945, both widespread state practice and a codified body of law have developed that address almost every aspect of refugee and displaced persons' rights.[4] A central premise is that all refugees, without distinction, have certain rights, and that states have concomitant obligations to respect, protect, and implement those rights. The core legal principles applicable in the search for durable solutions for mass refugee flows are: the right to return to one's home and place of origin in safety; the right to voluntarily choose among available resettlement options; the right to full restitution of property left behind; and the right to compensation for loss or damage to refugee property.[5] The right to protection for refugees and stateless persons, and the engagement of the international community in providing the benefits that are lost from failure of national protection, have been spelled out in explicit terms in several of the most widely ratified treaties that exist today, including the 1951 Refugee Convention and the 1954 Convention on Stateless Persons.[6] These treaties broaden the fundamental customary international law rights of return and restitution, incorporate what are considered binding international definitions of refugees and stateless persons, and expand international obligations to implement fundamental refugee and stateless persons' rights.[7]

These rights have not only been codified in widely ratified treaties, they have also been increasingly incorporated in peace agreements all over the world accompanying solutions for mass refugee flows. Peace agreements in the former Yugoslav states of Kosovo, Croatia, and Bosnia-Herzegovina recognize and implement refugee return and property restitution.[8] The same is true for peace agreements concerning Georgia; Tajikistan; the multistate CIREFCA agreement of Central America involving Guatemala, El Salvador, Honduras, and Mexico; and many African agreements such as in Sierra Leone, Rwanda, Burundi, Mozambique, and Liberia.[9] In Liberia, Angola, Rwanda, Georgia, Myanmar, Mozambique, Zimbabwe, Afghanistan, Iran, the Democratic Republic of Congo, Guatemala, Abkhazia, and the Russian Federation, negotiated agreements specifically require that refugees and displaced persons are to be permitted to return to their homes or former places of residence.[10] These and other agreements recognize and implement property restitution, including those for Bosnia, Kosovo, Cambodia, Guatemala, Mozambique, Rwanda, Croatia, Burundi, and Georgia.[11] These agreements not only spell out legal rights but also create implementing mechanisms to make the rights a reality. As Scott Leckie of the Center on Housing Rights and Evictions (COHRE) has remarked, "During the past two decades millions of people throughout the world have been able to formally exercise their housing, land, and property restitution rights and return home, from Tajikistan to Kosovo, from Mozambique to Liberia, and from Bosnia-Herzegovina to South Africa and beyond."[12] At the same time, there has been increased attention to addressing root causes of displacement, with an emphasis on restorative and sometimes retributive justice and security as essential elements of the durability of solutions.[13] This is not to say that such refugee solutions are perfect, or that they are always respected, or that the solutions always remain durable. The point is that in these cases there is greater attention to and awareness of the core rights and obligations that must be part of any postconflict refugee plan. In other words, there is a renewed focus on framing political solutions on rights grounded in international law.[14]

In sharp contrast is the Palestinian refugee case. Despite the development of a significant body of as-yet-unimplemented law on Palestinian refugee rights, the Palestinian case is characterized by exclusions. Exclusion clauses specifically directed at Palestinians appear in the major rights treaties and international agency mandates. The right of return, housing and property rights, and the principle that refugees should be permitted to choose their own solution have all been systematically excluded from the framework for discussion about solutions.[15] And issues like restorative and retributive justice or truth and reconciliation are not even on the horizon in plans for the end of conflict.[16]

Christine Bell's statement that "the Israel/Palestinian peace agreements demonstrate an almost complete divorce between the concept of peace and the concept of justice" could not be more apt.[17] Throughout the various peace negotiations and agreements between the Israelis and Palestinians, the core international legal principles governing refugee rights have been singularly absent. Over time, the most that can be said is that the principles of exclusion characterizing the Palestinian refugee case evolved into principles of ambiguity in the last unofficial negotiations, but with the same result: absolving the parties of incorporating rights and justice in the framework for resolution.

Thus, in contrast to the plethora of peace agreements requiring implementation of core refugee rights, the various negotiated arrangements (commonly called "agreements" in the Palestine-Israel situation), from Oslo to the Road Map, either omit any references to Palestinian or to international human rights law in general, or replace the understood international framework with a political framework that distorts the legal requirements themselves.[18] I will review how international law on individual Palestinian refugee rights has played out through the main negotiation processes and agreements, omitting discussion of proposals that were not substantive negotiations, such as the Arab Peace Initiative of 2002.

The Oslo Process

Although the Madrid negotiations preceded the Oslo process, Madrid did not result in any agreements, though its Letter of Invitation laid out a framework for the opening conference as well as for future bilateral and multi-lateral negotiations, and affirmed that negotiations would be based on UN Resolutions 242 and 338—the relevance of which will be discussed below. It is important to note that to date, the only real "agreements" reached on the Palestinian-Israeli conflict resulted from the Oslo process, but these are only interim and not final agreements or final peace treaties. A series of documents resulted from the Oslo process, but the most important ones concerning the key issues and claims were the 1993 Declaration of Principles (DOP), the 1994 Gaza-Jericho Agreement, and the 1995 Interim Agreement between Israel and the PLO.[19] In all of these instruments, there are limited references to human rights.

The 1993 Declaration of Principles, the initial framework agreement between the parties, states that its purpose is to recognize mutual legitimate and political rights to achieve a "just, lasting and comprehensive peace settlement and historic reconciliation through the agreed political process."[20] There is no reference to what will define the "legitimate rights" involved, let alone reference to any of the key instruments or customary law on refugee rights. The 1994 Gaza-Jericho Agreement refers generally to "internationally-accepted norms and principles of human rights" as governing the "powers and responsibilities" of the parties, but without any specification of what norms or rights apply, and without reference to treaties or UN Charter obligations.[21] In the 1995 Interim Agreement, there is a reference to "rights," but the only legal rights specified are those concerning government and absentee property acquired by *Israelis* in the Occupied Territories. This provision requires Palestinians to respect these rights; no parallel rights are recognized for Palestinian refugee or absentee property acquired by Israel, or any other individual Palestinian rights.[22] Both the Interim Agreement and the 1998 Wye River Memorandum imply that internationally accepted norms are subject to the agreements themselves, rather than that the agreements are governed by applicable international law, which is what law requires.[23]

Concerning key refugee rights, the Oslo process postponed discussion of the refugee issue until the final stage, which to date has never materialized. Thus, the main rights discussed above were not referenced at all.[24] However, the lack of commitment to an international legal framework as the reference for negotiations can be seen as a critical reason for the failure of the entire Oslo enterprise.[25]

Camp David and Taba

The talks at Camp David in 2000, though the subject of extensive publicity, did not result in any agreements. However, the parties did issue a trilateral statement reaffirming that the negotiations aimed at achieving "a just and lasting peace" were based on UN Security Council (UNSC) Resolutions 242 and 338.[26] Far more extensive were the negotiations between PLO and Israeli officials in January 2001 in Taba, Egypt. The Taba Summit resulted in two separate draft proposals published by the parties.[27] The proposals, one by the Palestinians and one by the Israelis, reflect a much deeper discussion of the Palestinian refugee issue than in prior negotiations, but also reflect two dramatically different approaches to refugee rights and legal principles.

The Palestinian proposal reflects a sophisticated understanding of the international law of Palestinian refugee rights and incorporates a sound legal framework, a refugee definition, mechanisms and modalities for implementing durable solutions for the refugees, and an "end of claims" clause.[28] The Palestinian proposal is consistent with the framework and principles underlying UN General Assembly (UNGA) Resolution 194, the core UN resolution incorporating refugee rights for the Palestinians, international law, and practice on refugee rights.[29] It focuses on the voluntary choice of the refugee to decide to return to home or land within 1948 Israeli borders, or to choose from available resettlement options. The Palestinian proposal discusses Israel's moral and legal responsibility for forced displacement and dispossession of Palestinian refugees in 1948 and for preventing their return.[30]

The Israeli proposal, called a "private non-paper draft," responded to the Palestinian proposal, and includes the Israeli narrative on the Palestinian refugee issue, a framework for a solution and a mechanism for implementation, modalities for compensation and rehabilitation, a special clause for Jewish refugees, and an "end of claims" clause. It does not have a refugee definition.[31] The five options set out in the Israeli proposal are: a limited number of refugees "returning" to Israel; a land swap; resettlement primarily in a Palestinian state; rehabilitation in Arab host countries; and some resettlement in third states.[32] The Israeli proposal does not acknowledge Israel's direct responsibility for the refugee issue or for implementing durable solutions, but states that Israel has indirect responsibility along with "all those parties directly or indirectly responsible."[33] The Israeli response is, in essence, a political framework, inconsistent with Resolution 194, in that although it lists five options for a solution, the solution is driven by Israel's concern for preservation of an institutionalized Jewish-privileged state including Jewish control of land, rather than implementation of individual refugee choice to return and obtain restitution of Palestinian property.[34]

The Geneva Initiative

The Geneva Initiative, a private, nongovernmental initiative made public in October 2003, much like the Israeli response in the Taba negotiations, reverses the international law framework.[35] The key UN resolutions referenced in Geneva are UNSC Resolutions 242 and 338. In Article 7 of Geneva, the main provision on refugees, the drafters state that "the parties recognize that UNGAR 194, UNSC Resolution 242, and the Arab Peace Initiative . . . concerning the rights of the Palestinian refugees represent the basis for resolving the refugee issue, and agree that these rights are fulfilled according to Article 7 of this Agreement."[36] In the Preamble, the drafters likewise reiterate their commitment to UNSC Resolutions 242 and 338 and state that "this Agreement is based on, will lead to, and—by its fulfillment—will constitute the full implementation of these resolutions."[37] In other words, 194, 242, and 338 mean what the drafters interpret them to mean, rather than what international legal consensus and state practice say they mean.

Article 7 presents five options for the refugees. They include "return" to "the state of Palestine," areas in Israel to be transferred to Palestine in a land swap, third-country resettlement, and limited "return" to Israel in a total number that Israel agrees to accept—but the latter would be part of a formula incorporating the fifth option, in which the largest proportion will be required to be resettled in third states and absorbed in Arab host states.[38] Although the return provision states that the solution process for refugees "shall entail an act of informed choice," the real choice of return at refugee discretion is not part of the formula.[39] Rather, property compensation is discussed and a mechanism for compensation through an International Commission is described. Israel would agree to a single "lump sum" contribution to an international fund, which would be the total accepted Israeli liability for the Palestinian refugee problem. Property of Israeli settlers left in the Occupied Territories would be used to offset Israeli payments to this fund. Israel would also contribute to a "refugeehood" fund to be distributed to refugee communities for development, but the details of this fund were never made public.[40]

The Road Map for Peace

In contrast to Taba and the Geneva efforts, the latest intergovernmental initiative, the Quartet's Performance-Based Road Map for Peace, issued in April 2003, does not refer to international law on individual refugee rights or to any outside framework besides what the parties agree upon.[41] The Road Map was preceded by a speech given on 24 June 2002 by President George W. Bush in which he called for a Palestinian state.[42] The Road Map attempts to provide conditions for realizing its creation and "propose[s] a phased time-table, putting the establishment of security before a final settlement. It is designed to create confidence, leading to final status talks."[43]

The Road Map, like Oslo, refers to the refugees as part of the third and final phase, when the parties are to "reach a final and comprehensive permanent status agreement that ends the Israel-Palestinian conflict in 2005, through a settlement negotiated between the parties based on UNSC Resolutions 242, 338, and 1397, that ends the occupation that began in 1967, and includes an agreed, just, fair, and realistic solution to the refugee issue."[44] The three Security Council resolutions referenced do not address any of the individual refugee rights at all. The language of 242 (para. 2), "Affirm[ing] further the necessity . . . For achieving a just settlement of the refugee problem," is simply recalled in 338 and 1397.[45] Although there is an argument that this language, by implication, must refer back to 194 because that is the international consensus for the resolution of the refugee problem, and this may have been the PLO's assumption, it is clearly not Israel's assumption or intention.[46] The absence of any reference to 194 appears quite deliberate.

These three resolutions—242 (1967), 338 (1973), and 1397 (2002)—set out an exchange solution, "land for peace," that is considered the basis of the two-state solution incorporated into 1397 as "a vision of a region where two States, Israel and Palestine, live side by side within secure and recognized borders."[47] This formula, however, leaves out the individual rights of Palestinians as refugees to return, restitution, and compensation, and appears to incorporate a trade-off between the "right" to a state and individual rights.[48] All of the negotiation processes thus far have been based on the formula of two ethno-national states in the Mandate Palestine area. Under such a plan, the refugees would be resettled in a future state of Palestine in the West Bank, Gaza, and East Jerusalem. As there is no explicit reference to the rights of Palestinian refugees and displaced persons to return to their homes or to housing and property restitution as understood under international law, the settlement of the refugee question could thus be based on some notion of humanitarian/political considerations, not legal principles.

Israeli Unilateral Withdrawal from Gaza

The last supposed gesture toward a peace plan was the unilateral Israeli withdrawal from Gaza in August 2005, with the claim that this effectively terminated Israeli occupation there. Under Israel's Revised Disengagement Plan of 6 June 2004, passed by the Knesset, Israel claimed that its intentions in withdrawing were to "dispel the claims regarding Israel's responsibility for the Palestinians within the Gaza Strip."[49] However, under the Disengagement Plan, Israel maintains the right to guard and monitor all of the external borders of Gaza, including Gazan airspace and coastal waters. Further, Israel reserves the right to use force of any kind in the Gaza Strip.[50] Under accepted legal consensus, an occupation terminates when the effective control of the occupier has ceased.[51] The cessation of occupation presupposes that sovereignty returns to the legitimate occupant, and the occupant can exercise self-determination and independence. None of these criteria are met in the situation in Gaza, and the continued and effective sealing-off of people and goods into and out of Gaza confirms that Israel remains firmly in control of the territory.[52] Moreover, as to the divestment of responsibility in Gaza, Israel's unilateral actions of formal withdrawal violate the language and intent of numerous provisions of the Oslo Agreements. For example, the 1995 Israel-PLO Interim Agreement on the West Bank and Gaza Strip states that "neither side shall initiate or take any step that will change the status of the West Bank and the Gaza Strip pending the outcome of the permanent status negotiations."[53] Nor is unilateral withdrawal consistent with Article I.1 of the Interim Agreement, which requires Israel to transfer powers and responsibilities to the Palestinian Council (the permanent successor to the Palestinian Authority), and until such time as that takes place, continue to exercise such powers and responsibilities itself.[54] Although Hamas has de facto, and possibly de jure, powers in Gaza, it is not the recognized sovereign or successor to the Palestinian Authority that can inherit the powers and responsibilities of the Oslo Agreements.[55] Although the Oslo Agreements have been materially breached by both sides, neither Israel nor the PLO has repudiated them, so provisions that can be executed remain the obligation of the parties.[56] Israel's obligations to respect and protect the Gazan population and territory as an occupying power under the Hague and Fourth Geneva Conventions should remain in force.[57]

Israel's other goal in withdrawal from Gaza is stated in Principle 3 of the Revised Disengagement Plan: "In any future permanent status arrangement, there will be no Israeli towns and villages in the Gaza Strip. On the other hand, it is clear that in the West Bank, there are areas which will be part of the State of Israel, including major Israeli population centers, cities, towns and villages, security areas, and other places of special interest to Israel."[58] The goal of dividing the territory over which Palestinians have a right to self-determination and a sovereign state runs afoul of customary law that requires that a single territorial unit for a people's self-determination must not be dismembered.[59] In the Declaration of Principles and the Interim Agreement on the West Bank and Gaza Strip, Israel and the PLO agreed that the West Bank and Gaza were a "single territorial unit . . . whose integrity is to be preserved pending the conclusion of permanent status negotiations."[60]

The recognition of Palestine as a non-member observer state by the UN General Assembly on 29 November 2012 has not materially changed this assessment of the legal framework applicable to the negotiated agreements and peace "process" between Israel and the Palestinians to date. The resolution requesting non-member observer statehood recognition references UNGA Resolution 194(III) in its preamble, and lists refugees, borders, settlements, Jerusalem, water, and security among the issues to be resolved in final status talks. At the same time, the resolution refers to the Arab Peace Initiative of 2002 as the basis for a "just and agreed upon" solution for the Palestinian refugees, rather than Resolution 194 as the framework for resolution. The Arab Peace Initiative's "agreed upon" language returns to the negotiation framework driven by Israel's Jewish-preferencing discussed above, and not to a legal framework.[61]

This brief mapping of the legal story of post-1948 Palestinian refugee rights shows that law has not served the Palestinians well—and not because of any paucity of applicable legal principles to their claims. The political project has been one of sustained and vigorous efforts to preclude the application of the plethora of legal rights and obligations that apply to the resolution of the conflict and the refugee problem—first through exclusion, and then through deliberate ambiguity. This story is one of the emasculation of legal rights, meaning rights devoid of content—an exercise in symbolism that fools the uninformed, but brings the parties no closer to a lasting peace than they have been for the last six decades.

Notes

The author thanks Boston University law students Robert Guth and Amber Camio for their excellent research assistance on this chapter. It could not have been completed without them.

1. BADIL Resource Center for Palestinian Residency and Refugee Rights, *Survey of Palestinian Refugees and Internally Displaced Persons: 2010-2012* (Bethlehem: BADIL, 2012), 2 (hereafter BADIL, 2010-2012 Survey). According to UNRWA, 4,797,723 Palestinian refugees were registered in its "area of operation" (West Bank, Gaza, Jordan, Syria, and Lebanon) as of 1 January 2012 (UNRWA Statistics, http://www.unrwa.org/etemplate.php?id=253).

2. Terry Rempel, "Housing and Property Restitution: The Palestinian Refugee Case," in *Returning Home: Housing and Property Restitution Rights of Refugees and Displaced Persons,* ed. Scott Leckie (Ardsley, NY: Transnational, 2003), 275.

3. See, e.g., Donna E. Arzt, *Refugees into Citizens* (New York: Council on Foreign Relations Press, 1997), 64, arguing that Israel can justly deprive right of return based on national security concerns; Marc Zell and Sonia Shnyder, "Palestinian Right of Return or Strategic Weapon?: A Historical, Legal and Moral-Political Analysis," *Nexus: a Journal of Opinion* 8 (2003): 100–104, arguing that repatriating Palestinian refugees is neither practical nor obligatory during Israel's state of public emergency; Joel Singer, "No Palestinian 'Return' to Israel," *ABA Journal* 87, no. 2 (2001): 14, arguing that once the PLO agreed to a two-state partition, Palestinians as a people forfeited claims to return to the Jewish state of Israel.

4. For further analysis of the development of the right of return and restitution in customary international law see John B. Quigley, "Repatriation of Displaced Palestinians as a Legal Right," *Nexus: a Journal of Opinion* (2003): 17, 18–19; Terry Rempel, "Housing and Property Restitution," 275, 308–311; Eric Rosand, "The Right to Return Under International Law Following Mass Dislocation: The Bosnia Precedent?," *Michigan Journal of International Law* 19 (Summer 1998): 1121–1139. See also Scott Leckie, ed., *Housing, Land, and Property Restitution Rights of Refugees and Displaced Persons* (Cambridge: Cambridge University Press, 2007), covering the breadth of black-letter and soft law, including conventions, peace agreements, declarations, and guiding principles, codifying and expanding the law on refugee and displaced persons' rights.

5. United Nations High Commissioner for Refugees (UNHCR) Executive Committee (EXCOM) Conclusion No. 67 (XLII), Resettlement as an Instrument of Protection (1991); UNHCR EXCOM Conclusion No. 40 (XXXVI), Voluntary Re-

patriation (1985); UNHCR EXCOM Conclusion No. 18 (XXXVI), Voluntary Repatriation (1980); UNHCR EXCOM Conclusion No. 15 (XXX), Refugees without an Asylum Country (1979); UNHCR EXCOM Conclusion No. 5 (XXVIII), Asylum (1977).

6. Convention relating to the Status of Stateless Persons (CSSP), 28 September 1954, 360 U.N.T.S. 117; Convention relating to the Status of Refugees (CSR), 28 July 1951, 189 U.N.T.S. 137.

7. For example, the well-established right of restitution was complemented by provisions that required states to recognize the refugee's right to own property, protected property claims by disregarding the refugee period for purposes of continuity of use and ownership, and guaranteed the refugee's right to consolidate property by transferring assets into and out of the state of refuge. CSSP, at arts. 10, 13, 14, 30; CSR, at arts. 10, 13, 14, 30. The right of return was complemented by a prohibition of involuntary return by the state of refuge (*refoulement*). CSR, at art. 33. See also Susan M. Akram and Terry Rempel, "Recommendations for Durable Solutions for Palestinian Refugees: A Challenge to the Oslo Framework," *Palestine Yearbook of International Law* 11, no. 1 (2000–2001): 9–15. For examples of these principles incorporated into peace agreements, see infra notes 8, 9, and 10, and accompanying text.

8. Protocol on Voluntary and Sustainable Return, Kosovo-Serb.-UN Interim Admin. in Kosovo, art. 1, 6 June 2006, http://www.unmikonline.org/pio/returns /Protocol-on-returns-eng.pdf; General Framework Agreement on Peace in Bosnia-Herzegovina (Dayton Peace Agreement), annex 7, ch. 1, art. 1, 14 December 1995, http://www.unhcr.org/refworld/docid/3de497992.html; Basic Agreement on the Region of Eastern Slavonia, Baranja, and Western Sirmium (The Erdut Agreement), paras. 9, 12, November 1995, as reprinted in Leckie, *Housing, Land, and Property Restitution Rights*, 37.

9. Comprehensive Peace Agreement between the Government of Liberia and Liberians United for Reconciliation and Democracy and the Movement for Democracy in Liberia and Political Parties, 18 August 2003, as reprinted in Leckie, *Housing, Land, and Property Restitution Rights*, 43; Arusha Peace and Reconciliation Agreement for Burundi, Protocol 4, ch. 1, art. 2, 28 August 2000, as reprinted in Leckie, *Housing, Land, and Property Restitution Rights*, 39; Tajikistan General Agreement on the Establishment of Peace and National Accord, Protocol on Refugee Issues, 27 June 1997, as reprinted in Leckie, *Housing, Land, and Property Restitution Rights*, 37; Tripartite Agreement on the Voluntary Repatriation of Rwandese Refugees from Tanzania, 12 April 1995, as reprinted in Leckie, *Housing, Land, and Property Restitution Rights*, 51; Tripartite Agreement between the Government of the Republic of Mozambique, the Government of Zimbabwe, and UN-HCR for the Voluntary Repatriation of Mozambican Refugees from Zimbabwe, 22 March 1993, http://www.unhcr.org/refworld/docid/3ee884a74.html; Declaration and Concerted Plan of Action in Favor of Central American Refugees, Returnees, and Displaced Persons, 31 May 1989, UN Doc. CIREFCA/89/14.

10. Scott Leckie, "New Directions in Housing and Property Restitution," in *Returning Home*, 3, 13–14.

11. The most detailed return and property restitution agreement for refugees and other returnees can be found in Annex VII of the Dayton Accords of 1995, in which the return of all property is a core requirement. Implementation of Dayton is particularly interesting because, to date, no compensation has been paid for property because all refugee property has been ordered restituted, with a primary focus on accommodating secondary occupants in other places rather than frustrating restitution to the original owners. See Paul Prettitore, "The Right to Housing and Property Restitution in Bosnia and Herzegovina: A Case Study," BADIL Resource Center for Palestinian Residency and Refugee Rights Working Paper No. 1, 2003.

12. Leckie, ed., *Housing, Land, and Property Restitution Rights,* xix.

13. "Recognizing that host States have the primary responsibility for the protection of and assistance to refugees on their territory, and the need to redouble efforts to develop and implement comprehensive durable solution strategies . . . [and] emphasizing that States have the primary responsibility to provide protection and assistance to internally displaced persons within their jurisdiction, as well as to address the root causes of the displacement problem." See G. A. Res. 63/149, paras. 6–7, UN Doc. A/RES/63/149, 18 December 2008; "Recogniz[ing] the importance of achieving durable solutions to refugee problems and . . . the need to address in this process the root causes of refugee movements in order to avert new flows of refugees . . . welcom[ing] the efforts under way, in cooperation with countries hosting refugees and countries of origin . . . to promote a framework for durable solutions, particularly in protracted refugee situations, which includes an approach to sustainable and timely return which encompasses repatriation, reintegration, rehabilitation and reconstruction activities." See G.A. Res. 63/148, paras. 18–19, UN Doc. A/RES/63/148, 18 December . . . 2008; "Emphasizing that States have the primary responsibility to provide protection and assistance to internally displaced persons within their jurisdiction as well as to address the root causes of the displacement problem . . . [and] noting the growing awareness of the international community of . . . the urgency of addressing the root causes of their displacement and finding durable solutions, including voluntary return in safety and with dignity, or local integration." See G. A. Res. 62/153, paras. 4–5, UN Doc. A/RES/62/153, 18 December 2007.

14. "Recognizing that the human rights machinery of the United Nations, including the mechanisms of the Commission on Human Rights and the human rights treaty bodies, has important capabilities to address human rights violations that cause movements of refugees and displaced persons or prevent durable solutions to their plight." See G. A. Res. 56/166, para. 10, UN Doc. A/RES/56/166, 19 December 2001; "Not[ing] that the Executive Committee . . . has specifically acknowledged the direct relationship between the observance of human rights standards, refugee movements, problems of protection and solutions." See G. A. Res. 48/139, para. 6, UN Doc. A/RES/48/139, 20 December 1993; "Emphasizing the need for States to assist the High Commissioner in her efforts to find durable and timely solutions to the problems of refugees based on new approaches that . . . are built on respect for fundamental freedoms and human rights and internationally agreed

protection principles and concerns." See G. A. Res. 47/105, para. 8, UN Doc. A/
RES/47/105, 16 December 1992; "Recognizing that the promotion of fundamental human rights is essential to the achievement of self-sufficiency and family security for refugees, as well as to the process of re-establishing the dignity of the human person and realizing durable solutions to refugee problems." See G. A. Res.
44/137, para. 10, UN Doc. A/RES/44/137, 15 December 1989. See also "Report of the
Representative of the Secretary-General on the Human Rights of Internally Displaced Persons," para. 2, UN Doc. A/62/227, 13 August 2007, explaining that the report details the activities of the Representative of the Secretary General, including "pursu[ing] dialogue with Governments and with regional organizations and
United Nations agencies in a common effort to ensure better mainstreaming of the
human rights of internally displaced persons into their activities"; UNHCR, "UN-
HCR Response to the Three Evaluations/Assessment of Refugee Women, Children
and the Community Services Function," para. 5, 8, May 2003, http://www.unhcr
.org/402211734.pdf, discussing UNHCR's increased focus on a rights-based approach for protection of displaced persons, including their Agenda for Protection,
which "has set out the strategic framework for UNHCR, Governments and NGOs
to address the international protection of refugees in a systematic way, informed
by international human rights law"; UNHCR Agenda for Protection, UN Doc A/
AC.96/965/Add.1, 26 June 2002.

   15. For further analysis of the "protection gap" and the instruments and agencies that create it, see Susan Akram and Terry Rempel, "Temporary Protection as
an Instrument for Implementing the Right of Return for Palestinian Refugees,"
Boston University International Law Journal 22, no. 1 (2004): 53–86; Susan Akram,
"Palestinian Refugees and their Legal Status: Rights, Politics, and Implications for
a Just Solution," *Journal of Palestine Studies* 31, no. 3 (Spring 2002): 36; Lex Takken-
berg, *The Status of Palestinian Refugees in International Law* (Oxford: Oxford University Press, 1998), 277–317. See also UNHCR, *State of the World's Refugees 2006:
Human Displacement in the New Millennium* (Oxford: Oxford University Press,
2006), 112–113, Box 5.1, discussing Palestinian refugees and the protection gap;
UNHCR, "Note on the Applicability of Article 1D of the 1951 Convention Relating
to the Status of Refugees to Palestinian Refugees," 2 October 2002, http://www
.unhcr.org/refworld/pdfid/3da192be4.pdf; G. A. Res. 39/99, para. 1, UN Doc. A/
Res/39/99, 14 December 1984, calling on the UN Secretary General in consultation
with the UNRWA "to undertake effective measures to guarantee the safety and security and the legal and human rights of the Palestine refugees in all the territories
under Israeli occupation in 1967 and thereafter."

   16. Public International Law and Policy Group, *Human Rights and Fundamental Freedoms, Peace Agreement Drafter's Handbook,* June 2005, summarizing the
core rights incorporated in all peace agreements, incorporated in national laws,
subject to monitoring, and part of truth and reconciliation mechanisms, http://
www.pilpg.org/areas/peacebuilding/peacehandbook/humanrights05.pdf; Public
International Law and Policy Group, *Refugee Return, Peace Agreement Drafter's
Handbook,* June 2005, summarizing five elements found in most agreements on
refugee return, including a preamble, definitions, language guaranteeing parties'

cooperation in the resettlement of refugees, language enumerating refugee rights, and language detailing the implementation process, http://www.pilpg.org/areas /peacebuilding/peacehandbook/refugeereturn.pdf; Public International Law and Policy Group, *Economic Restructuring, Peace Agreement Drafter's Handbook*, June 2005, summarizing eleven basic elements found in agreements on economic restructuring, based on language from prior agreements and including a section on reparations, http://www.pilpg.org/areas/peacebuilding/peacehandbook /econrest.pdf.

17. Christine Bell, *Peace Agreements and Human Rights* (Oxford: Oxford University Press, 2000), 205.

18. Following is a list of peace "negotiations" and agreements to date: Geneva Accord, Draft Permanent Status Agreement, October 2003, Isr.-PLO, reprinted in M. Cherif Bassiouni, ed., *Documents on the Arab-Israeli Conflict: The Palestinians and the Israeli-Palestinian Peace Process* (Ardsley, NY: Transnational, 2005), 1223 (hereafter Geneva Accord); Statement by the Quartet, New York, 26 September 2003, reprinted in Bassiouni, ed., *Documents*, 1221; Statement by the Quartet, Jordan, 22 June 2003, reprinted in Bassiouni, ed., *Documents*, 1220; Israel's Response to the Road Map, 25 May 2003, reprinted in Bassiouni, ed., *Documents*, 1218; A Performance-Based Road Map to a Permanent Two-state Solution to the Israeli-Palestinian Conflict, 15 October 2002, UN SCOR, Annex, UN Doc. S/2003/529, 2003, reprinted in Bassiouni, ed., *Documents*, 1214 (hereafter the Road Map); Nusseibeh-Ayalon Agreement, 6 August 2002, reprinted in Bassiouni, ed., *Documents*, 1211; Arab Peace Initiative Established at the Arab League Summit, 28 March 2002, reprinted in Bassiouni, ed., *Documents*, 1205; European Union Non-Paper on the Taba Conference, 2002, reprinted in Bassiouni, ed., *Documents*, 1169 (hereafter EU Non-Paper); Palestinian-Israeli Security Implementation Work Plan (Tenet Cease-Fire Plan), 14 June 2001, reprinted in Bassiouni, ed., *Documents*, 1202; Israeli-Palestinian Joint Statement of the Status Negotiations between Israel and the Palestinian Authority at Taba, 27 January 2001, reprinted in Bassiouni, ed., *Documents*, 1168 (hereafter Taba Joint Statement); Israeli Private Response to the Palestinian Refugee Proposal of 22 January 2001, "Non-Paper—Draft 2," 23 January 2001, Taba, reprinted in BADIL, *Occasional Bulletin No. 10 Annex*, http://www .badil.org/Publications/Bulletins/Bulletin-10a.htm (hereafter Israeli Non-Paper); Palestinian Proposal on Palestinian Refugees, 22 January 2001, Taba, reprinted in BADIL, *Occasional Bulletin No. 10 Annex*, http://www.badil.org/Publications /Bulletins/Bulletin-10a.htm (hereafter Palestinian Proposal); Trilateral Statement on the Middle East Peace Summit at Camp David (Camp David II), 25 July 2000, reprinted in Bassiouni, ed., *Documents*, 1159; Protocol Concerning Safe Passage between the West Bank and the Gaza Strip, 5 October 1999, Isr.-PLO, reprinted in Bassiouni, ed., *Documents*, 1153; Sharm el-Sheikh Memorandum, 4 September 1999, reprinted in Bassiouni, ed., *Documents*, 1149; Wye River Memorandum, 23 October 1998, Isr.-PLO, 37 I.L.M. 1251, reprinted in Bassiouni, ed., *Documents*, 1139; Protocol Concerning the Redeployment in Hebron between Israel and the PLO, 17 January 1997, reprinted in Bassiouni, ed., *Documents*, 1130; Agreement on Temporary International Presence in the City of Hebron, 9 May 1996, Isr.-PLO, 36 I.L.M.

650, reprinted in Bassiouni, ed., *Documents,* 1128; Final Statement, Summit of the Peacemakers at Sharm el-Sheikh, 13 March 1996, UN GAOR, 51st Sess., UN Doc. A/51/9, 1996, reprinted in Bassiouni, ed., *Documents,* 1124; Barcelona Declaration, Adopted at the Euro-Mediterranean Conference, 27–28 November 1995, reprinted in Bassiouni, ed., *Documents,* 1110; Framework for the Conclusion of a Final Status Agreement between Israel and the PLO (Beilin-Abu Mazen Document), 31 October 1995, reprinted in Bassiouni, ed., *Documents,* 1101; Interim Agreement on the West Bank and the Gaza Strip (Oslo II), 28 September 1995, Isr.-PLO, UN GAOR, 51st Sess., Agenda Item 10, Annex, UN Doc. A/51/889, 1997, reprinted in Bassiouni, ed. *Documents,* 975 (hereafter Interim Agreement); Agreement on Preparatory Transfer of Powers and Responsibilities, 29 August 1994, Isr.-PLO, reprinted in Bassiouni, ed., *Documents,* 954; Letters Exchanged between PLO Chairman Yasir Arafat and Prime Minister Yitzhak Rabin following the Signing of the Gaza-Jericho Agreement, 4 May 1994, reprinted in Bassiouni, ed., *Documents,* 950; Agreement on the Gaza Strip and the Jericho Area, 4 May 1994, Isr.-PLO, UN GAOR, 49th Sess., Annex, UN Doc. A/49/180, 1994, reprinted in Bassiouni, ed., *Documents,* 917 (hereafter the Gaza-Jericho Agreement); Protocol on Economic Relations between the Government of Israel and the PLO, 29 April 1994, reprinted in Bassiouni, ed., *Documents,* 899; Joint Statement following the First Meeting of the Israeli-Palestinian Economic Cooperation Committee, 17 November 1993, reprinted in Bassiouni, ed., *Documents,* 898; Declaration of Principles on Interim Self-Government Arrangements between Israel and the PLO, 13 September 1993, reprinted in Bassiouni, ed. *Documents,* 890 (hereafter Declaration of Principles); Letters Exchanged between PLO Chairman Yasir Arafat and Israeli Prime Minister Yitzhak Rabin Concerning Israel-PLO Recognition, 9 September 1993, reprinted in Bassiouni, ed., *Documents,* 888; Geneva Initiative Letter of Invitation to the Madrid Peace Conference, Issued by the United States and the Union of the Soviet Socialist Republics, 30 October 1991, reprinted in Bassiouni, ed., *Documents,* 88 (hereafter Letter of Invitation).

19. Interim Agreement; Gaza-Jericho Agreement; Declaration of Principles.

20. Declaration of Principles, pmbl.

21. Gaza-Jericho Agreement, art. 14.

22. Interim Agreement, art. 20, *passim.*

23. Lynn Welchman, "The Role of International Law and Human Rights in Peacemaking and Crafting Durable Solutions for Refugees," BADIL Resource Center for Palestinian Residency and Refugee Rights Working Paper No. 3, 2003, http://www.badil.org/Publications/Legal_Papers/WorkingPapers/WP-E-03.pdf. For a more detailed discussion of how international legal obligations such as the right to return have become bargaining chips in these peace agreements, see Bell, *Peace Agreements and Human Rights.*

24. See pages 1–5 in Bell, *Peace Agreements and Human Rights,* discussing the core refugee rights of return, property restitution, and compensation.

25. For unofficial/independent commentary see Nadim Shehadi, "Palestinian Refugees: The Regional Perspective," Chatham House Briefing Paper, April 2009; Rex Brynen, "The Past as Prelude? Negotiating the Palestinian Refugee Issue," Cha-

tham House Briefing Paper, June 2008; Haydar ʿAbd al-Shafi and Rashid Khalidi, "Looking Back, Looking Forward," *Journal of Palestine Studies* 32, no. 1 (Autumn 2002): 28; Rashid Khalidi, "Toward a Clear Palestinian Strategy," *Journal of Palestine Studies* 31, no. 4 (Summer 2002): 5; Jeff Halper, "No Return to Oslo," Palestine Center Information Brief, 5 October 2001, http://www.thejerusalemfund.org/ht /display/ContentDetails/i/2102/pid/2254; Rex Brynen, "Much Ado About Nothing? The Refugee Working Group and the Perils of Multilateral Quasi-negotiation," *International Negotiations* 2, no. 2 (November 1997); Center for Policy Analysis on Palestine, "Oslo's Final Status and the Future of the Middle East," August 1997; Omar M. Dajani, "Stalled Between Seasons: The International Legal Status of Palestine During the Interim Period," *Denver Journal of International Law and Policy* 26 (1997): 27; Abdel Monem, Said Aly, Rashid I. Khalidi, Ian S. Lustick, Camille Mansour, Moshe Maʿoz, Anthony Parsons et al., "Reflections on the Peace Process and a Durable Settlement: A Roundup of Views," *Journal of Palestine Studies* 26, no. 1 (Autumn 1996): 5, 7–9, 12–14; Eyal Benvenisti and Eyal Zamir, "Private Claims to Property Rights in the Future Israeli-Palestinian Settlement," *American Journal of International Law* 89 (1995): 295. For government commentary see Israel Ministry of Foreign Affairs, "Major PLO Violations of the Oslo Accords," 25 October 1996, http://www.mfa.gov.il/MFA/Archive/Peace+Process/1996/MAJOR+PLO+ VIOLATIONS+OF+THE+OSLO+ACCORDS+-+25-Oct-.htm; PLO's Negotiations Affairs Department, "Israel's Violations of the Oslo Agreements," http://www .nad-plo.org/inner.php?view=nego_nego_f16p. For commentary from the negotiators themselves, see Dennis Ross, *The Missing Peace* (New York: Farrar, Straus and Giroux, 2005); Uri Savir, *The Process* (New York: Random House, 1998); Ron Pundak, "From Oslo to Taba: What Went Wrong?," *Survival* 43, no. 4 (Autumn 2001): 31.

26. "The Security Council, Recalling all its previous relevant resolutions, in particular resolutions 242 (1967) and 338 (1973) . . . Calls upon the Israeli and Palestinian sides and their leaders to cooperate in the implementation of the Tenet work plan and Mitchell Report recommendations with the aim of resuming negotiations on a political settlement; Expresses support for the efforts of the Secretary-General and others to assist the parties to halt the violence and to resume the peace process; Decides to remain seized of the matter." UNSC Res. 1397, UN doc # S/ RES/1397, 2002; "The Security Council . . . Calls upon the parties concerned to start immediately after the cease-fire the implementation of Security Council resolution 242 (1967) in all of its parts." UNSC Res. 338, UN doc # S/RES/338, 1973; "The Security Council . . . Affirms further the necessity . . . For achieving a just settlement of the refugee problem." UNSC Res. 242, UN doc # S/RES/242, 1967. See also Shimon Shamir and Bruce Maddy-Weitzman, eds., *The Camp David Summit—What Went Wrong?* (Brighton: Sussex Academic, 2005), a collection of papers from an international conference entitled "The Camp David Summit, 2000: What Went Wrong—Lessons For the Future," held at Tel Aviv University in June 2003 and at which Israeli, Palestinian, and American negotiators and experts presented; Jeremy Pressman, "Visions in Collision: What Happened at Camp David and Taba?," *International Security* 28, no. 2 (Fall 2003): 5, discussing the inaccuracies of the

"dominant narrative" of what happened at Camp David and arguing that providing "a different understanding of Israeli-Palestinian relations in 2000 (and January 2001) . . . suggests that the door to Israeli-Palestinian political talks is open"; Pundak, "From Oslo to Taba," 32, 37–43, arguing that the common assertion that the summit involved a "near perfect offer which . . . Arafat lacked the courage to grasp" is "too simple and misleading"; Hussein Agha and Robert Malley, "Camp David: The Tragedy of Errors," *New York Review of Books*, 9 August 2001, 62, arguing that the common assertion that no agreements were reached at Camp David because of Arafat's unwillingness to compromise despite Barak's "unprecedented offer" is shallow; Robert Malley, "Fictions About the Failure At Camp David," *New York Times*, 8 July 2001, critiquing the common assertion that Camp David was "a test that Mr. Barak passed and Mr. Arafat failed" and summarizing myths about the summit; Bell, *Peace Agreements and Human Rights*, 86, noting President Bill Clinton's criticism that failure to reach an agreement was due to Arafat being unwilling to compromise as much as Barak and noting Arafat's "stated intent to unilaterally declare a Palestinian state on . . . the day by which final status agreement should have been reached" despite the parties' commitment in a trilateral statement to avoid acting unilaterally.

27. Israeli Non-Paper, Palestinian Proposal.

28. Palestinian Proposal, paras. 4–6, 23, 25–28, 30–37, 59–61, discussing international law in paras. 4–5, refugee definition in para. 6, repatriation commission in paras. 7–14, modalities of return in paras. 15–24, legal status of refugees in paras. 25–26, restitution of property in paras. 27–28, compensation for refugees in paras. 30–37, modification of internal laws in para. 23, 59, and end of claims clause in paras. 60–61. Adding an "end of claims" clause to any agreement represented a major point of contention during the negotiations between the PLO and Israeli officials. The Israelis insisted that any agreement between the parties must include a joint declaration stating that the agreement itself marked the "end of the conflict" and would resolve all claims between Israel and Palestinians. For their part, Palestinians would only accept an "end of conflict" clause stating that the actual *implementation* of the agreement would resolve all claims and represent the end of the conflict. Omar M. Dajani, "'End of Conflict' and Other Fictions: Competing Visions of Peace and Justice in the New Middle East" (paper presented at the conference Justice Across Cultures, Brandeis University, Waltham, MA, 8 March 2004), http://www.brandeis.edu/ethics/pdfs/internationaljustice/otheractivities/JAC_Dajani.pdf.

29. On 11 December 1948, UNGA Resolution 194(III), para. 11(a) affirmed the rights of displaced Palestinians to *safely* "return to their homes and live at peace with their neighbors . . . at the earliest practicable date." The Resolution insisted that the "governments or authorities responsible" pay compensation for any loss or damages to any refugee property, whether or not those refugees choose to return. Essentially, the Resolution affirms multiple rights for Palestinian refugees: the right of return, the right to housing and property restitution, and compensation for any damages. BADIL, 2010–2012 Survey, 37, 39–40. The Resolution also clearly states options for refugees not wishing to exercise their right of return, including resettlement and restitution and compensation of property. These core refugee rights in

UNGA Resolution 194 are not referenced in UNSC Resolutions 242 and 338, and the omission of any reference to Resolution 194 in the Security Council Resolutions as well as in most of the negotiations is a deliberate effort to keep these rights out of the framework of the current "peace process."

30. Palestinian Proposal, paras. 2–5, 19–21, 61, discussing Israel's legal and moral responsibility in paras. 2–3; UNGA Res. 194 in paras. 2, 4–5; and voluntary choice to return or choose from available resettlement options in paras. 19–21, 61.

31. Israeli Non-Paper.

32. Israeli Non-Paper, para. 8.

33. Israeli Non-Paper, para. 3.

34. For unofficial/independent commentary, see Pressman, "Visions in Collision"; Pundak, "From Oslo to Taba," 43–44. For government/official commentary see EU Non-Paper; Taba Joint Statement; Israeli Non-Paper; Palestinian Proposal.

35. Geneva Accord.

36. Geneva Accord, art. 7, para. 2.

37. Geneva Accord, Preamble.

38. Geneva Accord, art. 7, para. 4.

39. Geneva Accord, art. 7, para. 4, stating, "The solution to the [permanent place of residence] aspect of the refugee problem shall entail an act of informed choice on the part of the refugee to be exercised in accordance with the options and modalities set forth in this agreement." See also UNHCR, *Resettlement Handbook* (revised July 2009), II/2-II/6, 1 November 2004, http://www.unhcr.org/46f7c0ee2.pdf (chapter 2.1, "Voluntary Repatriation," discussing voluntary repatriation as the preferred solution and stating on p.II/3 that "whenever possible, UNHCR also advocates that returnees should be allowed to return to their place of former residence or any other place of their choice and that property rights are restored"); UNHCR EXCOM Conclusion No. 105 (LVII), Women and Girls at Risk (2006); UNHCR EXCOM Conclusion No. 102 (LVI), Local Integration (2005); UNHCR EXCOM Conclusion No. 101 (LV), Legal Safety Issues in the Context of Voluntary Repatriation of Refugees (2004); UNHCR EXCOM Conclusion No. 99 (LV), General Conclusion on International Protection (2004); UNHCR EXCOM Conclusion No. 96 (LIV), Return of Persons Found Not to be in Need of International Protection (2003); UNHCR EXCOM Conclusion No. 73 (XLIV), Refugee Protection and Sexual Violence (1993); UNHCR EXCOM Conclusion No. 47 (XXXVIII), Refugee Children (1987); UNHCR EXCOM Conclusion No. 18 (XXXI), Voluntary Repatriation (1980).

40. "The aggregate value agreed to by the Parties shall constitute the Israeli 'lump sum' contribution to the International Fund. No other financial claims arising from the Palestinian refugee problem may be raised against Israel." Geneva Accord, art. 7, para. 9(c); "The value of the Israeli fixed assets that shall remain intact in former settlements and transferred to the state of Palestine will be deducted from Israel's contribution to the International Fund. An estimation of this value shall be made by the International Fund, taking into account assessment of damage caused by the settlements." Geneva Accord, art. 7, para. 9(e); "A 'Refugeehood Fund' shall be established in recognition of each individual's refugeehood. The

Fund, to which Israel shall be a contributing party, shall be overseen by the International Commission." Geneva Accord, art. 7, para. 10.

41. Statement by the Quartet, New York; Statement by the Quartet, Jordan; Israel's Response to the Road Map; Road Map.

42. "My vision is two states, living side by side in peace and security. . . . Peace requires a new and different Palestinian leadership, so that a Palestinian state can be born." Speech by U.S. president George W. Bush on Middle East peace, 24 June 2002, reprinted in Bassiouni, *Documents*, 1208.

43. Paul Reynolds, "History of Failed Peace Talks," *BBC News*, 26 November 2007, http://news.bbc.co.uk/2/hi/middle_east/6666393.stm.

44. Road Map, 1218, para. 5.

45. See also note 26.

46. John B. Quigley, "Repatriation of the Displaced Arabs of Palestine: The Legal Requirement as Seen from the United Nations," Ohio State Public Law and Legal Theory Working Paper Series, Paper No. 60, 2006, http://ssrn.com/abstract =896915.

47. UNSC Res. 1397, recalling UNSC Resolutions 242 and 338 and "affirming a vision of a region where two States, Israel and Palestine, live side by side within secure and recognized borders"; UNSC Res. 338, calling for a ceasefire and implementation of UNSC Resolution 242 immediately following the ceasefire, presumably including that resolution's reference to refugees, and calling for negotiations to establish "a just and durable peace in the Middle East"; UNSC Res. 242, emphasizing the need to establish a "just and lasting peace" and affirming the necessity of "achieving a just settlement of the refugee problem" to do so, but without providing details as to how such a just settlement is to be achieved.

48. "The only resolutions specifically referenced in the Oslo agreements, and indeed in any of the Arab-Israeli treaties, are 242 and 338, the basis of the 'land-for-peace' formula. However, neither resolution has specific language referring to the framework of a just solution for the refugees. . . . By making explicit reference to only the resolutions embodying the 'land-for-peace' formula—in other words, satisfying the Palestinian collective demand for self-determination—but excluding reference to any resolutions delineating individual rights of the refugees, the Oslo framework legitimizes a tradeoff of the latter rights for the former." Akram, "Palestinian Refugees and their Legal Status: Rights, Politics, and Implications for a Just Solution," 47. Regarding Israel's demand for an "end of claims" clause, see Dajani, "'End of Conflict.'"

49. Government Resolution Regarding the Disengagement Plan, 6 June 2004, reprinted in Bassiouni, *Documents*, 1255 (Sec 1, Principle 6, "Political and Security Implications").

50. Government Resolution, 1257 (Sec 3.1, "Security Situation following the Relocation"). For the impact of the blockade of Gaza and the unilateral use of force by Israel against Gaza, see OCHA, "The Monthly Humanitarian Monitor: October-November 2012," 19 December 2012, http://unispal.un.org/unispal.nsf /b792301807650d6685256cef0073cb80/6ffa3f199915cd2585257ad9006dd704 ?OpenDocument (hereafter OCHA, Humanitarian Monitor); UNRWA, "Gaza in

2020: A Liveable Place?," 27 August 2012, http://www.unrwa.org/userfiles/file
/publications/gaza/Gaza%20in%202020.pdf; OCHA, "Easing the Blockade: As-
sessing the Humanitarian Impact on the Population of the Gaza Strip," March 2011,
http://www.ochaopt.org/documents/ocha_opt_special_easing_the_blockade
_2011_03_english.pdf (hereafter OCHA, Easing the Blockade); UN Human Rights
Council, "Human Rights Situation in Palestine and Other Occupied Arab Territories: Report of the United Nations Fact Finding Mission on the Gaza Conflict," UN
Doc. A/HRC/12/48, 15 September 2009, http://www2.ohchr.org/english/bodies
/hrcouncil/specialsession/9/docs/unffmgc_report.pdf. See also "Israel Breaches Truce
820 Times in Three Months," *MEMO Middle East Monitor,* 26 February 2013, http://
www.middleeastmonitor.com/news/middle-east/5329-israel-breaches-truce-820
-times-in-three-months; UNCTAD, "Development-centred Globalization: Towards
Inclusive and Sustainable Growth and Development," UN Doc. TD/INF.43, 1 February 2012, http://unispal.un.org/unispal.nsf/9a798adbf322aff38525617b006d88d7
/74ecff7fc4bb4b2b852579e500562cb8?OpenDocument&Highlight=0,oslo.

51. Lassa Oppenheim and Hersch Lauterpacht, *International Law, a Treatise,*
7th ed. (London: Longmans, 1952), 1905–06; Regulations Respecting the Laws and
Customs of War on Land Annexed to Convention (IV) Respecting the Laws and
Customs of War on Land (signed 18 October 1907, entered into force 26 January
1910), 205 CTS 277, art 42 (Hague Regulations).

52. OCHA, Easing the Blockade, 3, 20–21.

53. Interim Agreement, art. XXXI, para. 7.

54. Interim Agreement, art. XXXI, para. 7.

55. Iain Scobbie, "An Intimate Disengagement: Israel's Withdrawal from Gaza,
the Law of Occupation and of Self-Determination," *Yearbook of Islamic and Middle
Eastern Law,* 11 (2004–2005): 25–30.

56. "Violation of a treaty by one of the contracting States does not *ipso facto*
cancel such treaty, but it is in the discretion of the other party to cancel it on the
ground of violation." Oppenheim and Lauterpacht, *International Law,* § 547, at 555.

57. Richard Falk, "Statement on Gaza to the Human Rights Council," 23 March
2009, http://www.transnational.org/Area_MiddleEast/2009/Falk_OralStatement
_Gaza.html; Richard Falk, "Israel's War Crimes," *Le Monde Diplomatique,* March
2009, http://mondediplo.com/2009/03/03warcrimes; Richard Falk, "Report of the
Special Rapporteur on the Situation of Human Rights in the Palestinian Territo-
ries Occupied by Israel since 1967," UN Doc. A/63/326, 25 August 2008; Michael
Lynk, "Down by Law: The Israeli Supreme Court, International Law and the Separation Wall," *Journal of Palestine Studies* 40, no. 1 (Autumn 2005): 6; Michael Lynk,
"The Wall and the Settlements," United Nations International Meeting on the
Question of Palestine, 78, 8–9 March 2005, http://unispal.un.org/unispal.nsf
/eed216406b50bf6485256ce10072f637/1c08688d55a2d5ce8525700e00551745
?OpenDocument; "Legal Consequences of the Construction of a Wall in the Occu-
pied Palestinian Territory, Advisory Opinion," 2004 I.C.J. 136, 9 July.

58. Disengagement Plan of Prime Minister Ariel Sharon—Revised, 28 May
2004, http://www.knesset.gov.il/process/docs/DisengageSharon_eng_revised.htm.

59. Regarding the legal effect of Gaza disengagement, see Scobbie, "An Intimate Disengagement," 20–24; Harvard University, Program on Humanitarian Policy and Conflict Research, "Legal Aspects of Israel's Disengagement Plan Under International Humanitarian Law," Legal and Policy Brief, November 2004 (prepared by Claude Bruderlein).

60. Interim Agreement, art. XI, para. 1; Declaration of Principles, art. IV.

61. For legal opinions and commentary on Palestinian statehood recognition, compare Guy S. Goodwin-Gill, "Legal Opinion on the Palestine Liberation Organization, the Future State of Palestine, and the Question of Popular Representation," 31 August 2011, 4, para. 10, "If [the Palestinians] are 'disenfranchised' and lose their representation in the UN, it will not only prejudice their entitlement to equal representation, contrary to the will of the General Assembly, but also their ability to vocalise their views, to participate in matters of national governance, including the formation and political identity of the State, and to exercise the right of return," with James Crawford, *The Creation of Statehood in International Law* (New York: Oxford University Press, 2006), 18, questioning the value of statehood and stating that "the intimate connection established by nineteenth-century doctrine between recognition and statehood has done much harm." See also Julie Holm (for MIFTAH), "The Legal Ramifications of Palestinian Statehood," *MIFTAH's Special Studies,* 17 November 2011, http://www.miftah.org/Display.cfm?DocId=24120& CategoryId=21, explaining how recognizing Palestine statehood would provide Palestinians with increased "access to international courts and institutions," "leverage . . . to fight the occupation," and political support "needed to create a durable solution"; Nadia Hijab, "The Fine Print of Palestine Statehood," *Al Shabaka: The Palestinian Policy Network,* 5 December 2012, http://www.al-shabaka.org/node/539.

7. The Debate on Islamism and Secularism

The Case of Palestinian Women's Movements

ISLAH JAD

The "Ideal Woman": Between Secularism and Islamism

Conflict over the construction of gender and the ideal woman is not a neutral or primarily religious concern. Nationalists and Islamists alike seek to establish an ideal society that depends on a particular conception of womanhood.[1] The difference between the two conceptions is that religious or Islamist groups seek to restore a mythical age in which women were guardians of tradition,[2] whereas the nationalists tout the fertile, modest peasant as their epitome of the feminine. In both cases, the ideal woman embodies a past when "traditional family and moral values [built] 'our nation.'"[3]

Despite the similarities between them, the Islamist ideal woman is opposed to the "modern" ideal woman constructed by the secular nationalist discourse.[4] While nationalists consider the society Islamists strive to build as reactionary and antimodern,[5] Islamists view secularism as an unwanted colonial imposition, a worldview that gives precedence to the material over the spiritual, to a modern culture of alienation and unrestrained hedonism. The nationalists counter that secularism is central to universal humanism, a rational principle that calls for the suppression or restraint of religious passion so that intolerance and delusion can be controlled, and political unity, peace, and progress secured.[6]

In this essay, I aim to problematize the dichotomy that frames secularism and Islamism as opposing ideologies. By focusing on the Women's Action Department in the Khalas, or Islamic National Salvation Party (INSP), which was announced in 1995 as the political and legal party of Hamas, I examine the formal gender ideology of Hamas and how it is reconstructed, renarrated, and practiced by Islamist women. I argue that this ideology largely stems not from religious texts, but from accommodations to contending positions. The "traditions" that the Islamists, like the modernist nationalists, seek to revive are "invented" and modern constructs.[7] Furthermore, Hamas has generally become more like the nationalists by acquiring the political mission of national independence formerly dominated by Fatah, while Palestinian secularism, for its part, has historically invoked Islam as a means to propagate its legitimacy.[8]

Indeed, neither Islam nor nationalism is a fixed idiom, and the Islamist challenge to the Palestinian national movement is, to a great extent, a product of the failure of the secularists to deliver on their promises of independence and state building. As such, Hamas has identified itself with the struggle to gain Palestinian national rights. Yet one can travel further back in time to encounter the links between Islamism and secularism.

Some Definitional Issues: Who Are Islamist Women?

I am reserving the term "Islamist women" for those who belong to the Islamic movement and who are actively engaged through their activism in the public sphere in promoting what Keddie has called an "Islamic state that would enforce at least some Islamic laws and customs."[9] The different forms of Islamic dress signal the heterogeneity of the Islamist groups and their political projects in the Palestinian context. Hamas advocates the gradual Islamic re-education of the masses through da^cwa (proselytizing), until the masses themselves call for an Islamic government. The Islamic Jihad and Liberation Party (Hizb al-Tahrir) encourages the forceful seizure of state power as the main instrument of re-Islamization of the state and society.[10] However, all are united and agree on some form of Islamization, defined here as increasing Islamic consciousness and practice, of people and government (Islamization here refers to increasing Islamic consciousness and practice). These processes range from giving classes in mosques, universities, and homes to demanding the application of the shari^{c}a through various institutions.[11] This movement has developed against and in relation to secular nationalism.

The Shifting Nature of Palestinian Secularism:
History and Theory

Hajj Amin al-Husseini, the leader of the national movement during the British Mandate, and Shaykh ʿIzz al-Din al-Qassam, a political exile from Syria and the head of the Arab Higher Committee (the national leadership for the Palestinian people during the 1930s and 1940s), were also religious authorities. The Arab Higher Committee's ideology, however, was nationalist and secularist in the sense that it aimed to establish an independent Palestinian state that would include Arabs and Jews. It was also driven by a strong desire to modernize society and spread education and science through the British public school curriculum.[12] It was not hostile to Western culture and the West's enlightenment project; rather, its animosity was directed mainly toward the West's dominance and occupation of Palestine.

The Committee pursued a path of negotiation and diplomacy to seek independence, and, when this strategy did not work, destitute peasants pushed the Committee to use violence. Yet neither al-Qassam nor Hajj Amin formed Islamic organizations or movements to fight the British and Zionist movements. Akram Zuʿaytir's diary on the 1936–1939 revolt[13] mentions clearly that "the rebellion, [led] by the nationalists, mobilized religious clergy," and not vice versa.[14] Thus, Islam as a religion was a mobilizing factor and not a political movement taking Islam as its ideology.

In the years that followed, secular nationalism played an important role in the Palestine Liberation Organization (PLO), as well as across the Middle East. One thinks, for example, of Muhammad Mossadegh and the National Front in Iran and Gamal Abdel Nasser and Nasserism in Egypt. But these forms of nationalism struggled to produce liberation from foreign domination, not to mention that they failed to resolve the various other social and economic problems found in most of the Third World—thus opening a space for Islamism to flourish.

Of course, many of the nationalists were already religiously inclined. In their study of religion and the Fatah leadership, Jawad al-Hamad and Iyad al-Barghouti reveal that the majority (thirteen out of twenty-one) of the founding leaders of Fatah in the early 1950s were either members or sympathizers of the Muslim Brotherhood or the Islamic Liberation Party.[15] Fatah's first magazine, *Falastinuna* (Our Palestine), reflected the religious orientation of the nascent movement that helped to spread its agenda among refugees in Gaza who came from rural, conservative backgrounds. All of the founding leaders were Muslim, although Christians represented 20 percent of Fatah (whereas Christians did not exceed 11 percent of the Palestinian population).

In addition, in 1946 Jamal al-Husseini, one of the leading nationalist figures and Hajj Amin's aide, established the first group of Muslim Brothers as an Islamic movement in Jerusalem.[16] These linkages between nationalism and Islamism demonstrate that both movements were not wholly one ideology or the other.

Many have studied this phenomenon and put forth theories. Whether in its Baʿthist, Nasserist, or other forms, Arab nationalism incorporated Islam as part and parcel of its claims of difference and used it as a unifying ideology in the quest for building what Ghassan Salame calls a "state of legitimation"—which derives fortification from enduring social elements rather than from insisting on a vision for change and innovation.[17]

Sadiq Jalal al-Azm goes further to argue that the secular nationalist elites retained Islam as a nonrational practice by neglecting to make it a subject of scientific and social science inquiry. Rather, they used Islamic cultural heritage as a tool in the service of their regional, national, or party politics. As a result, when the nationalist waves faded, the uncritical approach to Islam and Islamic heritage remained and was easily presented as the untouchable core of Arab and Muslim identity.[18] Islamists have used this conception of Islam to their advantage.

Like nationalism, Islamism is interpreted as a political system and is used for political ends.[19] According to Talal Asad, both Arab nationalism and Islamism share a concern with the modernizing state because Islamism also seeks to work through the nation state. This is central to the predicament of Islamists, because they exist in a (national) system not of their own making. However, it is this statist project, Asad argues, and not the fusion of religious and political ideas that gives Islamism a nationalist cast.[20] He urges us not to focus on the "real motives" of Islamists, but rather to look for what circumstances oblige Islamism to emerge publicly as a political discourse, and how it challenges the deep structures of secularism.[21] Islamists seek to have a public space for Islam while secularists insist on "containing it" in the private sphere as faith that concerns the individual only. Asad stresses interconnections between religion and secularism by stating that

> although religion is regarded as alien to the secular, the latter is also seen to have generated religion, that in the pre-modern past, secular life created

superstitious and oppressive religion, and in the modern present secularism has produced enlightened and tolerant religion. Thus, the insistence on a sharp separation between the religious and the secular goes with the paradoxical claim that the latter continually produces the former.[22]

Two scholars have debated the linkages between religion and secularism in the construction of Palestinian nationalism. Musa Budeiri argues that the fact that Fatah "resort[s] to religious symbols and ideology to mobilize and enlist support casts doubt on the often repeated assertion that Fatah, and by implication the Palestinian national movement, is a secular force."[23] Fatah, for example, has always made extensive use of common Islamic concepts such as *jihad* (holy war) and *shahid* (martyr). Islam, Budeiri assures us, was and continues to be one of the paramount elements of Palestinian national identity, especially inside the Occupied Territories. He states that "the Islamic movement in Palestine was instrumental from the very beginning of the British Mandate in assimilating a nationalist discourse. It is indeed difficult to establish a demarcation line separating Islamists from their 'nationalist enemies.'"[24]

Budeiri comments that the fusion between Islam and nationalism denigrates the real meaning of secularism, which should be separate from religion. Yet he also perceives Islam and politics in terms of continuity rather than discontinuity. Islam, as a symbolic reference point, functions as a cultural reservoir to be drawn upon in the national call for resistance. This configuration of Islam as a political tool that appears cyclically or is more or less unchanging can be understood as a religious "resurgence," in other words, the coming back of the same old structure, as if it is an eternal, unchangeable entity.[25]

In contrast to Budeiri, Jamil Hilal does not recognize Islam as a central factor in the construction of Palestinian national identity, whether under the Mandate or in its modern formation in the 1960s. He defines secularism as a clear separation of political institutions from religious ones, saying that "in a national political field [secularism] implies that organizations, identities, and ideologies have distinct paradigms, dynamics, and determinants that differ from those pertaining to the religious field."[26] He believes that the confrontation with Zionist and British rule generated a secular dimension to Palestinian identity in the form of a *national* individuality transcending that of religion, sect, and locality.[27] According to Hilal, at no stage did Palestinian nationalism resort to religious discourse or mythology to maintain its hegemony.

Hilal also points out that leading Christian figures were members of the PLO, such as George Habash, head of the Popular Front for the Liberation of Palestine, and Nayef Hawatmeh, head of the Democratic Front for the Liberation of Palestine. "This does not contradict," he says, "the fact that most Palestinians have been and are still religious in the popular meaning of religiosity."[28] However, once Hamas established a "sort of cultural hegemony," Islam's dominance was reflected in the common mode of dress, in proposed curricula for government schools, in the increasing use of Qur'anic verses in official statements and speeches by the Palestinian Authority (PA), in the self-censorship of newspaper articles relating to religious issues, and in the Palestinian official media.[29]

The PLO accepted that marriage, divorce, and inheritance should be based on popular understandings of Islam. As such, gender relations within the Palestinian community under the political control of the PLO were governed by shariʿa and not secular law. Commentators on Islam and secularism failed to see that in matters of gender and the family, there was more continuity than discontinuity between the two ideologies. Hilal, for one, did not address why a mainly secular movement was in need of such religious idioms to legitimize itself. This confirms the view that the ambiguities of modernity are most apparent when it comes to the issue of the role of women in the body politic.[30] Yet, while one of the diagnostic criteria for unmasking the nature of a national project is to examine its construction of gender and gender relations, many writers and scholars who have written on Hamas and Palestinian nationalism are silent on this question.[31]

Likewise, those authors who insist that Palestinian national identity has been, until recently, mainly based on secular idioms avoid acknowledging how nationalism and its multiple identities are permeated by class, gender, and religion.[32] Some feminists, for example, demonstrate that "although many [nationalisms] were influenced by the ideas of the enlightenment and were of secular persuasion, they unwittingly endorsed the notion that any changes in the position of women could only be condoned in the national interest."[33] Nationalist ideologies thus need an "ideal woman." Fatah's ideal was often portrayed as the fertile, modest, and authentic peasant. At the same time, Fatah's "modern woman" was represented as the disciplined, de-eroticized body, the "sister of men." Through both these ideals, the Palestinian national movement portrayed women as the "privileged repository of uncontaminated national values."[34] This model has persisted in Fatah, the PLO, and the PA.

Furthermore, Fatah always resisted challenging the patriarchal control of women within the PLO. The many attempts by activists in the General Union of Palestinian Women (GUPW), the PLO-affiliated women's organization formed in 1965, to promote and protect women's rights in divorce, marriage, and inheritance failed. The activists attributed this failure to the refusal of the head of the PLO, Yasser Arafat, to endorse any such move or, according to Laila Khalid and Samira Salah, to the refusal of Fatah "to question the flagrant abuse and exploitation of some of the Fatah fighters, whether in the uncontrolled practices of polygamy, the failure to recognize their children from undeclared marriages, or the many cases of domestic violence."[35]

Fatah's failure to address women's rights might serve to explain the ease with which support for a secular PLO comprised of men and women was transformed into sympathy, and, in many cases, even allegiance, to the Islamic movement. The increasing politicization of gender and religious identities called into question the progressiveness of the secular Palestinian national unity and the unity of the Palestinian national identity. However, the increasing popularity of Islamists has its roots not only in these cultural or ideological premises, but also in the important changes that occurred in the West Bank and Gaza Strip after the Israeli occupation in 1967. After 1967 the Palestinian national movement emerged as a resistance movement, but when the PLO signed the Oslo Accords in 1993 and shifted to "peace" negotiations as the only strategy to achieve independence, the Islamists took up the banner of national resistance and began to emerge as a hegemonic political power.

Shariᶜa Politics and a Possible Common Ground

The Islamic Salvation Party, or Khalas, was established in 1995 as the first legitimate Islamist political party in Palestine and was a front for the underground movement of Hamas. What, then, were women's rights in the party agenda and program? Here the answer does not come from the male leadership of the party, but rather from the party's women. I draw on the contributions of three conferences and a workshop organized by the party's Women's Action Department that took place in the Gaza Strip between 1998 and 2003. These events illustrate the shift that has been taking place vis-à-vis Islamist women's experiences in the party as well as in their daily practices.[36]

The department organizes a one-day women's conference annually in which male and female attendees give papers on gender issues. The papers cover "hot topics" inspired by secular, nationalist women's groups or they address specific issues that women face in their fields of activity, such as work, politics, and culture. Some of the workshops are directed at the male members of the department and focus on topics such as socialization and discuss shariʿa family law. According to one participant, "Some topics elicit fierce resistance from men as in the discussion of shariʿa, while other topics such as the mixing of the sexes are [supported]."[37] As one male member of the party put it, "As a party keen for the development of women, we should abolish segregation in the party."[38]

The motivation behind the call to reform shariʿa is in essence to change the internal power relations between males and females within the family structure. Male members are receptive to change and support "mixing," which enhances the image of the party and its women as "modern," while they continue to object to significantly deeper changes within the family, such as the redivision of gender roles. Support for mixing is not shared by all Islamists, however, and many encourage segregation among students in the university, which suggests that even the veil is not enough to transcend sex barriers.

Since the conferences are a vehicle through which Islamists present their ideologies about gender, it is noteworthy that the highest level of Hamas leadership is keen to attend the conferences "to show its support" for what women do. For example, Shaykh Ahmad Yassin gave a speech at the first conference in 1998, and in 1999 the prominent Hamas leader Mahmoud al-Zahhar presented a paper.[39] At the fifth conference, Shaykh Ahmad Yassin was again present, as was Dr. ʿAbd al-ʿAziz al-Rantissi, and the establishment of the "Islamic Women's Movement in Palestine" was announced in the presence of more than 1,500 men and women. The goal of this movement was to link all Islamist women's institutions and thus channel efforts into representing an Islamic vision for women. This collaboration included eight women's organizations: the Muslim Women's Association, the Wom-

en's Action Department in the Salvation Party, the Women's Action De-
partment in al-Mujam'a al-Islami, the Islamic Bloc (female students), the
Female Student Council in the Islamic University, the Palestinian Mothers'
Society, the Family Care Society, the Women's Unit in the Arab Institute for
Study and Research, and the Mothers of Martyrs Society.

In the first conference, Islamist women concentrated on delegitimizing
other women's groups in order to present the Khalas party as the true and
authentic voice for Palestinian women's interests. In the second conference,
however, the presenters admitted that the Islamists had no unified vision or
agenda for women's issues. To address this problem, they attempted to re-
interpret religious texts to make a place for women's modern achievements.
Khitam Abu Musa, an Islamist woman, inverted the gender vision of the
Hamas Charter of 1988 in her paper by interpreting Islam as the religion
that gave woman all their rights, namely education, the free choice of a husband, inheritance (widely denied by custom), mobility (to participate in
the call for the rule of God and jihad), proselytizing, and social or professional work.[40] By stressing a more controversial issue—that of "mixing with
men"—the paper concludes that "now we can see that Muslim woman was
moved to prove herself in all aspects and fields of life. Islam allows women
to meet men (abah) and to exchange dialogue if she is committed to the
'adab shari'a (the conventions of shari'a)."[41] Yet surprisingly, in the process
of formulating this new reading of religious texts, a parallel process of "de-
Islamizing" the discourse on women's rights took place. For example, the
women of the Women's Action Department adopted new terms predominantly used by donors and feminist activists, such as "sustainable development." Also for the first time, they began to use a "modern" and "feminist"
critique of the liberal rights approach.

These first two conferences were landmarks in the transformation of
Hamas gender ideology from an utter rejection of feminism to borrow-
ing and selectively incorporating positions advocated by feminists. This co-
optation of feminist norms resulted in their Islamization, while at the same
time Islamic discourse was de-Islamized.

Two main points can be drawn from these conferences. The first is that
Islamists should take the lead in elevating (nahda) women through Islamic
reform (i.e., advocating for, organizing. educating, and mobilizing women);
otherwise, others will lead. Secondly, the task of liberation falls primarily

on women, as women must struggle and claim their rights in the context of a tolerant shariᶜa. Here, the Islamists, as did their nationalist predecessors, see women as an important factor in shaping a national identity and that women themselves must struggle for their rights.

The Women's Action Department then organized a final conference in 2003 that built on as well a workshop held in August and September 2000. It provided more thoughtful critiques of the discourses of women's rights as they figure in international conventions. For instance, in this conference, the concept of sustainable development and its applicability to Palestinian society was brought under scrutiny and questioned.

For the first time, the papers also questioned the viability of rights discourses due to their liberal, utilitarian, and individualistic Western base.[42] Amira Haroun's paper, for example, illustrates the tone of the conference as a whole: "The concept of rights was established (in the West) on utilitarianism; thus, utilitarian individualism supersedes rationality and engulfs all social relations. . . . This conception is false, since the individual was never an abstract being, the individual was always a social being."[43] Therefore she contests the discourses of women's NGOs, based on liberal rights, and she does so via another Western, feminist discourse based on the notion of active citizenship.[44] Islamist critiques of liberalism, like socialist feminist critiques, question the morality of narrowly defending the principle of individual rights and allowing it to take precedence over social responsibility. Western citizenship, according to the critique, is conceived of as rights alone, and in political terms it is reduced to the limited practice of voting, which reflects an impoverished view of social membership. Instead, Islamists argue for social citizenship, a more substantive version of citizenship that is based on participation and social responsibility.[45] Haroun asserts that "in our Islamic vision, the notion of the individual is seen in its relation to the collective. That is why the notion of individual rights, in Islam, is formed in the context of duties that help to awaken in the individual the incentives to give and not only to take."[46]

The stress in Islamic discourse on this give-and-take approach is linked to the specific situation of Palestinians, which is not cultural but national and conjunctural—a dimension missing in feminist NGO discourse. In the absence of a clear national agenda put forth by the nationalist, secularist women's movement, the Islamists thus link women's rights with the national and social needs of the Palestinian people. They do this by asking women, as did the old nationalists, to serve the nation by reproducing more men.[47]

Islamist discourse is determined not by religious text, but by political context. Hamas's shifting versions of shariᶜa raises two issues. First, it is a challenge to the secular feminist NGOs and the national women's movement, which are based on a liberal, individualistic notion of rights, and which ignore the plight of the nation under occupation. By putting Islam at the center of a modified notion of Palestinian nationalism, the Islamists have managed to delegitimize feminist discourse by portraying it as non-national and alien. Hamas's version of shariᶜa also poses a challenge to the rather ambivalent Palestinian secularism that has used Islam as a source of its legitimacy. By "Islamizing" Palestine and "nationalizing" Islam, the Islamists have proved successful in forging a brand of nationalism to which Islam is integral and constitutes a mobilizing force for the masses.

In such a context, the secularists, while challenging the Islamists, are losing ground by advocating rights in isolation from the national agenda and in the absence of a mobilizing organization. The national women's movement and NGO activism, with no organized constituency and based only on short-lived projects, does not have the potential to constitute an alternative. In addition, the little support they have is derived from a decaying, delegitimized authority. By becoming a movement opposed to all violations of civic and human rights, the Islamists have developed a political organization.

Islamist women have forged a space for educated women from poor, mainly refugee backgrounds whose families support their activity in all spheres of public life. These Islamists have managed to establish themselves by providing services and defending male prisoners' rights. This is an important addition for women's activism in a phase of national struggle.

Shariᶜa, as a guiding principle for women's rights, has at times been used in contradictory ways. Islamists initially employed it as a fixed, divine, and immutable idiom to delegitimize and to silence non-Islamic women's groups. Yet this debate on shariᶜa triggered a debate within the Islamic movement itself. Female Islamists' search for an alternative to the secular feminist platform brought them into continuous engagement with Islamic law. In some instances, highly educated and professional Islamist women called for equal rights in the public sphere, at least vis-à-vis work and activism.

The top male leadership reacted swiftly to both secular and Islamist calls for women's rights by attempting to "fix" shariʿa[48] vis-à-vis laws concerning the Penal Code. The Islamists refused to consider a change to the Code that would designate the "honor crime" as murder deserving a life sentence rather than a light punishment of a few months in prison. This again silenced feminist and secularist women's groups and discouraged them from suggesting reforms. The top male leadership's power not only applies to women's rights, but also asserts an Islamist hegemonic power in society and in regard to the PA. It also relates to the still-uncertain nature of any future Palestinian state (Islamist or nationalist) through a strategy of active citizenship.[49]

Secularist challengers pushed the Islamists to engage with such notions as pluralism, women's rights, public good, sustainable development, and the social self versus the individual self—and the Islamists borrowed and co-opted these notions from the secular context. Yet, while there are moments of engagement between Islamists and secularists, there are also indications that there may be a retreat into interpretations of Islam that would affect women negatively. The male Islamists of Hamas could return to the idea of women as reproducers of the nation. Their stand on polygamy is not yet clear. Heated debate has also occurred on the suitability of women for military action.

In sum, Islamist women's discourse does not stem only from the Qurʾan but also from positive engagement with other discourses, whether secular feminist or nationalist. This engagement incites Islamist women to return to religious texts to look for possible new readings in order to respond to the challenges posed by other women's groups. As a result, Islamist women's discourses rely on both religious texts and on what other women's activism and discourses provoke. This engagement could prove the common ground on which Islamist, secularist, and nationalist women unite by pushing for new interpretations of religious texts and advocating for better daily realities for women—all in the context of the unsolved national struggle. This mutual accommodation[50] requires each party to remain open to the approaches and discourses of the other, instead of adopting an attitude of total rejection, as was exemplified by the stance of some women's NGOs and the Islamists at the first conference.

Islamists have built on women's modern gains, such as education and work opportunities. Hence, the kind of state they might claim will depend not on the blueprint of a religious text, but to a great extent on what form of state and society they live in, as well as on the visions posed by other nationalist and secularist groups if sufficiently supported by a substantial majority.

Notes

1. Valentine Moghadam, "Introduction: Women and Identity Politics in Theoretical and Comparative Perspective," in *Identity Politics and Women: Cultural Reassertions, Gender and Feminisms in International Perspective,* ed. Valentine Moghadam (Boulder, CO: Westview, 1994), 3–26; Hanna Papanek, "The Ideal Woman and the Ideal Society: Control and Autonomy in the Construction of Identity," in *Identity Politics and Women,* 42–75; Deniz Kandiyoti, "Identity and Its Discontents: Women and the Nation," *Millennium: Journal of International Studies* 20, no. 3 (1991): 429–443.

2. Sami Zubaida, *Law and Power in the Islamic World* (London: I. B. Tauris, 2003); Sami Zubaida, "The Trajectories of Political Islam: Egypt, Iran and Turkey," *Political Quarterly* 71, no. s1 (2000): 60–78; Olivier Roy, *The Failure of Political Islam,* 2nd ed., trans. Carol Volk (London: I. B. Tauris, 1999); Sami Zubaida, "Religion, the State, and Democracy: Contrasting Conception of Society in Egypt," in *Political Islam: Essays from Middle East Report,* eds. Joel Beinin and Joe Stork (Berkeley: University of California Press, 1997), 51–63.

3. John Stratton Hawley, *Fundamentalism and Gender* (Oxford: Oxford University Press, 1994), 32.

4. Jenny White, *Islamist Mobilisation in Turkey: A Study in Vernacular Politics* (Seattle: University of Washington Press, 2002); Hawley, *Fundamentalism and Gender,* 30.

5. Roy, *The Failure of Political Islam;* Zubaida, "Religion, the State, and Democracy"; Aziz Al-Azmeh, *Islams and Modernities,* 2nd ed. (London: Verso, 1996).

6. El Messiri and Al-Azmeh cited in Talal Asad, *Formation of the Secular: Christianity, Islam, Modernity* (Stanford, CA: Stanford University Press, 2003), 21.

7. Eric Hobsbawm, "Introduction: Inventing Traditions," in *The Invention of Tradition,* eds. Eric Hobsbawm and Terence Ranger (Cambridge: Cambridge University Press, 1983), 2–3.

8. Yet it must be noted that real conflicts exist between Islamism and nationalism. In contemporary political Islamic movements, for example, and contrary to the meaning of Islam at its inception, Islam is inclusive of Muslims and exclusive of non-Muslims, unlike nationalism.

9. Keddie quoted in Azza Karam, *Women, Islamisms and the State: Contemporary Feminisms in Egypt* (New York: St. Martin's, 1998), 16.

10. Iyad al-Barghouti, *al-Islam al-Siyasi fi Filastin: Ma Wara al-Siyasa* [Political Islam in Palestine: beyond politics] (Jerusalem: Jerusalem Media and Communication Centre [JMCC], 2000), 43–46.

11. Karam, *Women, Islamisms and the State,* 235.

12. There was one exception. In Palestinian private schools, the Committee added a religion requirement that was not taught in the public schools. Abdel-Latif Tibawi, *Arab Education in Mandatory Palestine: A Study of Three Decades of British Administration* (London: Luzac, 1956).

13. Al-Thawra al-Kubra (the Great Revolt) of 1936–1939 started in April 1936 and was initiated by a six-month strike announced by various political and militant organizations.

14. Akram Zuʿaytir, *Yawmiyyat Akram Zuʿaytir: al-Haraka al-Wataniyya al-Filastiniyya 1935–1939* (Beirut: Palestine Studies Association, 1980), 411.

15. Jawad al-Hamad and Iyad al-Bargouthi, *Dirassa fi Fikr Harakat al-Muqawama al-Islamiyya Hamas* [A study in the political ideology of the Islamic Resistance Movement, Hamas 1987–1996] (Amman: Middle East Study Centre, 1997).

16. Amnon Cohen, *Political Parties in the West Bank under the Jordanian Regime, 1949–1967* (Ithaca, NY: Cornell University Press, 1982), 144.

17. Ghassan Salame, ed., *Democracy without Democrats? The Renewal of Politics in The Muslim World* (London: I. B. Tauris, 2001), 20; Al-Azmeh, *Islams and Modernities;* Eric Davis, "The Concept of Revival and the Study of Islam and Politics," in *The Islamic Impulse,* ed. Barbara Stowasser (Washington, DC,: Croom Helm in association with the Center for Contemporary Arab Studies, Georgetown University, 1987), 37–58; Bruce Lawrence, "Muslim Fundamentalist Movements: Reflections toward a New Approach," in *The Islamic Impulse,* 15–36; Bassam Tibi, "Islam and Arab Nationalism," in *The Islamic Impulse,* 59–75; Albert Hourani, *Arabic Thought in the Liberal Age 1798–1939,* 2nd ed. (Cambridge: Cambridge University Press, 1983).

18. Sadiq Jalal Al-Azm, "Hamlet wal-Hadatha" [Hamlet and modernity] (paper presented at the conference al-Hadatha wal-Hadatha al-ʿArabiyya [Modernity and Arab modernity], Markaz al-Dirassat wal-Abhath al-ʿAlmaniyya fil al-ʿAlam al-ʿArabi [Secular Studies and Research Centre in the Arab World, 2004).

19. Roy, *The Failure of Political Islam;* Al-Azmeh, *Islams and Modernities;* Tibi, "Islam and Arab Nationalism."

20. Asad, *Formation of the Secular,* 199.

21. Asad, *Formation of the Secular,* 199.

22. Asad, *Formation of the Secular,* 193.

23. Musa Budeiri, "The Nationalist Dimension of Islamic Movements in Palestinian Politics," *Journal of Palestine Studies* 24, no. 3 (1994): 12.

24. Budeiri, "The Nationalist Dimension of Islamic Movements in Palestinian Politics," 7.

25. Davis, "The Concept of Revival and the Study of Islam and Politics"; Barbara Stowasser, introduction to *The Islamic Impulse,* 1–14.

26. Jamil Hilal, "*Secularism in Palestinian Political Culture: A Tentative Discourse,*" in *International Social Science Review* 3, no. 1 (2002): 1.

27. Hilal, "*Secularism in Palestinian Political Culture,*" 1.

28. Hilal, "*Secularism in Palestinian Political Culture,*" 1.

29. Palestinian newspaper columnists have complained of frequent censorship by editors of articles that touch on religion for fear of provoking Islamists. Hilal, "*Secularism in Palestinian Political Culture,*" 1.

30. Deniz Kandiyoti, "Some Awkward Questions on Women and Modernity in Turkey," in *Remaking Women: Feminism and Modernity in the Middle East,* ed. Lila Abu-Lughod (Princeton, NJ: Princeton University Press, 1998), 283.

31. Henry Munson, "Islam, Nationalism and Resentment of Foreign Domination," *Middle East Policy* 10, no. 2 (Summer 2003): 40–53; Hilal, "*Secularism in Palestinian Political Culture*"; Khalid Hroub, *Hamas Political Thought and Practices* (Washington, DC: Institute of Palestine Studies, 2000); Khalid Abu al-ʿOmrayn, *Hamas: Harakat al-Muqawama al-Islamiyya fi Filastin* [Hamas: The Islamic Resistance Movement in Palestine] (Cairo: Markaz al-Hadara al-ʿArabiyya [Arab Civilization Center], 2000); Jawad al-Hamad and Iyad al-Barghouti, *Dirassa fi Fikr;* Meir Litvak, *The Islamisation of Palestinian Identity: The Case of Hamas* (Tel Aviv: Moshe Dayan Centre for Middle Eastern and African Studies, Tel Aviv University, 1996); Nur al-Din al-Tahiri, *Hamas: Harakat al-Muqawamah al-Islamiyya fi Falastin* [Hamas: The Islamic Resistance Movement in Palestine] (Casablanca: Dar al-ʿItissam, 1995); Ziad Abu-Amr, *Islamic Fundamentalism in the West Bank and Gaza* (Bloomington: Indiana University Press, 1994); Zeʾev Schiff and Ehud Yaʾari, *Intifada: The Inside Story of the Palestinian Uprising That Changed the Middle East Equation* (New York: Simon & Schuster, 1989).

32. Kandiyoti, "Identity and Its Discontents," 429–443; Floya Anthias and Nira Yuval-Davis, introduction to *Woman-Nation-State,* eds. Floya Anthias and Nira Yuval-Davis (London: MacMillan, 1989), 1–15.

33. Kandiyoti, "Identity and Its Discontents," 410.

34. Kandiyoti, "Identity and Its Discontents," 410.

35. Laila Khalid and Samira Salah (active members in the General Union of Palestinian Women representing the PFLP, or Popular Front for the Liberation of Palestine), interview with the author, 10 October 2003, Tehran.

36. For more details, see Islah Jad, "Islamist Women of Hamas: A New Women's Movement?," in *On Shifting Ground: Muslim Women in the Global Era,* ed. Fereshteh Nouraie-Simone (New York: Feminist Press, 2005), 94–111.

37. Amira Haroun, interview with the author, 30 April 2004, Gaza Strip.

38. Zayyad [pseud.], interview with the author, 2 March 2004, Gaza Strip.

39. Political leaders usually attend the conferences' inaugurations and then leave, and thus presenting a theoretical paper shows more involvement in the event.

40. Khitam Abu Musa, "al-Marʾa fil-Tasawwur al-Islami" [Women in Islamic thought] (paper presented at the workshop al-Marʾa al-Filastiniyya ila Ayn? [Palestinian woman: to where?], Gaza, April 1997), 17–21.

41. Khitam Abu Musa, "al-Marʾa fil-Tasawwur al-Islami," 21.

42. Anne Phillips, *Democracy and Difference* (Cambridge: Polity Press, 1993).

43. Amira Haroun, "Introduction" (paper presented at the conference al-Marʾa al-Filastiniyya wa al-Tahawullat al-Ijtimaʿiyya [Palestinian women and social change], Gaza Strip, 8–9 August 2000).

44. Some Islamist thinkers follow the critiques of the Enlightenment principles of universality and individualism offered by Marxist feminists and postmodernists. These critiques suggest that, if citizenship could be refashioned in a way that divested it from abstract universalism and "false egalitarianism," it could be a more effective tool in advancing gender justice. See, for example, Rashid al-Ghannouchi, "Muqarabat fil-ʿAlmaniyya wal-Mujtamaʿ al-Madani" [Approaches to secularism and civil society], 17 July 2003, http://www.islamonline.net; Abdel-Wahab el-Messiri, "Towards A New Islamic Discourse: Re-Capturing the Islamic," 17 July 2003, http://ikhwanmisr.net/article.php?id=4655; Azzam Tamimi, "Can Islam be Secularized?," November 2002, http://s14.zetaboards.com/uloomination/topic /407720/1/. Some authors have claimed that sex difference and the female body should be the proper basis of legal and political recognition. See, for example, Rian Voet, *Feminism and Citizenship* (London: Sage, 1998); Ruth Lister, *Citizenship: Feminist Perspectives* (New York: NYU Press, 1997); Anne Phillips, *Democracy and Difference*; Anne Phillips, *Engendering Democracy* (Cambridge: Polity Press, 1991); Anne Phillips, *Feminism and Equality* (New York: NYU Press, 1987).

45. Maxine Molyneux, "Women's Rights and the International Context in the Post-Communist States," in *Mapping the Women's Movement: Feminist Politics and Social Transformation in the North,* ed. M. Threlfall (London: Verso, 1996), 232–259.

46. Haroun, "Introduction," 5.

47. Anthias and Yuval-Davis, introduction.

48. Zubaida, *Law and Power in the Islamic World,* 1.

49. At the same time, Islamists discredit the notion of popular sovereignty advocated by the Palestinian Authority (PA) as the basis for new legislation. It is still uncertain whether the Islamists want instead to establish a sovereignty belonging to God, since their state project has yet to be spelled out.

50. Salame, *Democracy without Democrats?;* Michael Hudson, "Obstacles to Democratization in the Middle East," *Contention* 14 (1996): 81–106; Augustus Richard Norton, "The Future of Civil Society in the Middle East," *The Middle East Journal* 47, no. 2 (Spring 1993): 205–216.

8. Other Worlds to Live In

*Palestinian Retrievals of Religion
and Tradition under Conditions of
Chronic National Collapse*

LOREN D. LYBARGER

Today, perhaps more than ever, the question of Palestinian identity has become obvious and urgent. The always-fragile national consensus has ceded to open schism. In the wake of devastating interfactional bloodletting, the Islamic political movement, Hamas, now dominates the Gaza Strip while the weakened secular-nationalist Fatah movement putatively controls the West Bank. The choice for Palestinians, as it comes across in media analyses and think-tank position papers, seems stark: either an embattled secular-nationalist Fatah movement reasserts itself, or Palestine becomes "Hamastan."[1] But, even the very possibility of Palestine, or, for that matter, "Hamastan," seems ever more unrealizable. Israel, backed by the United States and the European Union, relentlessly presses its advantage. It has expanded its settlements and road networks while extending a system of walls, fences, and checkpoints that have isolated Palestinians within their towns, villages, and camps, and in the case of Gaza, within a besieged coastal strip subject to punishing bombardments from air, sea, and land. Negotiation and armed resistance have seemed to yield little more than cynicism, despair, and death. The parties backing these diverging approaches—Fatah and Hamas, primarily—have failed to galvanize consistent broad majority support. Neither secular nationalism nor Islamism in their current forms appear to offer any clear basis for political unity and collective action.[2] But if not these, then what?

This question is keenly ontological. The deep and chronic political divisions and concomitant collapse of the "plausibility structure"—the taken-for-granted institutions and legitimating discourses[3]—of Palestinian nationalism have produced what Catarina Kinvall, quoting Anthony Giddens, refers to as "existential anxiety" and corresponding attempts to "securitize the subject."[4] For Kinvall and Giddens, who follow Erikson here, existential anxiety results from a loss of a sense of "fundamental safety in the world" rooted in "a basic trust of other people."[5] Such loss is itself the consequence of an inability to sustain a "feeling of biographical continuity," that is to say, a coherent narrative of self in relation to others across time and space, a narrative often expressed in the category of home.[6] Violent displacement—an experience that Palestinians have suffered repeatedly—shatters the coherence of this category of home, leading individuals to attempt to retrieve, repair, or create a new canopy under which to shelter a singular, stable, and integrated self. Often this attempt to re-securitize the subject expresses itself in a "politics of resistance" and the "growth of local identities" that aim to "surpass the life of contradictions and anxieties of homelessness."[7]

Kinvall argues further that the sentiments and values mobilized within these politics often get expressed through the notions of nation and religion. They do so precisely because these symbolic-institutional complexes serve to stabilize a single, unified self within "an essentializing historical narrative."[8] Nation and religion "provide answers to questions concerning existence itself, the external world and human life, the existence of 'the other,' and what self-identity actually is."[9]

Yet, while they certainly may perform the locative, stabilizing functions that Kinvall describes, the reappropriation and revivification of religious and nationalist narratives, symbols, and structures can just as frequently dislocate, destabilize, and divide individuals and social groups. Because it concerns itself with the legitimacy and precariousness of social systems, religion often enters into direct competition with politics.[10] When the political order legitimizes itself with reference to religious conceptions and practices, then resistance and protest against the prevailing order, especially during periods of crisis, will likely take the form of either heterodox religious or explicitly anti-religious secular movements. Alternatively, when the political order is based on an ideology that negates or subordinates religious values and institutions within a secular or multisectarian conception of collective belonging, protest and resistance in periods of crisis quite often can manifest as politicized religion. In both cases, however, the "solutions" that religious or nationalist revivification provide are never automatic or self-evident. Rather, these "must be rediscovered, reinvented, and reconceptualized every time [they are] called upon as an answer to ontological insecurity."[11] This process is not a unitary one precisely because no society constitutes a single homogenous entity. Rather, various and conflicting interpretations of nation and religion will emerge in relation to the differing interests and needs of diverging class, status, gender, and generational milieus.

The dynamic, multivalent nature of identity is now a well-established principle within the social sciences. Too frequently, however, its relevance to Palestinian lives is lost. For example, the categorical oppositions that dominate analyses of Palestinian politics, principally the opposition between secularists and Islamists, exclude or devalue other modes of relationship and identity, modes more immediate and intimate than the nation. These other modes can shape the daily lives of Palestinians profoundly and in so doing give rise to diverse conceptions of belonging. At the level of the quotidian, the nation can sometimes seem distant or irrelevant or even invasive and threatening and thus something to shield oneself against. Other discourses, other practices, other conceptions, other canopies are available. They often elude detection because the national question is so all-pervasive and problematic. Yet, if we are to understand how Palestinian nationalism has changed in the last two decades, we must begin to view national groups, generally, and Palestinian society, particularly, not as monolithic wholes or simple dichotomous oppositions but rather as complexes in which diverse social groupings intersect and interact in ways that can potentially transform collective understandings of self and other under conditions of chronic national instability.

Within these dynamic social complexes religion can certainly play the stabilizing role that Kinvall, Giddens, and others have described, especially under conditions of chronic existential crisis. But the Palestinian case also demonstrates how processes of religious revitalization can, in their own right, generate or exacerbate social divisions and, in so doing, provoke countervailing responses rooted in alternative conceptions of belonging, heterodox and secular. The Palestinian case, consequently, forces us to reconsider the idea that religions *primarily* stabilize identity.

One must hasten to acknowledge that Palestinians have fought a long hard struggle to achieve recognition of their national existence; the persistence of alternative modes of identity and solidarity, such as religious ones, have seemed like false consciousness at best, treasonous sectarianism at worst. Anything that has threatened national unity has had to be resisted, and understandably so. One must also recognize that to direct attention to other forms of identity potentially plays into the "new Orientalism" that has reared its head in recent discussions about the Middle East—Iraq in particular, but also Lebanon, Palestine, Somalia, and Sudan.[12] The "tribe" has returned as a category of analysis with the implication that beneath the patina of nation-state structures one finds lurking age-old ethnic and religious proclivities that tend toward antidemocratic authoritarianism—an idea that echoes the trope of "Oriental despotism." Secularism, so goes the argument, is on the run, whether in Gaza, southern Lebanon, or Iraq. The justification for Lebanon 2006 or Gaza 2008–2009 and 2012, not to mention Afghanistan and Iraq, follows closely on the heels: a besieged liberal secular order must be defended at all costs. To raise the question of parallel social formations and their consequences for identity would seem to support this neo-Orientalist agenda and its call for reform of the Islamic other or, failing that, its violent suppression.[13]

How then to proceed? The answer surely is not to deny or negate other modes of identity and affiliation as false consciousness or mere fabrications of Orientalist fantasy. Sectarian formations are real, and regimes have mobilized them in the interest of establishing clients and undermining potential threats to the stability of their rule. Ignoring or devaluing such formations can only lead to serious distortions in analysis and understanding. Equally problematic, however, would be to privilege formations existing in parallel to the nation as the only relevant analytical category, denying thereby the basic fact of Palestinian national consciousness.

In what follows, I attempt to avoid both pitfalls by not losing sight of the broader context of occupation and the Palestinian struggle for national self-determination while nevertheless insisting that we see Palestinian society as a field of tension within which diverse social actors, possessing multiple affiliations, negotiate contending conceptions of belonging. What results from this approach is not the denial of the nation but rather a complex mapping of a continuum of identities that emerge in relation to the chronic destabilization of Palestinian social life.

The remainder of this essay depicts this continuum through an ethnographic analysis of three distinct institutional settings—a politically divided family in a large Gaza refugee camp; an Orthodox Christian youth group based at the Church of the Nativity in Bethlehem; and a small mosque in a Bethlehem-area refugee camp led by a shaykh with Muslim Brotherhood leanings. These examples derive from fieldwork carried out in the Gaza Strip and the West Bank in 1999–2000, the critical transition point between the rapidly imploding Oslo peace process and the outbreak of the al-Aqsa Intifada. The fieldwork built upon my prior years of experience of living in the West Bank from 1986 to 1989 and the Gaza Strip from 1991 to 1993. The data presented, therefore, capture the extended moment in which the secularist and Islamist divisions first emerged and then hardened in the struggles for factional dominance during the first Intifada and subsequent Oslo phase. As such, the data shed light on the identity dynamics that the Islamist-secularist tensions have engendered.

The analysis that follows focuses on the practices and discourses through which participants in the settings I describe internalized and expressed diverse notions of belonging. Sometimes these notions reflected the inherited ideological orientations of the dominant secular- and religio-nationalist formations, that is to say, Fatah and Hamas and their associated political tendencies. In other instances, they constituted alternative orientations rooted in the memory and institutions of the *hamula* (extended patriarchal family), religion, or neighborhood. In most cases, the interaction of these different levels produced hybrid identity conceptions that, depending on the intersubjective context, could either support or challenge the dominant frames in various ways. These complex processes offer us glimpses into how, at the level of the quotidian, Palestinians have attempted to "securitize the subject" in response to chronic ontological insecurity stemming from the contradictions, failures, and fragmentations of the secular-nationalist and religio-nationalist formations of Palestinian society since the late 1980s.

Family and Neighborhood in a Gaza Refugee Camp

Family and neighborhood constitute the primary institutional settings within which individuals live out their daily lives and forge their most immediate affiliations and value orientations. We see this especially in Palestinian refugee camps.[14] Rosemary Sayigh and Sara Roy have separately noted how after the massive forced displacements of the Nakba (the 1948 war) "the refugees turned inward, [clinging] to traditional forms of social organization and authority relations [so that] even today, the camps are divided into district quarters, each with its own *mukhtar*, or leader, which preserve the original village framework."[15] The persistence of family and traditional patriarchal social organization has had consequences for political identity. Individuals inherit faction loyalties through their families or adopt them through the influence of friends in their immediate neighborhood environs. The interaction among family, friends, and neighbors occurs through diverse mediating structures such as the exchange of social visits between homes, hanging out with one's *shilla* (an informal network of age-group peers who spend their free time together), going to markets on Friday, attending the local schools, and participating in prayer and study groups in neighborhood mosques and churches. These structures not only mediate social and political solidarities but also serve as sources of economic support, especially in impoverished refugee communities. Political factions have sought to secure loyalties by extending patronage. Observers have noted how the two dominant factions have mobilized support through a kind of rentier politics in which loyalties are secured in exchange for access to financial resources, jobs, or influence. Both Fatah and Hamas have pursued this type of politics by building extensive social service networks and cultivating links with traditional *hamula* institutions and religious organizations (mosques, churches). As a consequence, family and neighborhood ties become an extremely important means of access to aid, especially in communities like the refugee camps in Gaza that have struggled, since Israel's extended closure of the Strip beginning in the first Gulf War of 1990–1991, with intense long-term unemployment and the consequent chronic scarcity and poverty.

One of my informants in Gaza, a man I will call Latif, humorously expressed the importance of this basic reality by asking me if I had ever heard of "*ta'min waw*" (*waw* insurance). I replied I had not, thinking it was some new insurance company that had gotten established in Gaza along with the multiple other ventures that had appeared during the Oslo period. Latif laughed and then explained, "*ya zalameh, ta'min waw huwwa al-wasta!*" ("*Waw* insurance is connections, man!"[16]). He was referring to how he managed to land his job as head of maintenance in one of Gaza's new industrial parks near the Karni crossing point into Israel. The job was a reward from his Fatah contacts for his work in ferreting out collaborators with Israel during the first Intifada. Now he sat behind his desk and it was "*qahwah wa shay, shay wa qahwah kull yawm*" ("coffee and tea, tea and coffee every day"), he laughed. *Ta'min waw* was also how Latif's brother, whom I will refer to as Abu Jamil, had gotten his job as a maintenance supervisor in one of the headquarters of Fatah leader Muhammad Dahlan's Amn al-Wiqa'i, or Preventative Security. In this case, a family member with Fatah connections got Abu Jamil the job. The regular salary, the first he had ever received, enabled him to buy a beat-up car—a sign of a certain status in the camp. Abu Jamil's experience was hardly unique. Roy points out that by the late 1990s the Fatah-led Palestinian Authority (PA) had increasingly assumed the burden of employing Gazans. By 1998, PA wages accounted for 14 percent of the GDP in Gaza, twice the average of other developing economies. Two years later, the PA indicated that its expenditures on wages would "consume 60 percent of the $1 billion dollar budget."[17] These PA jobs were scarce for most Gazans, nonetheless, and thus the securing and manipulation of *wasta* (connections) remained an essential survival skill.

A third brother also relied on faction connections for economic security. However, this other brother, whom I will call ʿAbd al-Muʾmin, had loyalties to Hamas. He developed this orientation before the start of the first Intifada through his participation as a teenager in the *halaqat* (study circles) that Muslim Brotherhood activists organized in the mosque just down the road from their home in the camp. Through these connections, ʿAbd al-Muʾmin received support for computer training and eventually seed money to start an internet café in the camp's *suq*, or local business district and market area.[18] He would eventually marry into a family with strong Islamist orientations. His new wife, exploiting *mahram* injunctions,[19] would then insist on building a wall down the middle of the already cramped breeze-block and corrugated tin home, a move that caused a considerable degree of irritation and anger for Abu Jamil, who also lived with his family in this now partitioned structure.[20]

The tension between Abu Jamil and his brother and wife illustrated how the intersection of family and faction through the mediating structures of mosque and *shilla* (peer group) could reorient social and political solidarities. Such intersections had influenced a shift in Abu Jamil's loyalties. During the first Intifada, Abu Jamil had aligned with the Popular Front for the Liberation of Palestine. He had moved in this direction initially because of the influence of the *shilla* he was a part of in his camp neighborhood and also, perhaps, because being Popular Front distinguished him from his older brother, who, in aligning with Fatah, had continued the family's political tradition. During the Intifada, however, Abu Jamil became disenchanted with the Popular Front when he learned the faction had apparently not provided his wife and young children with any significant economic support after he was imprisoned on a six-month administrative detention charge. Before his release, he declared himself an independent. By the mid-1990s, however, he was working for the Fatah-aligned Amn al-Wiqaʾi (Preventative Security). In an alleyway conversation in the camp in 1996, an old friend from his boyhood *shilla,* an individual who had remained loyal to the Popular Front and was bitter about Fatah's crackdown on members of his faction, declared Fatah leader Yasser Arafat to be corrupt and autocratic. Abu Jamil reacted sharply, demanding that his childhood friend not make derogatory remarks about Abu ʿAmmar (Arafat's *nom de guerre*) in his presence. Patronage and integration into new faction structures had seemingly reoriented my friend, politically.

Three years later, however, I would learn that this loyalty shift was not as thoroughgoing as it might have seemed in that alleyway confrontation. Privately in 1999, Abu Jamil confided to me that if a new Intifada were to break out he would not go into the street and fight. Why die for a bunch of corrupt leaders from the "outside" who lived in ostentatious villas and hired Sri Lankan maids while everyone else was left to eke out a miserable existence in the camps, he asked rhetorically.[21] Abu Jamil was playing it safe, keeping a low profile in the camp and making sure he maintained good relationships in his neighborhood and with family members. One such friend owned a sewing workshop that produced clothes for the Israeli market. This friend would make clothes for Abu Jamil's family without Abu Jamil ever having to ask. In return, Abu Jamil performed electrical service and other maintenance work for the workshop. What counted in the end for Abu Jamil was this ethic of general reciprocity, an ethic he connected with the ʿadat wa taqalid ("customs and traditions") of traditional village society. If Abu Jamil identified with anything, it was with this notion of reciprocity and tradition in which family and friends assisted one another and deference was given to elders. Often during my visits with Abu Jamil, we would go to visit his aging uncle and hear his stories of fighting the British during the Mandate period.

We would sit on mats in an open-air patio, drinking bitter Bedouin coffee as the uncle lamented the loss of respect for family solidarity and the authority of elders.

The perceived failure of reciprocity—interpreted as rooted in a social and moral failure to adhere to the *ʿadat wa taqalid*—lay at the core of Abu Jamil's resentments toward his Hamas-oriented brother, ʿAbd al-Muʾmin. In opting for the Islamists, ʿAbd al-Muʾmin had effectively replaced his family with the faction. The wall his wife had driven down the center of the already tight quarters that she and her husband shared with Abu Jamil and his family symbolically signified this rupture. For Abu Jamil, this betrayal of fraternal loyalty and the consequent sundering of family unity amounted to a fundamental moral transgression, one that reduced the Islamists' rhetoric about brotherhood to sheer hypocrisy. Taken all together, thus, both the secular-nationalist and religio-nationalist options had become, for Abu Jamil, untenable and untrustworthy. The only authentic identity, the sole source of security, lay in familial and neighborly support systems founded on the ethic of reciprocity, an ethic that was at the core of the *ʿadat wa taqalid* of the *hamula* and its *fallahi* (peasant) ethos.

Christian Orthodox Flight from the Nation

The disenchantment among my Gaza contacts with secular-nationalist politics and factional rivalries, along with the perceived corruption within the leadership of the Fatah-led Palestinian Authority, had unexpected parallels in the Christian community. As with clan-based loyalties, Yasser Arafat and the PA leadership actively sought to mobilize the support of the traditional Christian leadership. In doing so, they played on Christian anxieties about the rapid demographic and social status decline of Christian communities in the West Bank and Jerusalem. In 1922, Christians comprised 11 percent of the total settled population of 649,048 living under British Mandatory rule. By 1946, the percentage of Christians had dropped to 8 percent of the total settled population of 1,845,559. Five and a half decades later, in 2000, Christians, estimating generously, barely comprised 1.5 percent (40,055) of the overall *Palestinian* population (2,597,616) in the West Bank and Gaza Strip.[22]

A similar pattern emerges in areas of strong Christian concentration. In Bethlehem, the largely middle-class Christian community confronted inexorable displacement as a consequence of the emigration of entire Christian families to Europe, Australia, and the Americas. In the wake of the departing Christians, a new Muslim middle class, mostly businesspeople from the southern West Bank, began settling within Bethlehem. Between 1946 and 1997, the percentage of Christians decreased from 78 percent to 56 percent of the total Palestinian population living within the Bethlehem urban area (comprising Bethlehem and the neighboring towns of Beit Sahur and Beit Jala).

The reasons for the demographic decline are numerous and described in detail elsewhere.[23] The fundamental point is that in 1999–2000 Palestinian Christians were experiencing severe existential anxiety on two levels: as members of a Palestinian national community under an aggressive colonizing occupation and as members of a rapidly shrinking minority within the besieged Palestinian community. Compounding this anxiety was the perception that the ideological and structural coherence of secular-nationalism, to which Palestinian Christians historically had provided important intellectual and political leadership, appeared to be unraveling. Many of my Christian interlocutors worried about the internal Islamization of Fatah and the PA, describing incidents of open discrimination and a discernible shift in the public symbols and rhetoric of leaders like Arafat. At the same time, the rising Islamist alternative presented a worse threat—a return to the days of *ahl al-dhimma*[24] and all that it implied for the reduction of the Christian community to second-class-citizen status. The sense of threat became palpable in the aftermath of the attempt in 2000 by the Islamic Movement in Nazareth to resurrect the burial site of a long-lost relative of Salah al-Din al-Ayyubi.[25] The Islamic Movement's fortuitous discovery of this tomb dramatized the increasing political strength of Palestinian Islamists in Nazareth. Located in the plaza of the Basilica of the Annunciation, an imposing structure that projects the prestige of the Catholic Church in the city, the tomb functioned symbolically to contest local Christian social and political dominance as well as Israeli assertions of power. (The Israeli government had planned to expand the basilica's plaza in preparation for large numbers of tourists who would come to the city to mark millennial celebration events, including the Pope's much-anticipated visit.) The events in Nazareth dramatized Christian vulnerability. Responding to these events and the Islamists' references to Christians as subordinate tribute-paying minorities (*ahl al-dhimma*), Bethlehem University sociologist Bernard Sabella stated, "At the dawn of the twenty-first century, the idea of *ahl al-dhimma* is no longer acceptable. I exist in Palestine not because Muslims or the PA or Israel 'protect me.' I exist here by virtue of my birth, and, above all, because I am a Palestinian."[26]

Yet, protection is precisely what Yasser Arafat and the PA sought to extend to the Christian community in an effort to play on fears of the loss of social and economic position in communities like Bethlehem and of Hamas's ascendancy—despite the fact that at that moment, the PA had succeeded in weakening Hamas militarily and isolating it politically.[27] In extending this protection Arafat and the PA leadership reached out to the traditional religious and social elites within the Christian community, offering them access and leadership positions within local councils and within the upper PA leadership. As Yezid Sayigh points out, this was standard procedure for Arafat, a master of rentier politics.[28] These tactics played out in plain view on 4 December 1999 during the inaugural celebration for Bethlehem 2000.

Bethlehem 2000 was a yearlong event meant to project the Palestinian Authority into various international forums and demonstrate to domestic constituencies its capacity to obtain international development assistance. Large sums of donor money funded a major facelift of Bethlehem's aging infrastructure. The din and dust of street and building repair became a constant of town life in the lead-up to the event. Church leaders and business elites hoped the improvements and publicity would attract world attention, thus amplifying the importance of the Christian community as well as securing an influx of tourism dollars.

The PA, for its part, desired to use the event to reinforce its position internally as the main conduit of patronage. At the opening celebration, the official invitation and program of events declared the ceremonies to be "under the patronage of His Excellency President Yasser Arafat." The events schedule indicated that Arafat would appear at eleven o'clock in the morning. On the appointed day, however, the president had still not made his much-anticipated entrance when dusk began to settle on the gathered crowd and heads of churches perched on the stage in Manger Square. With tension and anticipation growing, Latin patriarch Michel Sabbah began addressing the gathered crowd but was interrupted by a wail of sirens and a line of sport utility vehicles with security personnel hanging off the sides. The crowd jumped to its feet, stood on chairs, and began cheering as Arafat emerged and took the stage, embracing and kissing each church leader before finally standing with Patriarch Sabbah. In the aftermath of the Nazareth Basilica controversy, in which Arafat had intervened on the side of the churches, the Christians of Bethlehem had been feeling vulnerable and resentful toward what they saw as an ever-encroaching Islamic movement. Many privately criticized the PA for doing little to stem the Islamist advance. Arafat's appearance in Bethlehem, as well as his intervention in the Nazareth affair, sent a different signal. In standing on the stage with the gathered heads of the various churches, he symbolically reasserted the role he wished to claim as protector of the holy places and attentive father of the nation who included all Palestinians within his embrace. He, not the Islamists, he seemed to show, guaranteed the importance and presence of the Christian minority. The Christians gathered in Manger Square understood this message and shouted their approval.

If nothing else, the inaugural ceremonies of Bethlehem 2000 illustrated how state and quasi-state entities, in this case Arafat and the PA, sought to instrumentalize sectarian identities and loyalties in an effort to reinforce their control and legitimacy. The backing of church heads gave Arafat credibility abroad and the support of a wealthy minority at home. It also allowed him to project the image of an all-inclusive nationalism that contrasted with the exclusivity of both Zionism and Hamas's religio-nationalism. A closer analysis of the phenomenon, however, reveals that the retrieval of Christian sectarian identities was not simply a matter of top-down activation by movements or state entities. Church institutions as well as generational factors also played an important role in the process. From this angle of vision the appearance of Christian solidarity with Arafat-style nationalism gives way to a more complex picture. For some individuals, often the younger generation that came of age during and after the first Intifada, for example, the turn toward religion indexed disenchantment with the nation, not the affirmation of it that had been on display in Manger Square. For these individuals, the retreat into a Christian sectarian identity provided, in George Santayana's words, "another world to live in."[29]

During my fieldwork in 1999–2000, I spent considerable time getting to know members of the Greek Orthodox *shabiba,* or youth group. After a period of abeyance, the group became active again after a local doctor known for having strong pan-Arab nationalist sympathies revived it during the first Intifada (1987–1993). His intention had been to raise the nationalist consciousness of Orthodox youth in Bethlehem and provide them with an organizational outlet that reinterpreted religious sectarian orientations in terms of pan-Arab and multisectarian PLO nationalist sensibilities. As such, the church-based shabiba was meant to serve as an authentic nationalist Christian alternative to secular PLO faction organizations and also as a response to Muslim sectarian groups like Islamic Jihad and Hamas. Ironically, however, several of the core youth activists in the revived shabiba came to resist the nationalist emphasis, seeing it to be in significant contradiction with strict Orthodox identity and practice. These youths succeeded in eventually reorienting the purpose of the shabiba toward instilling a specifically Orthodox solidarity and religiosity among teens and young adults. Accordingly, shabiba activities shifted toward attendance at daily afternoon and evening liturgies, going to instructional talks focusing on Orthodox belief and practice, and participating in charitable work in the parishes. As I joined them in these activities, I increasingly realized that the built spaces, institutions, leadership, and practices of the church created an alternative canopy under which my interlocutors had found shelter in the midst of the turbulence of the unresolved struggle for a national existence.

The shabiba met often in the Basilica's main sanctuary or its various chapels. These spaces, redolent of centuries of Orthodox piety and community, hearkened to a religious identity that transcended the limited time and space of Palestinian nationalism. One entered the main sanctuary through a five-foot-high portal. Forcing those passing through it to bend at the waist, the door symbolically marked the transition from a profane space, the noise and bustle of Manger Square with its phalanxes of tour buses, pilgrims, souvenir shops, cafés, and peddlers, to a sacred temporal-spatial zone filled with incense and the hypnotic rhythms and quarter-tones of the Byzantine liturgy. After entering, one walked under the low ceiling of the narthex—a compressed space that then gave way instantly to the soaring ceiling of the main worship hall lined with orange marble columns. At the far, east end, there was a raised platform with high-backed wooden benches along the sides. An iconostasis rose up against the rear wall of the platform. Behind it rested an altar at which the priests, partially obscured from view, performed the Eucharistic mysteries. The spatial organization and iconography conveyed imperial power—the royal processions of the liturgy, the robed and mitered priests and monks, the iconic image of Christos Pantocrator ("Ruler of All"), the rising columns. To enter into this space was to enter into the nostalgic realm of Orthodoxy with its symbolic reconstitutions of

Constantinian imperial power and the long-departed Pax Christiana in the Holy Land.

The liturgical and didactic practices of the church reinforced the spatial contours within which this parallel nostalgic Orthodoxy came into being. The youth activists I came to know during the months I observed and participated in the work of the shabiba illustrated how these practices could shape a "physical *hexis*,"[30] an embodied cognitive-emotional disposition that signaled and shaped a distinct Arabo-Greco-"Orthodox" ethos and personality. This synthesized disposition was literally the work and product of the liturgy, in which Greek and Arabic became intertwined, as well as of an institutional structure in which Greek monks and Palestinian priests interacted with the shabiba youth to forge a trans-ethnic religious community whose primary external lines of distinction were religio-communal. To be part of this group was to define oneself in opposition to the non-Orthodox, that is, the various mutations of Latin Catholicism, the multiple manifestations of Protestantism, and of course Islam and Judaism. The Arabo-Greco synthesis discerned here might have been specifically distinctive of Bethlehem. The Orthodox groups in other centers with significant Christian populations—for example, Beit Jala, Beit Sahur, and Ramallah—evinced a contrasting phenomenon. In these other places, deep divisions between the local Arab Palestinian parishioners and the Greek-dominated hierarchy had developed over the course of a century and a half and were revived during the Oslo period. In the community that based itself at the Basilica of the Nativity in Bethlehem, however, the Greek hierarchy seemed to have forged a much closer bond with the Palestinian laity, especially with the youth. It is this integration and its implications for the creation of a counter- or transnational ethos—an alternative religious "world to live in"—that I will explore here.

During Lent in 2000, the Orthodox shabiba met each Friday at five o'clock in the evening for a liturgy in the Nativity Basilica's Mar Jiriyis Chapel.[31] To get to the chapel, one walked through the main worship space of the Basilica toward the raised platform, the *bema,* bearing the iconostasis and altar at the far, east end. To the right, a short set of stairs led up to a door that opened out onto a small plaza enclosed by the high walls of the Basilica and the adjoining structure containing the monk's living quarters and church offices. The entrance to the chapel was directly off of this enclosure. As with the Basilica's main entrance, the door leading into the chapel was barely five feet high, forcing everyone who passed through to bow at the waist in a symbolic gesture of submission to the royal authority of Christ and his priestly representatives. The contrast between the bright plaza and the cool, dark chapel was stark. The interior was close and intimate. High-backed wooden pews lined the facing wall. An iconostasis and altar rested against the back wall. To either side were low wooden benches.

On one April evening in 2000, I attended the weekly Lenten liturgy with the shabiba. Three of my contacts—Antun, George, and Sawsan (all pseudonyms)—were present. Antun, an Armenian who had converted to Orthodoxy recently, and George, the son of a deceased Bethlehem University professor, sat in the high-backed benches. They had been training as cantors under the guidance of the priests and monks at the Basilica and during these evening gatherings helped lead the congregation through the different tonal settings of the liturgy. As their position at the front indicated, Antun and George were leaders in the shabiba and both were considering careers within the church. Antun, following in his father's footsteps, had been developing a reputation locally as a skilled iconographer. He got his start in making icons during the first Intifada. His father, wishing to keep Antun out of harm's way, insisted his son help him with his work. He became absorbed in the craft and soon discovered he had a knack for painting. "I felt the Spirit had taken hold of my hands," he told me, adding, "This was the time that I began to turn away from politics and focus on religion exclusively." His shift to Orthodoxy came later through the influence of friends like George, who were connected to the newly formed shabiba.

George—departing sharply from his brother, who studied business administration at Bethlehem University, reveled in pop music, and ridiculed the priests—was planning to study theology in Lebanon and perhaps enter the priesthood. During the Intifada, he had been a student activist in a local cell of the Democratic Front for the Liberation of Palestine. He originally saw his involvement with the reconstituted Orthodox shabiba as merely an extension of his pan-Arab nationalist orientations. Later, though, under the influence of other activists like Sawsan as well as the priests and monks, he became instrumental in reorienting the shabiba away from political concerns and toward a specific Orthodox religious horizon.

In her late twenties, Sawsan was slightly older than George and Antun. She was one of the youth founders of the shabiba and, by all accounts, was the main force behind the reorienting of the group. Like George and Antun, she had undergone a reconversion to Orthodoxy after having become estranged from it. Her parents, according to her description, never attended the liturgies except for the major festivals—Easter and Christmas, primarily. Sawsan attended private Latin Catholic schools and had considered becoming Catholic. During the first Intifada, however, after the Israeli military forced the closing of all the schools, she began to participate in Orthodox liturgies with an aunt in Jerusalem and then started going to the Basilica in Bethlehem in the mornings. She also initiated meetings with a Greek monk for spiritual direction and, for a time, considered becoming a nun. After getting involved with the shabiba in Bethlehem, she quickly became embroiled in a conflict with the adult leader who had reconstituted the group soon after the start of the Intifada. This individual, as described earlier, held pan-Arab nationalist (*qawmi*) sympathies that he had acquired while studying in Iraq during the 1970s. Sawsan disagreed strongly with the politicization of the shabiba's meetings and insisted that the group focus strictly on discussions of theology, liturgy, and Orthodox history. She successfully convinced other youth leaders in the group of her views and together, with the support of the monks and priests, they reoriented the shabiba toward confessional, religious concerns.

After entering the Mar Jiriyis chapel that April evening, I noticed Antun and George had already arrived and had taken up positions in the high-backed wooden benches. Just after five o'clock, the presiding priest, a Palestinian from Beit Sahur, began intoning the opening lines of the liturgy. One of the Greek bishops was also present and traded off with the Palestinian priest in leading the chanting, with Antun and George serving as the choir. The bishop and priest alternated between Greek and Arabic. The youths followed along in their prayer manuals, and at the appropriate times, in imitation of the priest and bishop, would cross themselves by bending deeply at the waist, reaching to the floor with their right hands and then tracing a vertical line to their heads as they straightened, ending by sweeping their hands first to their right and then to their left shoulders. The Gospel reading also occurred in Greek and then Arabic, and it became apparent at this point that the Greek bishop also was fluent in Arabic. On this particular evening, the priests blessed a vessel of oil by making the sign of the cross over it with a copy of the New Testament while everyone else kneeled on the stone floor and bowed their heads. After this, the bishop and priest marked the foreheads, cheeks, forehands, and palms of the participants using what re-sembled a thick basting brush.

The Arabo-Greco integration so evident in the liturgical performance—especially in its linguistic hybridity and in the blending of Greek and Arab-Palestinian ethnicities within the authority structure, a blending symbolized by the Greek bishop and Palestinian priest serving together as co-officiators of the ritual—became further apparent in the semi-regular study sessions of the shabiba. On one June evening, I attended a study session led by the same Palestinian priest from Beit Sahur who had officiated at the liturgy described above, as well as by a Greek monk who was also a bishop from a parish in Kufr Kana in the Galilee. This monk-bishop was the guest lecturer. On this particular evening he spoke about the failure of the church to educate pa-rishioners on the importance of the liturgy and the Eucharist. He spoke in Greek, mostly, while the Palestinian priest translated into Arabic.

The monk-bishop claimed that the church's failure to educate its parish-ioners lay largely in the dilution of Orthodox-only schools. This dilution was, he said, the consequence of the enrollment of large numbers of Muslim students. In an effort not to offend its tuition-paying Muslim students, the schools had stopped explicit instruction in Orthodox theology and liturgical practice. As a result, the monk averred, Orthodox youth were susceptible to the corrupting influence of Western mass culture and conversion pressures from Catholic, Protestant, and Muslim groups. The youth were forgetting their Orthodox heritage and this fact threatened the future of the church. The church therefore needed to reach the youth and reorient them to the distinctions that mattered—that is, the distinctions between true Chris-tianity (Orthodoxy) and false Christianity (all other Christian confessions) as well as between Christian and non-Christian (the secular West, Islam).

The monk-bishop took particular aim at the expression "*kullu wahid*" ("All are one"). He claimed to have encountered this expression frequently, especially among Palestinian Christians. "All are *not* one!" he insisted. The idea of oneness, in his view, was a symptom of Western-style secularization and nationalism. "People don't want to confess their faith in front of Mus-lims. They prefer to say instead, 'We are all Palestinians.'" The church was not against nationalism (*al-qawmiyya*), he claimed, "but it is critical to maintain clear distinctions in matters of religion." The monk then launched into a de-tailed discussion of the Greek New Testament term *logos*—the uncreated Divine Word made human—and the notion of salvation and sanctification it implies. Using the Arabic word *ʿilaj,* he explained that *logos* was a type of "therapy." Only through Orthodoxy, he claimed, did this *ʿilaj* (therapy)—which he described as a thoroughgoing transformation ("sanctification") of the human being, who was subject to sin—become available to humanity. All other religions have "theoretical" notions of God, he said. None of them provided the actual, effective means, the *ʿilaj,* which could transform the soul through direct contact with the Holy Spirit. Only through the *ʿilaj* that Orthodoxy offered could humans achieve the transcendence of the human condition in the kingdom of God—a place beyond time and space. Only participation in the liturgy and the constant repetition of the phrase "*Ya rubb irhamna*" ("O Lord have mercy on us") could effect the transformation. "The West sees this and thinks we are mumbling nonsense," claimed the monk-bishop, "but we taste the Kingdom and ask God for help. We are not all one because not all paths lead to this salvation. There is only one true path, the path marked out by Orthodox piety and practice."

The monk-bishop's assertions—particularly his metaphor of *ʿilaj* ("cure" or "therapy")—resonated with the shabiba members in attendance. They peppered the bishop with questions about sanctification. His consistent response was that the youth needed to participate in the daily liturgy. Sanctification was not for cenobitic monks alone, but for all the laity as long as they were regularly present and took part in the liturgy. His insistence concerning the liturgy reflected the actual weekly practice of the shabiba. Through their recurring liturgical performances they forged a parallel social world structured along a divergent axis of memory and aspiration. The nation and its traumas and centripetal tensions receded within the space and time of the liturgy. The referents were to the Orthodox past and the work of sanctification through which that past became embodied in the physical-emotional-mental dispositions (*hexis*) of the shabiba youth. These dispositions not only made Orthodox memory present but also oriented those who now embodied it toward the task of recreating and reinforcing Orthodox solidarity into the future. The Kingdom of God, in the sense of Orthodox memory, practices, and structures, had become the primary cultural and institutional locus of identity for these youths. Figuratively understood, this Kingdom secured a transcendent Orthodox subject against an ontological destabilization resulting from a progressively precarious Palestinian national existence from which Christians, at least those Christians I interacted with in Bethlehem, increasingly felt excluded.

West Bank Camp Life and Islamist Re-Securitizing of the Subject

Christians were not the only group in Bethlehem to experience the ontological insecurity stemming from the indeterminacies that accompanied the
installation of the Palestinian Authority and the fraught negotiation process with Israel. Refugee communities in the area, too, grappled with the
implications of a peace deal that had given rise to a discourse of "normalization" (al-tatbi°)—the notion that because peace was imminent the refugees should end their insistence on the right of return (haqq al-°awda) to
the towns and villages from which they had been expelled in the 1948 war,
dismantle the refugee camps—long-established symbols of the injustice of
forced displacement—and resettle in new homes in the surrounding sub-
urbs. In Bethlehem-area camps, murals depicted the iconic skeleton key that
stood for the homes lost in 1948 and called upon residents to hold fast to the
right of return enshrined in UN Resolution 194, Article 11. These sentiments
found further expression in the repeated negative assessments and worries
of some of my contacts in the camps. Far from viewing the Palestinian Authority as a positive embodiment of their aspirations, these contacts, both
secularist and Islamist, saw the Oslo process and the PA as threats to their
collective existence. Many of them were former Intifada activists who felt
fundamentally betrayed by Oslo.

The depth and extent of these sentiments became clear to me on 22 March
2000, the day that Pope John Paul II visited Dheishe Camp as part of his
millennial tour of the Holy Land. This long-expected visit—an appearance
and short speech in the presence of President Arafat in the courtyard of the
camp's UN school that lasted barely thirty minutes—ended unexpectedly
in a violent Intifada-style clash between camp residents and the PA police
who had swept in with the president's entourage and flooded the camp.[32]
The clash began with fistfights between camp shabab (youth) volunteers re-
cruited to help provide order during the event and members of the PA police, whom camp residents subsequently identified as having come from the
Gaza Strip. Fistfights very quickly gave way to rock throwing between the
camp youth and the police, many of whom were young Intifada veterans
themselves. By midnight, camp activists had retrieved automatic rifles and
begun firing on the police station on the outskirts of the camp in an attempt
to free shabab detained during the melee. When I returned the next afternoon, I learned that the head of Preventative Security (the Amn al-Wiqaʾi),

a resident of the camp, had taken the side of the camp shabab. No one knew what would happen to those arrested. Dheishe residents called on Arafat to force the resignation of the police chief, who apparently insulted camp residents, calling them dogs. The camp itself lay under a carpet of rocks and shattered glass. I noticed the new traffic light installed at the camp's entrance just before the Pope's visit lying shattered in the road. One of my contacts commented, "I am sad the light was destroyed but thrilled we stood up to the police!"

What the *ishtibak* (clash) between Dheishe's former Intifada fighters and the PA police revealed was the fragility of Palestinian national unity. Long-simmering resentment against the PA could erupt instantly into open conflict. In the ensuing violence, other solidarities, subnational ones, could and did emerge. In the case of the post-Papal visit clashes in Dheishe, local camp solidarity prevailed—most vividly in the case mentioned earlier of the Preventative Security official who was also a resident of the camp—over loyalty to Arafat, the father of the nation, and his PA, the structural manifestation of the version of the nation Arafat putatively stood for. Yet camp solidarity, too, could be unstable. Oslo "normalization" had thrown the *raison-d'être* of the camps into serious question. Moreover, camp residents were as politically divided as any other Palestinian community. Traditionally leftist, Dheishe had witnessed the emergence of an influential Fatah presence, especially following the establishment of the PA in Bethlehem. It had also, during the first Intifada, seen the rise of a small Islamist contingent. What it meant to be a Dheishen, then, had become increasingly contested even if in moments of collective crisis, such as what transpired immediately following the Pope's departure, camp solidarity might briefly reassert itself.

I have examined elsewhere the secularist-Islamist tensions in the refugee camps in the Bethlehem area.[33] Here, I wish instead to focus on the institutions, practices, and conceptual categories through which Islamists in one of these camps, a community I will refer to as "Thawra Camp," built a parallel world to live in, one that provided shelter against the insecurities of camp life and the unpredictability of PA apparatuses increasingly seen as violent and corrupt.

My entrée into Thawra's small Islamist community[34] was through an individual I have named Shaykh Abu Banna, the founder of a mosque that stands some hundred meters from the community center and international guest house that institutionally anchors the dominant secular-leftist milieu. I first heard about the shaykh from his leftist detractors, who resented his preaching against the mixing of girls and boys in their community center activities. Born and raised in the camp, the shaykh had studied religious sciences at the University of Jordan in Amman during the late 1970s. He returned to Thawra in 1981 with strong Muslim Brotherhood leanings and began working for the *Awqaf* (Islamic Religious Endowment Authority) in Jerusalem. During the first Intifada, the shaykh found it increasingly difficult to travel to Jerusalem and so refocused his activities on the Bethlehem-area mosques and on Thawra in particular. He founded his mosque in Thawra during the Intifada as part of a long-term effort to reorient camp residents toward Islam through institution building and *da'wa* (missionary outreach that aims at reviving, reinforcing, and reforming the piety of Muslims, primarily).[35] The shaykh's interest in da'wa was strong, a fact that other Islamist activists that I came to know in Bethlehem attested to. My own interaction with the shaykh confirmed this interest. In every one of our meetings, the shaykh would turn our conversation from politics to the glorious contributions of Muslim converts as diverse as 'Umar Ibn al-Khattab and Yusuf Islam (Cat Stevens).

In describing his work to me, Shaykh Abu Banna drew stark dichotomies between those engaged in *jihad*—understood primarily as individuals who undertake the work of *da'wa*—and those who perpetuate terror and oppression. Within the latter category, he included anyone who opposed the advance of Islam—Israel, for an obvious example, but also, more pointedly, the secularists in the camp, fellow Thawrans, who abetted practices that undermined the collective moral order and thereby contributed to social chaos (*fitna*) among neighbors and between the sexes. In one of my earliest conversations with him, Shaykh Abu Banna likened his role in the camp to that of the Prophet Muhammad during his early preaching in Mecca. Thawra was like Mecca of that time, a community in crisis. It had lost its moral compass and cohesion. The strong exploited the weak. No one understood that humans had duties and responsibilities toward one another and ultimately toward God. Like the prophet, Shaykh Abu Banna sought to call his fellow Thawrans back to a consciousness of God embodied in the notion of *taqwa*—a unity of belief and practice grounded in Qur'anic dispensation.

Shaykh Abu Banna understood that to achieve this reorientation it was necessary to create an institutional structure that could support the emergence of an alternative religio-sociomoral milieu. The construction of his mosque during the Intifada along with a social outreach center that others in the camp identified as affiliated with the Muslim Brotherhood were signal events in this process. The development of these structures was controversial and resulted at one point in the mid-1980s just before the outbreak of the first Intifada in an open clash with leaders of the camp's Popular Front for the Liberation of Palestine faction. The clash, described initially as a fight between families, ended badly for the nascent Muslim Brotherhood contingent. Shaykh Abu Banna, however, led a recovery, and by the end of the 1990s he had clearly succeeded in establishing an Islamist presence in the camp.

I attended Shaykh Abu Banna's mosque several times during the summer of 2000. The structure was a small unassuming building that appeared still to be under construction. To enter, one had to step over mounds of sand and concrete blocks and around a cement mixer and other building tools and machines. The entrance, located off a narrow alley, led into a vestibule with shoulder-high wooden shelving subdivided into dozens of small boxes for shoes. A small set of stairs led up to a main worship space on the floor just above street level. Thin, flickering fluorescent tubes gave the space a dim, pale glow as rows of overhead fans stirred the hot, humid air. The walls were painted mint green and white. On the opposite wall stood a structure marking the *qibla* (prayer direction), a tall cabinet structure made of finished plywood with an arch cut out of it. The walls were barren except for a series of clocks indicating prayer times. A small room along the back wall contained the public address system. Covering the floor was a green all-purpose carpet with white strips of tape marking where worshipers should line up to form prayer ranks.

During the evenings I attended the mosque, approximately forty to forty-five camp residents ranging from teenagers to elderly men would come for the prayers. On one occasion, I entered into an extended discussion with an older gentleman active in daʿwa work. He recounted the glories of heaven, the reward for a pious life, as well as the necessity of faithful perseverance, like Joseph,[36] in the face of temptations and tribulations. These themes often appeared in Shaykh Abu Banna's homilies before the prayers. Shaykh Abu Banna never in my presence preached openly political sermons. Rather, as was his tendency, he focused on matters of piety, instructing worshipers in proper practice and discoursing on the importance of adhering to this practice as an example to others. As noted earlier, he would echo these themes in conversation with me, recounting the heroic piety of Islam's most prominent champions, each of whom responded to the Prophet's summons to abandon prior commitments and join the nascent Muslim community. Upon completion of his remarks, Shaykh Abu Banna, dressed in his *jalabiyya* (full-length white tunic) and red-checkered *hatta*,[37] would stand in the *qibla* to lead the series of invocations, recitations, and prostrations of the formal *salat* prayer. The ritual reinforced the discourse of piety in the shaykh's homilies. As with the Orthodox liturgies in the Christian community, it served to inculcate a distinctive bodily *hexis* and the attendant mental and emotional orientations that marked an individual as a member of the camp's Islamic milieu. This milieu defined itself through expressions of piety in personal and group demeanor, expressions that gave rise among those integrated within the group to a sense of difference relative to the dominant secularist ethos of the camp.

This sense of distinction and the ethos it rested in marked the orientations of a young married couple I came to know as a result of my visits to Shaykh Abu Banna's mosque. This couple had been supporters of Fatah during the first Intifada but had subsequently shifted their allegiances to the Islamic Movement. I had immediately noticed Majdi, the husband, at the mosque because when he prayed he was unable to bend his right leg when kneeling for the *raka'at*. I later learned he had broken the leg while running from soldiers during the first Intifada. The leg never healed properly. In my extensive conversations with Majdi and his wife, Amal, the couple were at pains to make clear to me that their embrace of Islam did not entail a rejection of modernity per se but rather of certain aspects of secularism they perceived as damaging to camp solidarity and morality. They lamented the deterioration of neighborly relationships. One of the neighboring families was building an addition to their home in the camp, for example, but, in doing so, had taken little care to keep the building materials out of the shared alleyway. This family also worked on the construction during hours when others were trying to rest or sleep. Had their neighbors possessed a stronger sense of piety, Majdi commented, they would have taken care to contain the construction and respect the needs of those around them. In the absence of a shared commitment to Islam, however, the community lacked not only basic decorum but also the conflict-resolution mechanisms that the shari'a provided. What prevailed, they told me, was a situation of each individual seeking his own gain at the expense of others. For Majdi and Amal, this reality stood for the general anomic condition of Palestinian society in the post-Intifada Oslo period.

Majdi and Amal listed many other social problems—for example, improper relations between the sexes and the divorce and marital strife that it produced, harassment of women in the streets by shabab, and the building of a casino in Jericho that promoted economic exploitation. What they desired was a return to a sense of proper limits in interpersonal interactions and institutional structures. At the same time, however, they argued for a "modern Islam" that supported the right of women to pursue a career. Majdi and Amal, as members of an emerging professional class in the camp—they both worked as schoolteachers—sought to ground their middle-class aspirations in an Islamic moral framework that stood in opposition to what they saw as the increasing secularization and consequent erosion of the moral foundations of camp solidarity.

Conclusion

As the ethnographic examples in this essay make clear, the recourse to religion and tradition often entails an attempt to resituate a subject that has become dislocated under chronic anomic conditions. A number of classical and contemporary theorists have stressed this locative (or re-locative) function as the core feature of religious institutions and practices.[38] According to this view, the primary purpose of religious myths, discourses, symbols, rituals, and institutions is to situate individuals and groups within a cosmos and to preserve and defend this situatedness through appeals to transcendent and timeless order. Even when inverted in "religions of rebellion" or "religions of revolution,"[39] the act of rebellion often simply reverses the terms of transcendence rather than overcoming them: heterodoxy inversely mirrors the claims of orthodoxy, reflecting a basic homologous relation and dialectic between the two.[40]

Yet, even as the Palestinian case recounted here would seem to confirm these insights, it also reveals the polyvalent, multidirectional, and contradictory character of any attempt to stabilize the subject through a retrieval of religion or tradition. Palestinian society, like all contemporary societies, has undergone significant institutional and sociomoral differentiation under the pressures of secularization, urbanization, industrialization, mass displacement, and mass politicization. A retrieval of the religious or "traditional" past under such circumstances can become a factor of destabilization and division as much as it can serve to unify and ground individual or collective identity. As the case of Abu Jamil in Gaza demonstrates, attempts to impose religious solidarities can split families, already shot through with diverging faction loyalties that have developed with the rise of mass politics. They can also provoke counter-retrievals and assertions of "secular" identities, sometimes in "retraditionalized" forms, as with Abu Jamil's appeal to the *fallahi* (peasant) ethic of general reciprocity contained in the *ʿadat wa taqalid* (customs and traditions). These dynamics can extend into the wider society, engendering opposing religious and "secular" identity subcultures within and across the secularist-Islamist divide.

Of course, these identity processes become comprehensible only under the conditions of perceived crisis such as have existed in Palestine and the wider Middle East since at least 1967. For many people, and not just Palestinians, secularism has proven to be deceptive and damaging. The religious return indexes this disenchantment with secularism and the corresponding search for other possibilities that this disillusionment has generated. And, yet, as Olivier Roy and Martin Riesebrodt have pointed out, albeit in different ways, the recourse to religion in the search for a comprehensive alternative to the secular nation-state has equally failed to overcome the underlying structural determinants that have produced the very conditions against which religious retrievals respond in the first place.[41] Such retrievals often devolve into forms of religious nationalism, protesting the symbols of secularism and secularity while accommodating the insurmountable structural foundations of the secular order.

Given this fact, and given their capacity to destabilize even as they attempt to re-securitize the subject, it is not clear at all that religious retrievals can succeed in stemming the ontological insecurity that arises under conditions of chronic destabilization. Indeed, they might even exacerbate insecurity by deepening existing lines of division. Hamas is ascendant, at least among certain significant segments of Palestinian society, but so far it appears incapable of forging a new foundation for collective solidarity that can repair the secularist-Islamist rift and mark out a new path for Palestinians to follow in their struggle against Israeli domination. If anything, the sociomoral and political split and concomitant sense of crisis have become sharper in the face of secularist resistance to Hamas's ascendancy and unrestrained Israeli use of force to suppress the emergence of a non-quiescent religio-political alternative. If neither nation nor religion can offer any real hope of ending the crisis and achieving some kind of shared vision and coherent sense of collective self, then what other options do Palestinians have? Could exile be a permanent condition? Could it be tolerated? Could it lead to other ways of being a people? What would it mean to renounce the singular nation *and* the one *umma* or ecclesia as realizable possibilities for collective life and instead embrace binational, religiously plural identities within the reigning structures? Would this signal defeat or would it open a path to the transformation and transcendence of these structures, especially within Israel? These questions lie at the heart of the still unresolved contradictions of Zionism and Palestine.

Notes

1. Michael Moran, "'Hamastan' Takes Shape on the Gaza Strip," Council on Foreign Relations, 17 June 2007; Dennis Ross, "The Specter of 'Hamastan': More Must Be Done to Counter Islamist Gains in Gaza," *Washington Post*, 4 June 2007; Brig.-Gen. (res.) Shalom Harari, "Iran Is Building 'Hamastan' in Gaza," Jerusalem Center for Public Affairs, 11 March 2007.

2. The most recent poll, as of this writing, from the Palestinian Center for Policy and Survey Research indicates that if elections were held today Hamas leader and elected Palestinian Authority prime minister in Gaza Ismail Haniyeh would defeat Fatah leader and Palestinian Authority president in Ramallah Mahmoud Abbas by a margin of 48 percent to 45 percent. Just three months prior to this survey, however, Abbas would have defeated Haniyeh by 51 percent to 40 percent, respectively. The authors of the survey suggest that the reason for this dramatic reversal lies in the public perception that Hamas won the military engagement with Israel in Gaza during March 2012: 81 percent say Hamas was the winner. This perception, they say, also correlates with public support for "Hamas's way" of armed resistance (41 percent support) as opposed to "Abbas's way" of negotiation (30 percent) or nonviolent resistance (24 percent). Note that these figures, whether those pertaining to Haniyeh's lead over Abbas or those referring to support for violence, represent a plurality, not a "majority," as the study's authors claim. Moreover, if support for negotiation is combined with support for nonviolent resistance, then 54 percent of Palestinians appear to back approaches at odds with Hamas's emphasis on armed violence. Interestingly, if an election were held today between the imprisoned younger Fatah leader, Marwan Barghouti, and Ismail Haniyeh, Barghouti would win by a clear majority of 51 percent to 42 percent, respectively. (This figure, however, represents a significant decline from three months ago, when Barghouti trumped Haniyeh by 61 percent to 32 percent.) Finally, if parliamentary elections were held, 35 percent say they would vote for Hamas while 36 percent

would cast ballots for Fatah. Taken together, these results continue to reflect deep and fluctuating political divisions in the Palestinian population. Neither Hamas nor Fatah, under Abbas's leadership, at least, appears capable of achieving clear majority backing for either violent resistance or negotiations despite the apparent findings that currently show a plurality of support for Haniyeh and "Hamas's way" (but see the qualification noted above). For the full survey, Palestinian Center for Policy and Survey Research (PSR), "Palestinian Public Opinion Poll No (46): In the Aftermath of the Gaza War: Hamas' way is preferred by the majority over Abbas' way as the most effective in ending occupation and building a Palestinian state and Haniyeh defeats Abbas in a presidential election," 13–15 December 2012, http://www.pcpsr.org/survey/polls/2012/p46e.html.

3. Peter Berger, *The Sacred Canopy: Elements of a Sociology of Religion* (New York: Anchor Books, 1967).

4. Catarina Kinvall, "Globalization and Religious Nationalism: Self, Identity, and theSearch for Ontological Security," *Political Psychology* 25, no. 5 (2004): 741–767; Anthony Giddens, *Modernity and Self-Identity: Self and Society in the Late Modern Age* (Cambridge: Polity, 1991).

5. Giddens, *Modernity and Self-Identity,* 38–39.

6. Kinvall, "Globalization and Religious Nationalism," 746–747.

7. Kinvall, "Globalization and Religious Nationalism," 747. The reference here is to the concept of "homesteading" as discussed in Annica Kronsell, "Homeless in Academia: Homesteading as a Strategy for Change in a World of Hegemonic Masculinity," in *Women in Higher Education: Empowering Change,* ed. JoAnn DiGeorgio-Lutz (Westport, CT: Greenwood, 2002), 37–56, and Christine Sylvester, *Feminist Theory and International Relations in a Postmodern Era* (Cambridge: Cambridge University Press, 1994).

8. Kinvall, "Globalization and Religious Nationalism," 758, quoting Stephen D. Reicher and Nick Hopkins, *Self and Nation* (London: Sage, 2001), 51.

9. Kinvall, "Globalization and Religious Nationalism," 759, quoting Stephen D. Reicher and Nick Hopkins, *Self and Nation,* 51.

10. Martin Riesebrodt, "Theses on a Theory of Religion," *International Political Anthropology* 1, no. 1 (2008): 39–40.

11. Kinvall, "Globalization and Religious Nationalism," 760.

12. Julie Peteet, "Pensee 1: Imagining the 'New Middle East,'" *International Journal of Middle East Studies* 40, no. 4 (2008): 550–552; Suad Joseph, "Pensee 2: Sectarianism as Imagined Sociological Concept and as Imagined Social Formation," *International Journal of Middle East Studies* 40, no. 4 (2008): 553–554; Eric Davis, "Pensee 3: A Sectarian Middle East?," *International Journal of Middle East Studies* 40, no. 4 (2008): 555–558; Usama Makdisi, "Pensee 4: Moving Beyond Orientalist Fantasy, Sectarian Polemic, and Nationalist Denial," *International Journal of Middle East Studies* 40, no. 4 (2008): 559–560.

13. Saba Mahmood, "Secularism, Hermeneutics, and Empire: The Politics of Islamic Reformation," *Public Culture* 18, no. 2 (2006): 323–347.

14. The material for the following discussion of Gaza derives from the section of my book focusing on the pseudonymously named "Karama Camp." See *Identity*

and Religion in Palestine: The Struggle between Islamism and Secularism in the Occupied Territories (Princeton, NJ: Princeton University Press, 2007), 179–232.

15. Sara Roy, *The Gaza Strip: The Political Economy of De-Development* (Washington, DC: Institute for Palestine Studies, 1995; repr., 2001), 19, 23–24; Rosemary Sayigh, *Palestinians: From Peasants to Revolutionaries* (London: Zed Books, 1979).

16. The term for "connections" is "*wasta,*" which begins with the Arabic letter "*waw.*"

17. Roy, *The Gaza Strip,* 370.

18. Numerous studies have documented the importance of Hamas's extensive social service network for integrating individuals into the Islamist sociopolitical milieu. See, inter alia, Jeroen Gunning, *Hamas in Politics: Democracy, Religion, Violence* (New York: Columbia University Press, 2008); Shaul Mishal and Avraham Sela, *The Palestinian Hamas: Vision, Violence, and Coexistence* (New York: Columbia University Press, 2006); Sara Roy, "Hamas and the Transformation(s) of Political Islam in Palestine," *Current History* 102, no. 660 (January 2003): 13–20; Beverley Milton-Edwards, *Islamic Politics in Palestine* (London: Tauris Academic Studies, 1996).

19. A *mahram* is a person one is prohibited from marrying because of consanguinity. Thus, for example, one is not allowed to marry one's mother, father, brother, or sister. A brother-in-law, however, could potentially become a marriage partner in the event of divorce or the death of one's husband. In this case, a new marriage contract and dowry would have to be negotiated. One may have unrestricted social interaction with mahrams because marriage is not possible with these individuals. Interactions with non-mahrams, however, must be supervised, hedged by observance of the commandment to cover one's ʿawra—parts of the body that one must clothe when in the presence of non-mahrams, or interdicted unless and until a formal marriage contract is concluded. See Qur'an 4:19–25 and the discussion at http://www.islamonline.net/servlet/Satellite?cid=1235628821068& pagename=IslamOnline-English-Ask_Scholar%2FFatwaE%2FfatwaEAskTheScholar.

20. I discuss this incident in greater detail elsewhere in relation to the concept of "moral familism." See Loren Lybarger, *Identity and Religion in Palestine,* 215–216n50.

21. On the phenomenon of Sri Lankan maids and the PA elite, see Mary Abowd, "In Service to the Movement," *Palestine Report Online,* ed. Ghassan Khatib, Jerusalem Media and Communications Centre, 6 September 2000, http://www .jmcc.org/media/report/2000/Sep/1.htm#feature.

22. Loren Lybarger, "For Church or Nation? Islamism, Secular-Nationalism, and the Transformation of Christian Identities in Palestine," *Journal of the American Academy of Religion* 75, no. 4 (December 2007): 707, 777–813.

23. Lybarger, "For Church or Nation?"; Lybarger, *Identity and Religion in Palestine;* Michael Dumper, "Faith and Statecraft: Church-State Relations in Jerusalem after 1948," in *Palestinian Christians: Religion, Politics, and Society in the Holy Land,* ed. Anthony O'Mahoney (London: Melisende, 1999), 74–80; Bernard Sabella, "Socio-Economic Characteristics and the Challenges to Palestinian Christians in the Holy Land," in *Christians in the Holy Land,* eds. Michael Prior and William

Taylor (London: World of Islam Festival Trust, 1994), 31–44; Daphne Tsimhoni, *Christian Communities in Jerusalem and the West Bank since 1948* (Westport, CT: Praeger, 1993).

24. *Ahl al-dhimma* is the Islamic legal convention that extends toleration to religious minorities—Jews and Christians, primarily—in exchange for agreement to pay special taxes (the *jizya*) and acceptance of certain social disabilities (wearing distinctive clothes, limitations on building churches, exclusion from military service) that mark non-Muslims as a subordinate group.

25. Salah al-Din, known in the West as "Saladin," was the Muslim leader who fought a series of successful campaigns against the European Crusaders, leading ultimately to the capture of Jerusalem in 1187.

26. Dr. Sabella made this comment to me in a taped interview soon after the Nazareth events had exploded and become an international affair involving the Vatican and Israeli government as well as the Palestinian Authority.

27. Roy, "Hamas and the Transformation(s) of Political Islam in Palestine."

28. Yezid Sayigh, *Armed Struggle and the Search for State: The Palestinian National Movement, 1949–1993* (Oxford: Oxford University Press, 1997), 635.

29. Clifford Geertz, *The Interpretation of Cultures* (New York: Basic Books, 1973); George Santayana, *Reason in Religion* (New York: Dover, 1930; repr., 1982).

30. Pierre Bourdieu, "Genesis and Structure of the Religious Field," *Comparative Social Research: A Research Annual,* ed. Craig Calhoun, 13 (1991): 1–44, 82–83.

31. Mar Jiriyis, or St. George, is considered the patron saint of Bethlehem. Iconic representations of the saint appear in stone panels affixed above the entrances to the homes of Christians in the area and in iconographic paintings in Christian business establishments.

32. I attended the Pope's visit and witnessed the ensuing violence, staying late into the night with friends. Our group initially fled to the rooftop of an apartment building across from the main entrance to Dheishe. We later managed to get back inside the camp as the violence continued. I left for Bethlehem as the clashes subsided in the early hours of the morning. I returned later that day to follow up on the events. This account derives from the fieldnotes I composed in the aftermath of the events.

33. Lybarger, "For Church or Nation?"; Lybarger, "Palestinian Political Identities during the Post-Oslo Period: A Case Study of Generation Effects in a West Bank Refugee Camp," *Social Compass* 52, no. 5 (2005):143–156.

34. The account that follows draws from ethnographic data first presented in my book, *Identity and Religion in Palestine: The Struggle between Islamism and Secularism in the Occupied Territories,* and an earlier article, "Palestinian Political Identities during the Post-Oslo Period: A Case Study of Generation Effects in a West Bank Refugee Camp."

35. The Muslim Brotherhood in the West Bank had long structured itself as primarily a *da'wa* organization, eschewing direct involvement in nationalist politics. Beverley Milton-Edwards, *Islamic Politics in Palestine* (London: Tauris Academic Studies, 1996), 55–59.

36. The story of Joseph, recounted also in the Bible, constitutes one of the most sustained and coherent narratives in the Qur'an. In the Qur'anic version, Joseph is sold into slavery in Egypt and is tempted by his master's wife. Sorely tempted, Joseph resists the invitation of a sexual liaison and is exonerated of the charge of molestation that the master's wife attempts to place upon him when they are caught together. God is credited in the narrative for undermining the schemes of the wife and protecting Joseph. Thrown into prison nonetheless, Joseph becomes known for dream interpretation and subsequently gains a prominent place as an advisor in the imperial Egyptian court. See Qur'an 12 in its entirety.

37. A thick cotton scarf that men (and sometimes women) wear over their heads or shoulders, the *hatta* (or *kufiyya*) has served as a secular-nationalist symbol linking the struggle for a state with the effort to reconquer the land and nostalgically preserve "authentic" collective values linked to the peasant village culture that existed before the creation of Israel in 1948. The color of the hatta that one wears can indicate distinctions in affiliation. Black-checkered hattas, for example, might indicate support for Fatah. Yasser Arafat invariably appeared in public wearing a black-checkered hatta shaped to appear like the map of British Mandate Palestine. By contrast, a red-checkered hatta can signify alignment with the leftist organizations or, alternatively, with Hamas and the Hashemites of Jordan. In adopting the red hatta, the latter two groups have contested nationalist attempts to monopolize *fallahi* (peasant) and Bedouin "tradition" as a legitimating discourse. (The Hashemite monarchy, seeking to domesticate Islamist opposition and achieve Islamist recognition of its claims to Sharifian status, has allowed the Muslim Brotherhood, the parent organization of Hamas, to continue to exist as a political party and run for parliament even as the regime has outlawed other opposition movements opposed to Hashemite rule.) One should bear in mind that there is nothing inevitable in this color symbolism. Palestinians will wear hattas of different colors without necessarily intending any particular political alignment.

38. Tyler Roberts, "All Work and No Play: Chaos, Incongruity, and Difference in The Study of Religion," *Journal of the American Academy of Religion* 77, no. 1 (March 2009): 81–104.

39. Bruce Lincoln, *Religion, Rebellion, Revolution* (New York: St. Martin's, 1985).

40. Bourdieu, "Genesis and Structure of the Religious Field," 1–44.

41. Olivier Roy, *The Failure of Political Islam,* trans. Carol Volk (Cambridge, MA: Harvard University Press, 1998); Martin Riesebrodt, *Pious Passion: The Emergence of Modern Fundamentalism in the United States and Iran,* trans. Don Reneau (Berkeley, CA: University of California Press, 1993).

PART 3

Trajectories for the Future,
Solutions for a State

9. Palestine in the American Political Arena

Is a "Reset" Possible?

MICHAEL C. HUDSON

There are two competing narratives about America and Palestine. One derives from the Protestant missionaries who early in the nineteenth century went to the "Holy Land" to convert the "natives" (an impossible task) and who ended up as educators. The descendants of these hardy and talented people not only established impressive schools and colleges, many of which thrive today, but also went on to become diplomats—the fabled and maligned "State Department Arabists"—as well as business-people and development professionals. They were genuinely attached to the Arabs of Palestine. After World War II, when the United States elected to support the Jewish nationalist, or Zionist, project in Palestine, which led in 1948 to the forced displacement of some 750,000 Palestinians from their homes, they supported the Palestinian cause. But these people constituted a small minority.

The other narrative, which has come to frame America's collective understanding of the Middle East, is the story of Zionism, which from its European origins succeeded in establishing Israel in historic Palestine. This is a story, celebrated in novels and films, of European Jews fleeing discriminatory European pogroms and ultimately the Holocaust, braving callous British officialdom, and creating a safe haven for a people uniquely persecuted in the West. To most Americans the Israelis were pioneers (like American whites) settling undeveloped territory, making the desert bloom, and fighting off or educating the "backward" natives. Israel became an extension of the "Judeo-Christian civilization" of which Americans were a part. It is this narrative to which most American elected politicians have subscribed up to this day.

A Short History of U.S. Palestine Policy

The expulsion of the Palestinians in 1948 and again after the 1967 war triggered the world's longest-running regional conflict. Arab-Israeli wars, in one form or another, erupt every five to ten years. The U.S. government, which has interests in Arab oil, has tried repeatedly to settle the conflict but has been unsuccessful thus far. It would not be unreasonable to expect that the most powerful nation in the world, if it put its collective mind and muscle to the issue, might by now have been able to move affairs toward the "prominent solution" that most academic and professional observers of the situation have long identified as the two-state solution. The history of this idea goes back to debates during the British mandate era over the binational versus the two-state approach. The 1947 UN partition resolution consecrated the "victory" of the two-state solution, but only one state emerged: Israel. For well over two decades the Palestinians were effectively out of the picture. Even the landmark 1967 UN Security Council Resolution 242, calling for "land for peace," did not squarely call for the Palestinians as a nation to be in charge of the land that Israel had occupied in the Six-Day War; it only referred to the rights of the "refugees." But with the reemergence of the Palestinians as a distinct political actor, starting in the late 1960s, the notion of two states—Palestine and Israel—also reemerged. Walid Khalidi's seminal article in *Foreign Affairs* in July 1978, "Thinking the Unthinkable: A Sovereign Palestinian State," was arguably instrumental in reframing the Palestine question for the American foreign policy elite.[1] And when the PLO in 1988 finally bought into the idea of sharing historic Palestine with Israel (albeit on very unequal terms), it became even clearer what the ultimate achievable solution would be. To be sure, the ascendancy of the right wing in Israel in the late 1970s gave impetus to Vladimir Jabotinsky's "greater Israel" project. But the realities of the regional situation—underlined by Israel's failed wars in Lebanon—effectively marginalized the expansionists on the Zionist side. What, then, is the record of American policy in trying to bring the two-state idea to fruition?

Confronted with the idea of American fatigue on Palestine, retired American diplomats will rightly point out that the United States engaged in dozens of diplomatic initiatives over the period of the mid-1940s through the final days of the Clinton administration in 2000. Yet only two of these initiatives achieved tangible results: President Jimmy Carter's Camp David diplomacy in 1978 and President Bill Clinton's "peace process" in the 1990s—and neither ultimately succeeded in putting a Palestinian state in place alongside Israel. With the coming of the George W. Bush administration in 2001, the president's initial declaration that he would support a Palestinian state alongside Israel was almost immediately sidetracked and then buried under the rubble of the attacks of September 11 and the debacle of the American intervention in Iraq. For six years Palestine was once again "on the back burner." To be sure, in a belated effort to revive the "peace process," Secretary of State Condoleezza Rice launched a hastily organized and poorly prepared multinational conference in Annapolis, Maryland, in November 2007, but in the following months little was accomplished. And during the 2008 American presidential election campaign, while all the candidates expressed effusive support for Israel, the Palestine-Israel conflict did not figure among the major foreign policy issues being debated.

Domestic Political Constraints

One of the strengths of the American political system is the existence of multiple points of access. This means that many different actors can participate in the discussion of policy issues. The separation of powers and federal structure of government have helped develop this process, as have the guarantees of civil rights and free speech. The tradition of a relatively free mass media and a multiplicity of print and electronic outlets has further protected this "free marketplace of ideas." Unfortunately, this liberal ideal is sometimes distorted in practice. Powerful lobbies, both in domestic and in foreign policy, can skew the discussion. In an earlier era foreign policy debates were the province of a small, self-selected, well-educated East Coast elite, symbolized best by the Council on Foreign Relations. This elite helped shape politicians' understanding of the national interest. But its somewhat inbred nature gave rise to what the social psychologist Irving Janis called "groupthink" and helped account for America's misbegotten adventure in Vietnam.[2]

Another kind of distortion has affected Middle East policy. Unlike most other foreign policy issues, the Middle East has been a salient domestic political issue since the Zionist movement decided to shape American power to support its project for a Jewish state in Palestine. There is no need here to retrace the development of the "Israel lobby" in American politics, except to note that the influence of this lobby expanded exponentially after the 1967 Arab-Israeli war and continues to shape Americans' understanding of the Palestine conflict. The idea of a morally pure, vulnerable Jewish state confronting a vastly more numerous and powerful Arab enemy remains the dominant narrative, whereas the idea of the Palestinians as victims, or even the idea of the conflict as a complex affair with rights and wrongs on both sides, is less accepted.

The organizations that together comprise the Israel lobby include, at the top, AIPAC—the American Israel Public Affairs Committee. But it is underpinned by scores of political action committees at the national, state, and local levels, and by thousands of "nonpolitical" organizations like synagogues. Non-Jewish organizations also figure in the mixture, including in recent years large Christian evangelical congregations. The "Israel lobby" (often ranked by American political analysts as the most powerful lobby in Washington, along with the National Rifle Association), is not just a debating society; it can reward or punish politicians in the most tangible of ways, such as through campaign funding, the mobilization of sizable voting blocs, and by promoting (or blackening) reputations through its access to the mass media. The lobby not only offers highly attractive incentives to politicians if they will support pro-Israel policies (even if they are one-sided), but it can also threaten to undermine politicians who might be intellectually inclined to support a more even-handed American stance. Unfortunately, there are no Arab or Palestinian lobbies that are remotely as powerful, and the business community (including even the oil companies) is extremely reluctant to take on the Israel lobby.

Members of Congress—Democrats and Republicans alike—are particularly vulnerable to this kind of pressure, as they are almost constantly running for election or reelection, but even the White House bends, because no president wants to alienate a major voting bloc that can be mobilized by this well-organized, well-funded, and militant lobby. Congress has "the power of the purse" by authorizing the spending of public money, which gives it serious leverage over whether or how an administration can exercise American power. This explains, then, why the United States, despite the formidable power, influence, and resources that it could deploy in support of its diplomacy, in fact rarely does so, owing to the political constraints imposed by the lobby. As the 2008 presidential election campaign got under way, it was noteworthy that all of the major candidates felt obliged to address AIPAC and attest to their pro-Israel credentials. When one of the candidates, Barack Obama, stated that "no one is suffering more than the Palestinian people," he was warned that he might be ceding pro-Israel votes to his main rival, Hillary Clinton, who was unstinting in her support for Israel. Obama immediately qualified his statement by saying that Palestinian suffering was due to "the failure of the Palestinian leadership to recognize Israel, to renounce violence, and to get serious about negotiating peace and security for the region."[3]

Changing U.S., Regional, and Global Conditions

Students of U.S. policy in the Arab-Israel dispute might be forgiven for becoming bored with their subject because nothing seems to change. Ever since 1948, American officials have been charged with supporting Israel even when Israel carries out policies that weaken, or at least complicate, America's broader regional interests. Occasionally the United States clashes with its headstrong client—as in the Sinai-Suez war of 1956–1957, when President Dwight Eisenhower forced Israel, Britain, and France to withdraw from the Sinai Peninsula—but the disputes are invariably temporary. American policy seems permanently bound in the straitjacket of the powerful Israel lobby. "Realistic" analysts are therefore inclined to think that a fundamental reset of U.S. policy is virtually impossible. And yet we know that conditions can change. As the United States contemplates its position in the Middle East over the next decades, are there factors that might persuade or require it to change its policy regarding the Arab-Israeli dispute? The answer is not clear, but if we look at some remarkable developments on three levels—the U.S., the regional, and the world—perhaps the situation is not as static as generally believed.

The U.S. Level

When Israeli prime minister Benjamin Netanyahu can generate some twenty-eight standing ovations during a speech (rejecting Obama's focus on the 1967 lines) to a joint session of the U.S. Congress (as happened on 24 May 2011) one might reasonably conclude that the domestic terrain remains unshakably favorable to Israel. But there are certain trends worth noting. In American public discourse, the Israel lobby—powerful as it is—no longer remains unchallenged. The 2007 landmark book *The Israel Lobby and U.S. Foreign Policy* by Stephen Walt and John Mearsheimer broke the taboo on public criticism of Israel and of the lobby itself.[4] The emergence of the Jewish lobbying group J Street as a centrist alternative to AIPAC indicates that American Jewish opinion is not monolithic in its support for right-wing Israeli government policies.[5] In June 2010 an article by Peter Beinart in the *New York Review of Books* entitled "The Failure of the American Jewish Establishment"[6] generated an ongoing debate in Jewish and U.S. foreign policy circles. Beinart accused the Zionist establishment not just of avoiding criticism of Israeli policies but also of trying to prevent others from criticizing them. He claimed that the establishment Zionist organizations were seriously out of touch with a younger generation of liberal American Jews whose views clash with the traditional Zionist narrative. But he also warned about the demographic growth of the Orthodox Jewish community, which displays chauvinistic and hostile views toward the Palestinians—views that are increasingly at variance with the growing public understanding of the Palestinian tragedy.

Another notable trend is visible among what the political scientist Gabriel Almond long ago described as "the attentive publics" on foreign policy issues.[7] The attentive publics are composed of journalism and media communities, think tanks, academic Middle East specialists, and NGOs focused on Middle East development and human rights issues. Arguably these attentive publics, which shape public discourse and frame issues on the Middle East, have increased both the quantity and the quality of debate. It is no longer correct to contend that the media and public intellectuals are uniformly pro-Israel.

To be sure, a number of advocacy think tanks in Washington are inclined to present Israel in a favorable light, including the Washington Institute for Near East Policy, the American Enterprise Institute, and the Hudson Institute, among others. And an avowedly partisan Zionist businessman established and funded the Saban Center for Middle East Policy at the Brookings Institution. But these organizations do not have the field to themselves. Alternative analyses come from the Carnegie Endowment for International Peace, the New America Foundation, and the Institute for Policy Studies, among others. There is even a think tank, the Palestine Center, and an academic research institute, the Institute for Palestine Studies, in Washington. Mainline foreign policy publications such as *Foreign Policy* and *Foreign Affairs* now have dedicated Middle East websites. The American Middle East academic community, though regularly targeted by pro-Israel "watchdog" organizations, has lost much of its fear of dealing with the "controversial" Palestine issue. Moreover, a few prominent public figures and intellectuals, such as former president Carter and former National Security Council advisors Zbigniew Brzezinski and Brent Scowcroft, have emerged to advocate a "balanced" U.S. approach.

The Regional Level

There was a time not so long ago—the last half of the twentieth century—when American policymakers could think of the Middle East as "theirs." Washington built up an impressive array of authoritarian allies, military bases, commercial connections, and even a degree of cultural hegemony. The twenty-first century is a different matter. U.S. policies and diplomatic failings over Palestine and Israel have steadily eroded American credibility and respect—what some people call soft power—among the people of the region. Even the closest of allies—Israel—feels no compulsion to follow American wishes. Saudi Arabia, another close ally, has appeared to lose patience with Washington's less-than-vigorous efforts to maintain the regional authoritarian status quo. And America's vaunted military superiority is dimmed by its wars of choice in Iraq and Afghanistan that have not yielded clear victories. America's inability to stop Israel's deepening presence in the West Bank has led many Palestinians and thoughtful foreign observers (but very few Israelis) to advocate a "one-state" solution on the empirically well-grounded belief that a meaningful Palestinian state is now a physical and political impossibility. The resignation of Obama's special envoy George Mitchell in May 2011 after years of fruitless shuttle diplomacy symbolized the impotence of American policy. Hence an important regional trend to consider is the decline of American influence.

What decisions might the Palestinians make as a result of this apparent decline? The most obvious one would be to distance themselves from an American-led "peace process." This would not be just because the Americans are biased toward Israel; that has been well-known for a half-century and more. Now, in addition, the perception exists that the United States is no longer "the only game in town." The Americans are too weak to influence

Israel; in fact, their leverage in countries throughout the region seems to be shrinking fast. Thus it is entirely understandable that the beleaguered Palestinian Authority leadership should threaten to take its case for declaring a Palestinian state to the world community instead, through the UN General Assembly. Several Latin American countries have already declared their support. For Israel, American decline also poses problems. If the Israeli right thinks Obama is going wobbly on defending Israel, the response might be that Israel should take matters into its own hands. That could mean annexing the entire West Bank, or expelling Palestinians living in Israel, or attacking Iran.

Another trend is the recent and dramatic "Arab Awakening." Within the space of only a few months in 2011 two of America's autocratic allies, Ben Ali in Tunisia and Mubarak in Egypt, fell in the face of popular uprisings. Two more, Saleh in Yemen and Qaddafi in Libya, were on their way out. Two other regimes in the oil-rich Gulf, in Bahrain and Oman, were shaken, as were two friendly non-oil monarchies, Jordan and Morocco. Even the regime of Bashar al-Asad in Syria, certainly no ally but strategically useful nonetheless, was experiencing a massive popular revolt. Known adversaries such as Iran and its nonstate allies, as well as the transnational radical Islamist movements (still intact despite the killing of Osama Bin Laden) might benefit from the messy aftermaths of popular revolts. What impact, if any, might the Arab Awakening have on America's Palestine policy?

Obama, to his credit, seemed to sense that transitions to more participatory governments would pose new challenges, even threats, to Israel as long as it continued in its obstinate and provocative ways toward the Palestinians and others in the region.[8] If Arab public opinion were to play a stronger role, the threat to peace would increase. Even such (waning) protection that Washington might offer might not ease Israel's growing insecurity. In a rational world, the Arab Awakening, then, might focus America's energies on reaching a settlement even if it meant "pressuring" Israel. But is it a rational world? As the discussion below suggests, rationality may be in short supply in Washington.

The Global Level

It is a slow-moving trend, and anyone familiar with the vast American military presence across the greater Middle East would find it difficult to believe. But the decline of the United States is now a topic of regular debate not just in Asia, where the refrain "Asia rising" is ubiquitous, but also in American circles. The global financial crisis of 2008–2009 originated in the United States, and it certainly dealt a blow to traditional American notions of global superiority. Contemporaneously, tectonic shifts in the global balance of power are driven by the astounding economic development of China, India, South Korea, and other Asian nations even as the United States and Europe struggle. America's scores on global indices of development, such as educational accomplishment, have declined. Shrinkage in the manufacturing sector, loss of dominance in some high-tech areas, and an economy unbalanced by excessive consumption and insufficient savings and investment render hollow the declaration of some American politicians in the 1990s, after the collapse of the Soviet Union, that America was the "indispensable nation."

Today the world observes the new influence of the "BRICS" (Brazil, Russia, India, China, and South Africa) and hears demands to restructure the UN Security Council. Regional organizations such as the G-8, the G-20, the Association of Southeast Asian Nations (ASEAN), the Asia-Pacific Economic Cooperation (APEC), and the European Union suggest that the global order is changing in ways not envisaged in realist international relations theory. Even in the Middle East, where regional organizations like the League of Arab States have languished, at least one organization—the Gulf Cooperation Council—has been relatively successful, and there are efforts to strengthen Euro-Mediterranean linkages and to envision larger structures that would accommodate major regional players such as Turkey, Iran, and even Israel. Breaking down regional barriers to economic and social interaction will be essential to stimulate the sluggish economies in much of the region.[9]

What might the decline of America and the gradual reemergence of a multipolar world mean for the Palestine question? It could mean good news. If one concludes from the long and fruitless history of Arab-Israeli diplomacy, dominated as it has been by the United States, that the Americans have lacked the ability to bring matters to a conclusion, then perhaps it is time for others to try. Ideally, of course, Middle East issues ought to be settled by Middle Easterners. In the region Turkey presents itself as a credible interlocutor, as might a newly independent regime in Egypt. From outside the region, "others" might mean the three junior members of the nearly forgotten "Quartet" (the UN, the EU, and Russia) playing leading rather than supporting roles. But more significantly, perhaps it is time for Asian and other

Middle Eastern players to become involved. China, India, and other Asian powers are rapidly strengthening their economic presence in the Middle East, and they do not bring the same colonial or neoimperialist baggage to the table. While they are not yet projecting much "hard power" into the region, they are certainly capable of exercising creative diplomacy and organizing peacekeeping missions. Perhaps it is time for the emerging Asian and Latin American giants to lend a hand instead of standing by while others try to settle problems in a region whose stability, after all, is bound to be in their interest.

What Would a Proper "Reset" Look Like?

An American administration cognizant of these new conditions might indeed contemplate a change of course. To his credit, at the beginning of his first term President Obama seemed intellectually committed to a "reset." But what would a proper reset actually entail? It might involve taking a series of steps such as the following:

Get a new team of advisors. The old ones are too partisan and are locked into a simplistic understanding of the Middle East.

Be multilateral. The United States cannot and should not arrogate "management" of this diplomacy to itself. It should genuinely share an international initiative including the Arab League, Europe, Russia, China, Japan, India, and Brazil.

Significantly increase economic and humanitarian assistance to the Palestinians, in conjunction with the international community.

Do not be intimidated by the Israel lobby. Also listen to liberal voices in the American Jewish community, and urge them to use their influence in Israel.

Offer "tough love" to Israel, including a warning that the historic aid relationship might be reviewed.

Offer security guarantees to both Israel and the Palestinian state. Intrusions and violence, governmental or irregular, from either side must be prohibited.

Ease Israel's onerous restrictions on the Palestinians. Insist on an immediate removal of most West Bank checkpoints, and enable Palestinians to visit Jerusalem more easily.

Do not move the U.S. embassy to Jerusalem until an overall agreement on Jerusalem's status has been reached.

Insist on an immediate and significant reduction of settlement expansion and an eventual complete removal of West Bank settlements. Special status should be negotiated for the settlements in and around Jerusalem.

Support a significant Palestinian presence in East Jerusalem, including unequivocal backing for a Palestinian capital and Palestinian authority in East Jerusalem.

Support the creation of a genuinely sovereign Palestinian state. Going back to the terms of UN Security Council Resolution 242, only minor territorial changes should be contemplated. The next president should reiterate that the Palestinian state must have territorial coherence and integrity. He or she should declare that Palestinians must have direct and unimpeded access to the outside world through Jordan and Egypt and by sea at Gaza and by air in the West Bank. A secure land corridor must be established between the West Bank and Gaza.

Accept the internationally recognized right of return for Palestinians displaced in 1948 and 1967. Admit this in principle, recognizing that in practice few would want to return to Israel proper, and press energetically for a compensation regime for Palestinians who lost their property and valuables.

Deal with the legitimate Palestinian authorities. Be prepared to deal with whoever the legitimately elected representatives in the Palestinian territories may be, including politicians from Hamas.

Encourage, rather than discourage, Israeli-Syrian negotiation over the Golan Heights, and be prepared to lift sanctions and the terrorist label from Syria if these negotiations prove fruitful.

If the points listed above constitute an "ideal" reset, and if U.S., regional, and global conditions are changing in such a way as to make a reset more thinkable, to what extent was the Obama administration after three years in office able to undertake the reset that the president himself claimed to want?

Obama's Missed Opportunity

The election of Barack Obama in 2008 raised hopes among those sympathetic to the Palestinian situation that things might change. And there were some encouraging signs. That he had actually had contact with a prominent Palestinian-American intellectual, Dr. Rashid Khalidi, when he was a community organizer in Chicago led observers to infer that he had at least heard "the other side of the story." In a 2008 campaign speech before AIPAC he plainly endorsed a two-state solution: "a Jewish state of Israel and a Palestinian state living side by side in peace and security." And he went on to assert the seriousness of his commitment: "And I won't wait until the waning days of my presidency. I will take an active role, and make a personal commitment to do all I can to advance the cause of peace from the start of my administration."[10] After his election he gave his first interview to the Arabic satellite channel al-Arabiyya and signaled his intention to deal with the Arab and Muslim worlds with respect and a willingness to listen. Another positive sign was his appointment of former senator George Mitchell as his special representative for the Middle East. Mitchell, of Lebanese descent on his mother's side, was regarded as relatively balanced on the Arab-Israeli conflict, compared to most members of the Washington political elite, especially members of Congress. Mitchell was received with suspicion by the Israel lobby as "pro-Palestinian." And in June 2009, Obama delivered an eloquent address at Cairo University elaborating the same themes. It seemed clear that he wished to undo the serious damage to America's credibility and influence in the region done by his neoconservative predecessor George W. Bush.

Yet at the same time the new president was sending seemingly contradictory signals. He was unwilling to forthrightly criticize Israel for the brutalities it inflicted on Gaza in December 2008, a month before he took office. He elevated a hard-line Middle East advisor, Dennis Ross, who had arguably contributed significantly to the ultimate failure of the Oslo process of the 1990s. He chose as his secretary of state Hillary Clinton, whose enthusiasm for Israel knew no bounds when she was a senator from New York, and who proceeded to take a hard line on Hamas's credible claims to be an authentic part of the Palestinian body politic. Symptomatic of the administration's skittishness on Israel was its embarrassing failure to stand up to AIPAC's attack on Ambassador Chas Freeman, Obama's choice to head the National Intelligence Council, who was forced to withdraw his name from consideration. In May 2009 Obama courageously declared that Israel's policy of settlement expansion was not conducive to resolving the conflict, and when Netanyahu defiantly ordered up new settlement projects on the eve of a visit to Israel by Vice President Joe Biden in March 2010, the president was reportedly furious but did nothing concrete to show his displeasure. Rather, in February 2011 he ordered the United States to veto a Security Council resolution condemning the settlements. Meanwhile, special envoy George Mitchell continued to shuttle between Israel and the Palestinian Authority, nominally under the aegis of the "Quartet," pursuing the "Road Map for Peace" first outlined by President George W. Bush in 2002, but nobody seemed to notice.

On 20 May 2011 President Obama delivered what was widely touted as a "reset" speech on U.S. Middle East policy at the State Department. The president proclaimed "a new chapter in American diplomacy" intended to respond to "the extraordinary change" taking place in the region: "The people," he said, "have risen up to demand their basic human rights." Admitting that America had in the past concentrated too narrowly on the pursuit of its basic interests—countering terrorism, trying to stop nuclear proliferation, securing the free flow of commerce, safeguarding the security of the region—Obama now asserted that America faced "a historic opportunity" to support popular aspirations. What forms would this support take? The president offered verbal support for the popular uprisings in Tunisia, Egypt, Libya, Syria, Yemen, and (in a more qualified way) Bahrain. He also promised financial and economic assistance for the new regimes in Tunisia and Egypt, and a trade and investment partnership initiative for the entire Middle East and North African region.

Obama concluded his speech by returning to "another cornerstone of our approach to the region," the Arab-Israeli conflict. Observers everywhere watched carefully to see whether he would announce a new American approach to a struggle that decades of diplomacy had failed to end. Would the "reset" in U.S. Middle East policy extend to this issue? And if it didn't, would

America be able to make good on its "historic opportunity" to align with the new popular forces shaping the region? If one were to judge on the basis of Netanyahu's furious reaction to what Obama then said—"The borders of Israel and Palestine should be based on the 1967 lines with mutually agreed swaps"—one might have answered, "Yes." Israel's many supporters in Congress rallied behind Netanyahu's defiant declaration that Israel would accept no such thing. But instead of standing up to Netanyahu, Obama once again hastened to assure him that he was leaving Israel plenty of room for maneuver in the negotiating process and that the United States would not pressure Israel to do anything that Israel might decide was against its interests. Thus the president continued to respond with meekness and weakness to Israel's rejection of what he rightly remarked was a fundamental parameter for peace dating back to UN Security Council Resolution 242 in 1967.

To be fair, President Obama continued to insist that the United States supported a meaningful, contiguous (though demilitarized) Palestinian state alongside Israel. Moreover, as Henry Siegman noted, the speech was important because it laid down certain markers. . . .

> 1. The time to press for a peace accord is now, not some time in the indeterminate future.
>
> 2. Putting forward American parameters for bilateral talks is not an imposition on the parties. The parameters are essential terms of reference for successful talks.
>
> 3. The starting point for talks about mutually agreed-upon territorial swaps must be the 1967 lines.
>
> 4. A peace accord must provide credible security arrangements for both parties and "full and phased" withdrawal of Israel's military forces from the West Bank."[11]

But on the negative side, it was notable that Obama adopted the right-wing Israeli government's new emphasis on the Jewishness of Israel, without regard for the large non-Jewish (Palestinian Arab) minority—some 1.2 million people, or nearly 25 percent of Israel's population. Crucially, Obama's speech sidestepped the key issues of Jerusalem and the Palestinian right of return. He also berated the Palestinians for proposing to go to the UN and seek international recognition for a Palestinian state, as if the UN were enemy territory rather than the source of the international consensus embodied in Security Council Resolutions 242 and 338. Little wonder that there was certainly no effort to rectify the previous U.S. official references to the "disputed" territories with the correct term—"occupied." It was therefore hardly surprising that reaction in the region to Obama's comments on Palestine-Israel was for the most part tepid. The speech ended with a whimper, not a bang, thus diluting its intended "reset" tone. And as if to undercut the positive aspects further, Obama addressed AIPAC a few days later and insisted that U.S. ties to Israel were "ironclad." As Siegman observed, "The fatal flaw in Obama's proposal is that it does not state clearly that rejecting his parameters will have consequences." Notwithstanding his initial effort at a reset, by the end of his first term Obama had failed to steer the United States toward a more balanced position on the Palestine-Israel conflict.

As he began his second term in 2013, Obama faced ongoing political deadlock at home, with no letup in Congressional pressure to support Netanyahu's provocative policies. In the Middle East the Islamist direction of the Arab uprisings was rekindling support for the Palestine cause and hostility toward Israel. While Obama's new foreign policy officials—John Kerry as secretary of state and Chuck Hagel as secretary of defense—were considered more balanced than some others on this issue, Obama himself was probably reluctant to invest political capital in Palestine, considering his bitter experience in his first term. As the columnist Roger Cohen observed, "President Obama . . . has zero cause for hope. Peace lies beyond the eye of a rusty needle. The limitlessness of Israeli strength and of Palestinian victimhood has narrowed the path to the well-known compromises needed to end the conflict."[12]

Notes

1. Walid Khalidi, "Thinking the Unthinkable: A Sovereign Palestinian State," *Foreign Affairs* (July 1978): 695–713.

2. Irving L Janis, *Victims of Groupthink: A Psychological Study of Foreign-Policy Decisions and Fiascos* (Oxford: Houghton Mifflin, 1972).

3. Lawahez Jabari, "Obama's AIPAC Speech Riles Palestinians," 5 June 2008, http://worldblog.msnbc.msn.com/_news/2008/06/05/4376646-obamas-aipac-speech-riles-palestinians?lite.

4. John J. Mearsheimer and Stephen M. Walt, *The Israel Lobby and U.S. Foreign Policy* (New York: Farrar, Straus and Giroux, 2007).

5. See, e.g., Edward Witten, "The New J-Lobby for Peace," *New York Review of Books*, 5 November 2009.

6. Peter Beinart, "The Failure of the American Jewish Establishment," *New York Review of Books*, 10 June 2010.

7. Gabriel A. Almond, *The American People and Foreign Policy* (New York: Harcourt, Brace, 1950).

8. See Ryan Lizza, "The Consequentialist: How the Arab Spring Remade Obama's Foreign Policy," *New Yorker,* 2 May 2011.

9. For further reading on regional integration in the Middle East, see Adeel Malik and Bassem Awadallah, "After the Arab Spring: Creating Economic Commons," Middle East Institute Insight Series, National University of Singapore, February 2012, http://www.mei.nus.edu.sg/publications/after-the-arab-spring-creating-economic-commons; Michael C. Hudson, ed., *Middle East Dilemma: The Politics and Economics of Arab Integration* (New York: Columbia University Press, 1998).

10. Obama speech to AIPAC, 4 June 2008, http://www.npr.org/templates/story/story.php?storyId=91150432.

11. Henry Siegman, "Can Obama Beat the Israel Lobby?," *The Nation,* 25 May 2011.

12. Roger Cohen, "Zero Dark Zero," *New York Times,* 28 February 2013.

10. Human Rights and the Rule of Law

NOURA ERAKAT

Between 27 December 2008 and 18 January 2009, Israel embarked on an unprecedented aerial and ground offensive against the Gaza Strip. In a span of twenty-two days, Israeli ground and aerial forces demolished 2,400 homes, 21 schools, and 60 police stations, and killed approximately 1,300 civilians, 280 of them children. The onslaught was particularly egregious because of the means employed. For eighteen months prior to the attack, Israel had imposed a debilitating naval blockade and ground siege that increased food dependency for survival to 56 percent and increased unemployment to nearly 40 percent. Moreover, Israel prevented Palestinians from fleeing the attack by sealing the borders, thereby preventing Palestinians from becoming refugees. Finally, Israeli forces obstructed the movement of medical personnel and used white phosphorous against heavily populated civilian areas. The horrific stories documented by Amnesty International, Human Rights Watch, Physicians for Human Rights-Israel, and the National Lawyers' Guild confirmed that war crimes were indeed committed and that the rule of law had been subverted in the name of national security underpinned by international complicity.

Rather than review the litany of violations and add to the chorus of indignant proponents of justice, this chapter ventures into territories imagined by advocates but rarely articulated due to our cynical and legitimate critiques of the centers of power. My point, then, is to discuss the relevance of international law in U.S. congressional advocacy. This means several things: conveying atrocities, making claims, and, not least of all, politely requesting a change in the scorching legacy of U.S. foreign policy in the Middle East.

And yet the United States as a superpower has a particular aversion to international law, which it sees as an unwanted intrusion. But to disavow the very law that human rights advocates and practitioners locally and globally seek to strengthen is counterproductive. How then do advocates engage effectively with federal policy lawmakers while maintaining and affirming principles of international law? To interrogate this question, this chapter addresses three major subjects: U.S. and international law, U.S. law and Gaza, and finally Congress and the Arab-Israeli conflict.

International Law and the United States

In regard to the Arab-Israeli conflict, international law is controversial in the United States not simply because of our government's unique relationship to Israel but also because of the United States' terse relationship to international law. While in international legal parlance the rule of law refers to the supplanting of the rule of force to solve conflict and avoid catastrophe, in the United States the rule of law has a wholly different meaning; namely, it refers to the rule by popular sovereignty. This concept constitutes a central tenet of U.S. political identity and it informs the U.S. relationship to the Constitution and, by extension, to all other legal documents including international ones.[1] As Thomas Jefferson wrote, "The will of the people . . . is the only legitimate foundation of any government, and to protect its free expression should be our first object."[2]

The Relationship of U.S. Political Identity and the Constitution

As Americans, we conceive of ourselves as a nation governed by self-imposed rules to which we collectively, and separately, adhere. Our condition of being ruled by law is not drawn from natural law or customary norms but rather from a political process in which our Founding Fathers engaged. This process culminated in the drafting and ratification of the Constitution, which is not only a source of all lawmaking power in the United States but also the self-expression of popular sovereignty. It remains binding because it was the product of self-creation. Effectively, as Paul Kahn, professor at Yale Law School, has captured, it defines the American citizen as a political being, which inspires patriotism for the nation and reverence for the document. He observes, "The rule of law is not a moral norm; rather, it is an existential condition signifying the continuing existence of the popular sovereign."[3]

Constitution as Sacred

This existential condition also represents a historical experience that defines our political identity in immutable ways. Kahn asks us to consider our judicial review of constitutional law. The process begins with the text itself, then examines the historical intent of the framers, and finally examines the judicial interpretation of the text in case law. Notwithstanding the two centuries that divide its drafting and our application, the intent of the framers is not anachronistic. The reason: the Constitution still embodies our popular sovereignty, and the judicial practice is in essence a practice of interpreting that principle or spirit. Therefore we read the text strictly and conservatively in order to keep its character intact.

The legal scholar Thomas Grey has observed that the U.S. Constitution is not simply a "hierarchically superior statute," but "a sacred symbol, the most potent emblem (along with the flag) of the nation itself." Ann Elizabeth Meyer illustrates the sacred nature of the Constitution in her treatment of the preservation of the original document in the National Archives. She writes, "Given the attention that is paid to preserving the documents, one could argue that the Constitution is treated more like a holy relic, such as the Shroud of Turin, than like a secular document laying out a scheme of government. Americans deem this normal."[4] In fairness, American reverence for its Constitution is due in part to the fact that unlike other nations that have witnessed several iterations of their founding documents, the United States has had only a single unique document. France, for example, has had some fifteen constitutions.

The Constitution, the United States, and the ICC

The veneration of our Constitution informs our relationship to international law. If the Constitution is a product of self-creation and establishes the rule of law as the popular sovereign, then international law would represent an intrusion rather than the evolution of the law of nations. Nothing demonstrates this point better than the United States' hostile rejection of and opposition to the establishment of the International Criminal Court (ICC). The ICC represents the triumph of human rights champions who, especially since the end of World War II, have sought to establish an international court empowered to pierce the veil of state sovereignty on behalf of humanity. Spurred by the atrocities wrought in internal conflicts in Yugoslavia and Rwanda, state parties negotiated a treaty to prosecute war crimes, genocide, crimes against humanity, and other international crimes. The treaty, better known as the Rome Statute, was completed in 1998. Only seven countries voted against the Statute: Israel, China, Yemen, Qatar, Libya, and the United States.[5] The Statute came into force in 2002 when sixty countries ratified it and became parties to it. Since its establishment the ICC has only initiated investigations and issued warrants to cases and persons in Africa. Nevertheless, the court still represents a belief among the community of nations that the unregulated use of force by states, within a state's own boundaries or outside of them, for the sake of self-defense, self-preservation, or otherwise, will not be tolerated. Therefore, despite its weaknesses, the Rome Statute represents a threat to strong countries engaged in armed conflict.

For this reason, the Clinton administration worked tirelessly to lobby the UN Security Council to secure a veto over any case it opposed, especially those cases involving U.S. leaders and/or servicemen. Although President Clinton supported the Court's purpose, the U.S. Congress vehemently opposed it for posing a threat to U.S. sovereignty and superiority. As put by then State Department spokesman Richard Boucher,

> Certainly, we share many of the concerns that are expressed by people in Congress, and we do not wish this to turn into some device that could be used against U.S. leaders or U.S. soldiers or U.S. military people who are acting within the authority of the U.S. government. And we think that we have clarified things in that direction, and that more needs to be done. So certainly those fundamental concerns are shared. Second of all, the President made quite clear that there are flaws that need to continue to be addressed and that we are not seeking ratification until those concerns that we have are satisfied. There were, in fact, 18 senators from both parties and 28 representatives who sent letters to the President urging him to sign. So we realize there are different opinions up on the Hill, in addition to the opposition. But, as I said, there are concerns that are well-founded that we share, and we would not think anyone would seek ratification without seeing them clarified.[6]

The Bush administration was not so refined in its opposition. Upon assuming power, Bush's Washington began to negotiate bilateral agreements with other countries, ensuring immunity of U.S. nationals from prosecution by the Court. As leverage, Washington threatened termination of economic aid, withdrawal of military assistance, and other painful measures.

But resistance didn't come just from the Bush administration—the House of Representatives also actively opposed the ICC. In 2005, in its FY06 Foreign Operations Appropriations Act, the House adopted a bill that prohibited the U.S. government from granting Economic Support Funds (ESF), or funding for development and infrastructure projects in regions where the United States has special security interests, to countries that had not agreed to a bilateral agreement providing immunity for U.S. citizens from the International Criminal Court. The message was clear from both Bush and Clinton: only U.S. officials can police U.S. civilians and military personnel.

U.S. Law and Gaza

Despite the United States' aversion to international accountability, U.S. law embodies several statutes that reflect principles of international law that may be useful for purposes of advocacy. These are the Arms Export Control Act, the Foreign Assistance Agreement, and the Mutual Defense Agreement with Israel.

Arms Export Control Act

The U.S. Arms Export Control Act (AECA) dictates the limited circumstances under which the United States may provide arms to other countries. The purpose of the AECA is to "strengthen the security of the United States and promote world peace," as well as to further "the purposes and principles of the United Nations Charter."[7] The statute mandates that the United States provide defense articles and services to friendly countries solely for internal security or legitimate self-defense. The AECA also requires the president, upon receipt of information of a violation, to notify Congress.[8] Effectively, the benefactor of the arms sales must be deemed ineligible to receive further defense articles and services until such violations cease and the United States receives satisfactory assurances that the violations will not recur.[9]

Foreign Assistance Act

The Foreign Assistance Act prohibits assistance to the government of any country that "engages in a consistent pattern of gross violations of internationally recognized human rights."[10] In order to receive assistance under the AECA, foreign countries are required to agree not to use military assistance for purposes other than for internal security, legitimate self-defense, the promotion of peacekeeping efforts endorsed by the United Nations Charter, and the development of infrastructure for friendly underdeveloped nations. Using United States military assistance inconsistent with the Foreign Assistance Act will lead to a "substantial violation," thereby terminating military assistance to the violator.

Mutual Defense Agreement of 1952

A bilateral arrangement between the United States and Israel restricts Israel's use of U.S.-supplied weapons. The 1952 Mutual Defense Agreement dictates that Israel may use U.S. military assistance for only the following purposes: to maintain its "internal security," for legitimate self-defense, or to permit it to participate in a United Nations peacekeeping endeavor.

While these domestic legal provisions abstain from providing an unfettered submission to international law and hence international interpretation, they provide a powerful resource, one that allows proponents of international law to shape, by advocacy, the limits of U.S. political interpretation.

Presumably by design, the AECA does not define the meaning of "legitimate self-defense" or "internal security" and, as demonstrated by the seemingly unanimous passage in January 2009 of Bill H.Res. 34, which recognizes Israel's right to defend itself against attacks from Gaza, our federal policymakers are certain that Israel's aggression against a defenseless population is "legitimate self-defense." Still, without challenge, the meaning remains entrenched in the convenient rapture of Orwellian realities. We, as a human rights community, have purposefully distanced ourselves from the halls of power that protect imperial interests at the expense of human ones. And yet that self-imposed exile has worked to reinforce a dangerous and self-fulfilling prophecy.

Congress and the Arab-Israeli Conflict

It is beneficial to consider the ways in which the Arab-Israeli conflict is handled in Washington today to narrow down ways in which to approach advocacy. At present, the primary motivating factor in Congress is Iran. In large part because of its explicit threat to the Israeli state but also because other Arab regimes would also like to see Iran militarily neutered, our government has responded eagerly to the preoccupation with Iran.

By its own means, the Bush administration saw to the creation of a "new Middle East." Then secretary of state Condoleezza Rice signaled its arrival when in opposing a ceasefire in southern Lebanon in 2006 she described the mounting death toll as "birth pangs." Now fully delivered, the configuration situates the U.S. allies of Jordan, Egypt, Saudi Arabia, Lebanon's March 14 Movement or Coalition, and Fatah at ideological odds with Iran, Syria, Hamas, and Hizbullah. In 2009, Seymour Hersh reported on the United States' advances to rapprochement with Syria, presumably in its effort to further isolate the Islamic Republic. He quoted Martin Indyck, former U.S. ambassador to Israel, American Israel Public Affairs Committee (AIPAC) employee, and current director of the Brookings Institution, who explained that

> the return of the Golan Heights is part of a broader strategy for peace in the Middle East that includes countering Iran's influence. . . . Syria is a strategic linchpin for dealing with Iran and the Palestinian issue. Don't forget, everything in the Middle East is connected, as Obama once said.[11]

Clearly, rapprochement has since collapsed and this point has been made moot by the imminent fall of the Syrian regime. Still, it continues to reflect the United States' broader Middle East strategy, which aims to mute opposition to its ubiquitous reach.

The pro-Israel lobby no longer shapes its Congressional advocacy by simply propagandizing Israel as a David among a sea of Arab enemies. Instead, it also describes Israel as being in alliance with its Arab friends against the encroachment of a menacing Iran. As much is indicated by Palestinian president Mahmoud Abbas, who, rather than condemn Israel for its flagrant violations and contempt for the rule of law in the aftermath of the war on Gaza, criticized Iran for its backing of Hamas. Abbas accused Tehran of trying to deepen the Palestinian split, saying, "Iran needs to take care of its own issues and stay away from intervening in Palestinian affairs."[12]

In effect, Palestine and Palestinians have been bifurcated into the good Palestinian on the one hand and the bad Palestinian on the other. Therefore approaching the conflict in a business-as-usual manner will not be very effective—questions will arise over "which Palestinians," "which loyalties"—and suddenly the human rights of Palestinians are subject to regional considerations that eclipse concerns over their subjugated status.

To avoid this trap in Congress and to advance human rights principles, the need to employ new paradigms in the entreaty to the safekeepers of Israel's financial capability seems obvious. Such new paradigms include the lexicon of religious morality and the logic of global economics—but while plausible, each is limited by its seemingly narrow appeal. Alternatively, the exaltation of individual rights and U.S. superiority may have universal appeal in an institution that enshrines the nation's political identity as the popular sovereign.

In this vein, I suggest several possible policy alternatives:

An emphasis on civil and political rights as enshrined in the Constitution and reified in the International Covenant on Civil and Political Rights.

An emphasis on U.S. superiority by framing grievances in the form of violations of U.S. domestic law—the AECA, the FAA, and the Mutual Assistance Agreement.

A reliance on liberal reverence for process by emphasizing the United States' long-standing policy toward settlements.

International Covenant on Civil and Political Rights

Civil and political rights both epitomize the sanctity of the individual, a resonant theme to policymakers who deem the Constitution sacred, and comport with one legacy of the Universal Declaration of Human Rights. Unfortunately, the violation of these rights is abundantly apparent among Palestinians—consider the denial of due process, the structural application of collective punishment, the obstruction of the right to assembly, and the prohibition on the right to movement. While addressing these violations would not remedy the depth of colonial occupation, they would work to chip away at the edifice of Israeli apartheid.[13]

On Military Funding: AECA and the Primacy of U.S. Law

By emphasizing the violation of U.S. laws and, by extension, an affront to its hegemony, the AECA and its counterparts may prove an effective tool. Its potential is underscored by its past success. In 1982, the Reagan administration determined that Israel "may" have violated its 1952 Mutual Defense Assistance Agreement with the United States by reportedly using U.S.-supplied antipersonnel cluster bombs against civilian targets during its military operations in Lebanon and the siege of Beirut. As a result, the Reagan administration prohibited U.S. export of cluster bombs to Israel for six years.

Far from signaling its irrelevance when export of cluster munitions resumed, the ban's legacy has continued to impact U.S. policy on the sale of cluster munitions. In reaction to their use in southern Lebanon in 2006, the State Department conducted an investigation and issued a report finding that Israel may have violated U.S.-Israeli procurement agreements on the use of cluster munitions. As a result, the FY2008 Consolidated Appropriations bill significantly restricted the export of U.S.-manufactured cluster munitions.[14] Section 646 (b) of the bill states that "no military assistance shall be furnished for cluster munitions, no defense export license for cluster munitions may be issued, and no cluster munitions or cluster munitions technology shall be sold or transferred, unless the agreement for the sale mandates that the cluster munitions will only be used against clearly defined military targets and will not be used where civilians are known to be present." While the standards are clearly far from adequate, they effectively serve as a wedge with the potential to deepen incrementally.

On Settlement Construction: The United States' Own Policies

Finally, in drawing on U.S. precedent and appealing to its liberal deference to process, it may be beneficial to highlight U.S. policy on settlements. In 1992, the United States legislated its opposition to settlements and settlement expansion in the form of Title VI of P.L. 102–391 (signed into law 6 October 1992). The bill states that U.S. funds may not be used in the Occupied Territories. In the mid-1990s and again in 2003, the United States reduced its loan guarantees to Israel by an amount equal to Israel's settlement construction. In 2003, the State Department reduced its $3 billion loan guarantees to Israel by $289.5 million due to Israel's continued construction of settlements.

Although the United States vetoed the February 2011 Security Council Resolution condemning settlements, the Obama administration made clear that its opposition was to the multilateral venue and not the substance of the initiative. Ambassador Susan Rice explained, "[U.S.] opposition to the resolution before this council today should . . . not be misunderstood to mean we support settlement activity. . . . On the contrary, we reject in the strongest terms the legitimacy of continued Israeli settlement activity."[15] Emphasizing U.S. historical opposition continues to be as relevant as ever as Israel's settler-colonial expansion continues unabated. Consider that population growth within settlements is not natural. As approximately one-twentieth of Israel's Jewish population, the settlers' numbers have grown by over 5 percent a year, some three times the national average. In 1977, the West Bank's

Jewish population was barely 7,000.[16] As of 2012 that number had reached 650,000.[17]

By no means am I suggesting a revolutionary approach to advocacy efforts. To the contrary, I have attempted to unpack the loaded practice of Congressional advocacy in relation to Palestinian human rights, and in effect I have outlined the broad parameters of a shifting paradigm—one that does not appeal to U.S. imperial interests in the name of pragmatism but instead appeals to its sense of national self and identity. This may benefit human rights advocates who, driven by conviction, may be willing to make the same deafening and unsuccessful appeals until incapacitated. We can continue to do so or we may consider amenable alternatives. Whatever the choice may be, the choice to disengage is not ours. Perhaps then, despite its self-interested motivations, the United States can help promote, rather than pummel, the rule of law in the region.

Three Years Later: A Forward-Looking Prologue

Three years later in 2013, it is worth reflecting on the developments, globally and in Washington in particular, that impact this analysis. It was not as clear in 2010 as it is today that what is in the United States' best interest, imperial though it may be, is not in perfect harmony with Israel's interests. It has thus appeared striking when, notwithstanding this divergence, U.S. lawmakers have used their authority to uphold Israel's interests without particular regard to U.S. foreign policy interests in the Middle East.

Perhaps the first rupture in this presumed synergy was Vice President Joseph Biden's 2010 visit to the Middle East when he called for an Israeli settlement freeze. Though it fit seamlessly into a U.S. foreign policy that sought to establish two states for two peoples in Israel and the Occupied Palestinian Territories, U.S. lawmakers fervently opposed their own executive in support of Israeli prime minister Benjamin Netanyahu's appeal for unchecked Israeli settlement expansion. Scores of Congressional members from both sides of the aisle lined up to chastise the Obama administration for its public handling of the affair. No fewer than twenty-three members expressed terse disapproval either in press statements or from the House floor. Several dozen other members sent four open letters to the Obama administration as well. Significantly, the lawmakers' choice of language mirrors an

AIPAC press release dated 14 March 2010 and therefore nearly every member echoed the sentiment that Israel should not be treated like any other country but rather with heightened sensitivity and special regard. Representative Todd Tiahrt described Obama's public position as "disrespectful" and characterized Secretary of State Hillary Clinton's decision to "openly question" Israeli policies as "inappropriate," as the United States has a "moral and strategic obligation to support this beacon of democracy in the Middle East."

The events precipitated a new rupture, not within the U.S. political establishment but rather within the formidable Israel lobby. Individuals and bodies who considered the failed U.S. initiative to thwart Israeli settlement expansion a missed opportunity formed the organization J Street, a liberal alternative to AIPAC. J Street's concern, however, is not just one missed opportunity; rather, it has sought to create a new home for "pro-Israel, pro-peace Americans." Unlike AIPAC, J Street would support U.S. efforts to achieve a two-state solution even if it meant curbing Israeli sovereign prerogative. Notably, J Street's advocacy conformed to AIPAC's own approach in that it drew a red line at the boundaries of accountability. The United States, it declared, should support Israel to establish a two-state solution, but it should not impose any economic or political pressure to do so.

In response to this development as well as to what appeared to be a nascent rift between American and Israeli interests, another set of individuals and organizations established themselves in a body to the right of AIPAC. The Emergency Committee for Israel exerted its collective influence to campaign against U.S. lawmakers in the 2010 midterm elections who expressed the slightest admonition to Israel during Operation Cast Lead or the settlement row. Its targets who lost that year included House Democrats Glenn Nye and Mary Jo Kilroy as well as Pennsylvania Senate candidate Joe Sestak. Headed by William Kristol, a prominent neoconservative with strong ties to the Republican establishment, the Emergency Committee for Israel has worked to make Israel a partisan issue in the Beltway. While the emergence of J Street and the Emergency Committee for Israel, both at odds with the long-standing AIPAC, does not suggest a move away from fundamental support for Israel, it has signaled a significant shift in a hitherto monolithic discourse. The shift has created some room where none previously existed to discuss what exactly is in the United States' best interest in the Middle East.

By winter 2012, the expanse between U.S. and Israeli interests became a matter of mainstream public discourse, as evidenced by the response to

Israel's 2012 military offense against Gaza, Operation Pillar of Cloud. Unlike the most recent instance of Israel's pummeling of Gaza only four years prior, the mainstream media responded to this offensive with heightened skepticism. Rather than accept, as a matter of fact, that Israel conducted its operation for the sake of self-preservation, a broad swath of mainstream media institutions asked whether this offensive was indeed necessary, and if so, whether it was not excessive and disproportionate to the threat posed by Hamas and Palestinians generally.

The apex of this divergence between U.S. and Israeli interests as well as within the Israel lobby establishment became evident in the disturbing confirmation hearings for the U.S. secretary of defense in February 2013. Indeed, during the eight-hour confirmation hearing of former senator Chuck Hagel, the Senate Armed Services Committee grilled Hagel about his commitment to Israel as a concept and a state in gross disproportion to more salient U.S. defense matters, including sexual harassment in the military and the Obama administration's use of drones. The strange spectacle was not lost on observers beyond the Beltway who ridiculed the episode in satirical form.[18] The committee ultimately confirmed Hagel in a 58–41 vote, but not before forcing him to pledge his allegiance to a Washington orthodoxy that may or may not have any practical relevance to U.S. foreign policy and security concerns in the Middle East or beyond.

These intervening events during a relatively short time span indicate a striking phenomenon: the U.S. political establishment may not be acting to further its own imperial interests at all. Instead, its elected officials, from congressional representatives to the head of its executive branch, are all arguably vulnerable to domestic political considerations. The problem, if there is only one, is not in the influence that human rights advocates can exert on the U.S. political establishment but in whether or not the political establishment has the wherewithal to respond to it at all. Unless human rights advocates organize themselves as a special interest group with the constituency and/or financial resources to shape electoral outcomes, they may not be able to penetrate a dynamic establishment that contemplates new foreign policy possibilities. If this trajectory is any indication of the dead ends in store for the efficacy of the U.S. political establishment, then the lost opportunity for human rights, writ large, may not be as devastating as one would imagine. Instead, there will likely be new opportunities worth seizing when, inevitably, the political establishment's interests again come into direct conflict with U.S. foreign policy interests. At that time, human rights organizations need only prepare themselves to highlight these divergences and make their case for a new way forward.

Notes

1. See Edmund S. Morgan, "The Problem of Popular Sovereignty," *Aspects of American Liberty: Philosophical, Historical and Political* (Philadelphia: American Philosophical Society, 1977), 101, in which the author concludes that the American Revolution marks the "subordination of government to the will of the people."

2. Thomas Jefferson to Benjamin Waring, 1801, in *The Jeffersonian Cyclopedia*, ed. John P. Foley (New York: Funk & Wagnalls, 1900), 387.

3. Paul W. Kahn, "Why the United States Is So Opposed to the International Criminal Court," *Crimes of War Project Magazine*, December 2003.

4. Ann Elizabeth Meyer, "Clashing Human Rights Priorities: How the United States and Muslim Countries Selectively Use Provisions of International Human Rights Law," *Satya Nilayam: Chennai Journal of Intercultural Philosophy* 44 (2006): 44–77.

5. Michael Scharf, "Results of the Rome Conference for an International Criminal Court," August 1998, accessed 9 July 2012, http://www.asil.org/insigh23.cfm.

6. Richard Boucher, State Department regular briefing, 2 January 2001, http://www.amicc.org/docs/Jan2_01.pdf.

7. Arms Export Control Act, 22 U.S.C. §§ 2751–2799aa-2 (2009). For a thorough discussion of the AECA in the context of Israeli actions during the al-Aqsa Intifada, see National Lawyers Guild, *The Al Aqsa Intifada and Israel's Apartheid: The U.S. Military and Economic Role in the Violation of Palestinian Human Rights*, January 2001, http://nlg.org/resources/delegations/al_aqsa_intifada.pdf.

8. 22 U.S.C. § 2753(c)(2).

9. 22 U.S.C. § 2753(c)(4).

10. Foreign Assistance Act of 1961 (P.L. 87–195), Sec. 116 Human Rights, http://transition.usaid.gov/policy/ads/faa.pdf.

11. Seymour Hersh, "Syria Calling," *New Yorker*, 6 April 2009.

12. Barak Ravid, "Clinton: Israel's Demolition of East Jerusalem Homes Harms Peace Efforts, *Haaretz*, 4 March 2009, http://www.haaretz.com/print-edition/news/clinton-israel-s-demolition-of-east-jerusalem-homes-harms-peace-efforts-1.271377.

13. In 2012, the Eightieth Session of the Committee for the Elimination of Racial Discrimination held that Israel's policies constitute a de facto policy of segregation and discrimination between Jews and non-Jews within the Occupied Territories, which is tantamount to apartheid. Committee on the Elimination of Racial Discrimination, Eightieth Session, *Concluding Observations of the Committee on the Elimination of Racial Discrimination—Israel*, CERD/C/ISR/CO/14–16, 9 March 2012.

14. Consolidated Appropriations Act, 2008 (P.L. 110–161), enacted on 26 December 2007.

15. Brad Knickerbocker, "If Obama Opposes Israeli Settlement Activity, Why did US Veto UN Vote?," *Christian Science Monitor*, 18 February 2011, http://www.csmonitor.com/USA/Foreign-Policy/2011/0218/If-Obama-opposes-Israeli-settlement-activity-why-did-US-veto-UN-vote.

16. Hillel Halkin, "What To Do With the Settlements," *Wall Street Journal*, 4 February 2010, http://online.wsj.com/article/SB10001424052748704259304575043101789714506.html.

17. Hagit Ofran via Eyes on the Ground in East Jerusalem, "How Many Settlers Are There?," 24 July 2012, http://settlementwatcheastjerusalem.wordpress.com/2012/07/24/how-many-settlers-are-there/.

18. *Saturday Night Live* sketch on Chuck Hagel's confirmation hearing, 11 February 2013, http://www.washingtonpost.com/blogs/the-fix/wp/2013/02/11/saturday-night-live-on-chuck-hagels-confirmation-hearing-video/.

11. Lessons for Palestine from Northern Ireland

Why George Mitchell Couldn't Turn Jerusalem into Belfast

ALI ABUNIMAH

> I formed the conviction that there is no such thing as a conflict that can't be ended. Conflicts are created, conducted, and sustained by human beings. They can be ended by human beings. I saw it happen in Northern Ireland, although, admittedly, it took a very long time. I believe deeply that with committed, persevering, and patient diplomacy, it can happen in the Middle East.
>
> —*George Mitchell, Obama administration Middle East envoy, 22 January 2009*

During Israel's December 2008/January 2009 invasion of the Gaza Strip, which killed more than 1,400 Palestinians, the vast majority civilians,[1] veteran Irish journalist Patrick Cockburn reported that Israeli society reminded him "more than ever of the unionists in Northern Ireland in the late 1960s." Like Israelis, he wrote, unionists were a community "with a highly developed siege mentality which led them always to see themselves as victims even when they were killing other people. There were no regrets or even knowledge of what they inflicted on others and therefore any retaliation by the other side appeared as unprovoked aggression inspired by unreasoning hate."[2]

Today, more than a decade after the 1998 Belfast Agreement, the Northern Ireland political settlement appears to be holding up, although it continues to face tests and its long-term viability is by no means assured. Irish nationalists share power with pro-British unionists in what is in effect a binational state. Political violence has virtually ended. When two British soldiers and a police officer were allegedly killed by Irish nationalists known as "dissident republicans" in March 2009, in the first of such attacks in more than twelve years, the deaths were met with unprecedented displays of unity and appeals for calm by former enemies.[3] People in Northern Ireland are far from coming to terms with the consequences of their long civil war, and the Agreement did not definitively settle the status of Northern Ireland, but a generation of children, now teenagers, has no memory of the pervasive violence that traumatized their society for decades. That alone is no small achievement.

President Barack Obama's appointment of former senator George Mitchell as his Middle East envoy within days of taking office brought renewed speculation that despite unprecedented levels of violence and an entrenched political stalemate, American intervention could bring about a two-state solution to the Palestinian-Israeli conflict. Mitchell's own optimism was borne out of his experience as chair of the excruciatingly difficult negotiations that led to the Belfast Agreement.[4]

Mitchell was not the only participant in the current Middle East peace process to draw direct parallels with his experience in Northern Ireland. Former British prime minister Tony Blair was appointed in July 2007 as the envoy of the Quartet, the ad hoc, self-appointed group of American, European, Russian, and UN officials that monopolizes the Middle East peace process agenda. As prime minister, Blair devoted intensive personal efforts to Northern Ireland, often comparing the Belfast negotiations to the Middle East. "The unionists were the Israelis and the republicans [Irish nationalists who want a united Ireland] were the Palestinians," Blair has said, and the British "were the Americans trying to bring the two sides together and get them to trust each other, while also having cards in our hands."[5]

This essay argues that principles and strategies adapted from those applied in Ireland would produce a better outcome for Palestine/Israel than the failed approach taken by every American administration—including through its first year the Obama administration—as well as the "international community" since the Middle East peace process began with the 1991 Madrid Conference and the 1993 Oslo Accords. Of course, every situation is unique, but there are nevertheless significant historic and structural parallels—many long-recognized by scholars and members of both communities—that make Ireland and Palestine suitable for comparison.

Both conflicts have at times been described as "intractable," not least because of the intensity of the enmity that appeared to motivate the antago-
nists. The discussion proceeds with brief histories of both conflicts and then
examines the outcomes, processes, and limitations of the Northern Ireland
settlement and highlights lessons for Palestine/Israel.

U.S. and International Intervention

Much of the optimism generated by Mitchell's appointment reflected a consensus that it signaled a commitment by President Obama to the kind of
early and sustained engagement that previous administrations had repeatedly, and with tragic consequences, failed to deliver. But the problem has
never been a lack of American engagement. Rather, it has been too much of
the wrong kind. Aaron David Miller, a former top State Department official,
succinctly summed up the American role in Arab-Israeli diplomacy over the
past quarter century as "Israel's attorney, catering and coordinating with the
Israelis at the expense of successful peace negotiations."[6]

Earlier administrations, whether or not they actively encouraged negotiations, had been heavily involved in Palestine/Israel and the broader region. Since 1967, the United States has given growing military, economic,
and diplomatic support to Israel—in effect intervening heavily on one side.
The George W. Bush administration took American engagement to unprecedented levels. It pushed for Palestinian legislative elections in 2006,
and then when Hamas defeated the U.S.-backed Fatah faction, it immediately attempted to overturn the result through overt political and financial
pressure on the Palestinian Authority and a covert scheme supervised by
Secretary of State Condoleezza Rice to overthrow the Hamas-led Authority
with the help of U.S.-backed Palestinian individuals and groups.[7] The administration dispatched Lieutenant General Keith Dayton to help train U.S.-
supplied and -financed Palestinian militias opposed to Hamas, and through
direct pressure on Palestinian Authority president Mahmoud Abbas it effectively vetoed a Palestinian "national unity government."[8] The Bush administration and many Congressional leaders supported the Israeli blockade
of the Gaza Strip and used financial aid to bolster client Palestinian leaders
and in effect subsidize the Israeli military occupation. These policies were
backed by the Quartet and some Western-allied Arab states and were maintained intact after the Obama administration took office in January 2009.

Along with all these interventions, sponsorship of peace negotiations has probably been the least significant form of international engagement. While Mitchell is held in high esteem for his personal role as a mediator in Ireland, it was not his skills alone that led to a successful outcome. He was backed by an administration ready to act in ways that have been anathema to American policymakers dealing with Palestine/Israel. While these realities are often ignored, exploring them is nonetheless essential to understanding how international intervention would have to change for the United States and other actors to start to play a constructive role in fostering a just, sustainable, and agreed peace. Such changes would involve a transformation not only in tactics but also in conceptions of what might constitute workable principles for a political agreement, whether it takes the form of a "two-state solution" or any other arrangement.

Parallel Histories: From Settler-Colonialism to Partition

Underpinning the conflicts in Ireland and Palestine are settler-colonial interventions whose legacy in each case has been to create two mutually exclusive claims to sovereignty, legitimacy, and self-determination underpinned by two diametrically opposed narratives, and a material reality of one community long monopolizing state power, resources, and symbols to dominate and denigrate the other.[9] Each country was partitioned as British forces withdrew to allow the community that enjoyed a privileged position in the prepartition colonial state to continue to exercise power afterward. The resulting state arrangements failed to gain legitimacy and instead generated resistance—expressed as indigenous nationalism—among a significant part of the population. Lacking sufficient consent, the partitioned entities—Israel and Northern Ireland—could only be sustained with massive and escalating use of state violence. In Northern Ireland's case, the 1998 Belfast Agreement created the democratic framework necessary for a new political dispensation based on consent rather than domination.

Ireland

Irish nationalists point to an eight-hundred-year history of English colonialism, but the taproot of the modern conflict was the Plantation of Ulster— the colonization of the northeast part of the island, beginning in the early

1600s. As English authorities granted land to Protestant settlers from England and Scotland, native Catholics were forcibly displaced in large numbers.

The chief British negotiator at the Northern Ireland peace talks, Jonathan Powell, observed that the planters "regarded themselves in much the same way as early Israeli settlers."[10] The consequences of their actions—forced displacement and subordination of the existing population—can also be compared to what happened in Palestine. Settlement in Ireland, Michael MacDonald has explained, "did not merely disrupt, but obliterated traditional Ireland, imposing over the ruins a colonial order that, though enduring, was—and in Northern Ireland still is—bitterly, even violently, resisted."[11]

Although Britain annexed Ireland in 1801, repeated Irish nationalist rebellions made the question of granting Irish "home rule" the central controversy in British politics through much of the nineteenth century. Unionists were generally comprised of the ascendant and long-settled Protestant population and were opposed to home rule, fearing it would threaten their privileged status. After the British Parliament passed a home rule bill in 1912, some 240,000 men, three quarters of the unionist adult male population, signed the "Ulster Covenant," pledging to "us[e] all means which may be found necessary" to prevent any form of Irish self-government. Their organized militias paraded through Belfast tens of thousands strong and imported large quantities of weapons, all of which succeeded in heading off implementation of home rule.

On Easter day in 1916 a few hundred Irish nationalists staged an armed uprising in Dublin and proclaimed an independent Irish Republic. The Easter Rising initially had little popular support and was easily crushed by the British. But it is regarded as a turning point in nationalist history, as the brutal British response, including the execution of the republican leaders, spurred growing support for the nationalist cause. In the 1918 election to the British Parliament, the republican party Sinn Fein won a landslide on a platform of total independence from Britain. Sinn Fein deputies refused to take their seats in the British Parliament, but met in Dublin and ratified the 1916 independence proclamation.

Following a guerilla war between British and republican forces that ended in stalemate, the sides signed the 1921 Anglo-Irish Treaty establishing the Irish Free State, an autonomous "dominion" of the British Empire. But its territory covered only twenty-six of Ireland's thirty-two counties. To appease unionists, the British simultaneously partitioned the island, forming Northern Ireland, an autonomous self-governing state linked to Britain, with a two-thirds Protestant majority.

The Northern Ireland state reproduced the pattern of relationships that had been established by settler colonialism, but it allowed unionists to present their dominance as the legitimate result of democratic majoritarianism. As Michael MacDonald explains,

> The contradiction of settlers to natives survived and structured three centuries of Irish history: partition acknowledged as much. Rather than fading away, the original conflict was institutionalized in political, social, and religious relations. Politically the natives were nationalists and the settlers unionists; socially, the nationalists were deprived and the unionists privileged; and religiously the deprived were Catholic and the privileged Protestant.[12]

As we shall see, this scheme can be easily transposed to Palestine after partition, where politically the natives are Palestinian nationalists and the settlers Zionists; socially the Palestinians are deprived and Israeli Jews privileged; and religiously the deprived are Muslim and Christian and the privileged Jewish.

Northern Ireland became a unionist-run, one-party state. Nationalist resistance to partition was violently suppressed by British forces and unionist militias.[13] Within a year, hundreds of Catholics were killed in Belfast, 11,000 were forced from their jobs, and 22,000—a quarter of the city's Catholic population—were driven from their homes.[14] The state institutionalized a recently invented "Ulster" Protestant culture and violently suppressed expressions of nationalist identity.[15] In the widely quoted formula attributed to Northern Ireland's first prime minister Sir James Craig, the state's seat of government at Stormont Castle was a "Protestant parliament for a Protestant people."[16]

Nationalists continued to view Northern Ireland as illegitimate, but they did not have the strength to end partition and found little practical support from their compatriots in the south who, though nominally committed to reunification, were focused on consolidating the Free State that eventually became the Republic of Ireland. In the mid-1960s, after almost fifty years of unionist rule, nationalists mobilized a civil rights movement modeled on the one in the United States—demanding equal citizenship and an end to systematic employment and housing discrimination against Catholics. This represented a departure from traditional republicanism, which focused on ending partition, but the unionist state perceived even demands for liberal rights "not as an enhancement of democracy . . . but as an attack on Protestant identity and on the very existence of the Northern [Ireland] state."[17] Unionists responded with violence and, as in the 1920s, Catholics were once again subjected to pogroms.

These events inaugurated the three-decade low-level civil war known as "the Troubles" in which more than 3,500 people were killed and 50,000 injured—nearly 2 percent of Northern Ireland's population.[18] As violence escalated, the British government abolished the unionist Stormont government, imposed direct rule, and sent in the army. The unionist state had collapsed, but the unionist-dominated status quo was preserved, as the army, initially sent in to protect Catholics, quickly began to act and be seen by them as an occupying force.[19] A reconstituted Irish Republican Army (IRA) resumed armed struggle, initially in defense of Catholic communities, but later went on the offensive against the police, army, and unionist militias (known as "loyalists"). The IRA and other republican armed groups also carried out bomb attacks and political assassinations. By default, the IRA began to serve social functions such as policing and administering the allocation of housing and other resources in neglected Catholic enclaves where state forces were regarded as the armed wing of unionism. British tactics included curfews, internment (imprisonment without charge or trial), assassinations, and extrajudicial executions, and there was extensive collusion between state forces and loyalist militias that killed hundreds of Catholics in sectarian attacks.[20]

Although the civil rights movement had failed to achieve reform of the state and equal rights (the British did gradually introduce limited reforms), Michael MacDonald argues that it broke the traditional solidarity within the unionist community between those who saw any concession as leading down a slippery slope toward a united Ireland (and a total loss of unionist power) and those arguing that modest reforms could render the Northern Ireland state acceptable to nationalists or at least weaken support for republicanism.[21]

Unionism viewed efforts to create a united Ireland as a mortal threat. In 1990, for example, James Molyneaux, leader of the then-dominant Ulster

Unionist Party, described the Republic of Ireland's constitutional claim to the north as "a demand for the destruction of Northern Ireland" that was "equivalent to Hitler's claim over Czechoslovakia."[22] Fear of a high Catholic birth rate—which could provide the Catholic majority needed to reunify Ireland—has been a recurrent theme in unionist discourse, just as a Palestinian "demographic threat" generates much anxiety among Israeli Jews. "The basic fear of Protestants in Northern Ireland," a former unionist prime minister said, "is that they will be outbred by the Roman Catholics. It is simple as that."[23]

While proclaiming their undying loyalty to the British crown, the unionist siege mentality was fed by the constant fear of "betrayal" and abandonment by the British. This led a small number of unionists to call for independence for Northern Ireland, but this never caught on, most likely because without British backing, Northern Ireland would be unlikely to have the resources to survive a sustained nationalist challenge. Unionists therefore insisted that maintaining Northern Ireland as part of the United Kingdom was the only means to protect their identity and way of life against a Catholic and Celtic-identified nationalist majority on the island of Ireland, whose culture unionists typically characterized as theocratic, backward, and inferior to their own.[24]

Palestine

Beginning in the late nineteenth century, Palestine was the target of Zionist settler-colonialism whose openly declared purpose was to transform Palestine into a Jewish "national home."[25] From the outset, the Zionist movement understood that this could not be achieved without the involuntary removal of the native Arab population.[26] The partition of Palestine was accompanied by the expulsion and flight of 750,000 Palestinians in the months preceding and following the declaration of the State of Israel in May 1948 as the British prepared to withdraw.[27] Palestinians, who were two-thirds of Palestine's two million inhabitants on the eve of partition, became a minority within the area on which Israel was established.

Within its borders, Israel accorded Jews political, economic, symbolic, and military dominance. The Palestinian population remaining inside the new state found itself, like nationalists in Northern Ireland, involuntarily subject to a regime that claimed moral and cultural superiority and democratic legitimacy because the dominant group, a minority in the prepartition colonial state, now constituted a majority and could continuously endorse its own power through elections. Like Irish nationalists, Palestinians did not have the means to challenge partition directly. Those forced out were disorganized and dispersed, while those inside Israel lived under military rule until 1966 and were largely isolated from the mainstream Palestinian national movement that began to emerge in the diaspora in the 1950s. Palestinian citizens of Israel set out on their own political trajectory, resisting Israel by demanding that it live up to its claims to be a liberal state. Without abandoning an identification with Palestinian nationalism, they accepted their status as citizens but demanded that Israel transform itself into a "state of all its citizens"—an approach reminiscent of the Northern Ireland civil rights movement.[28]

Israel's reaction to Palestinian demands for equal citizenship mimics the unionist response to the nationalist campaign for equality in Northern Ireland. Israel also characterized these demands as an existential threat, a tacit acknowledgment that inequality and discrimination are foundational elements of the Israeli state, not incidental to it. Proposals for a liberal democratic constitution published by Palestinian citizens of Israel,[29] for instance, prompted the head of Israel's Shin Bet intelligence service to warn that his agency would "foil the activity of anyone seeking to harm Israel's Jewish or democratic character, even if that activity was carried out by legal means."[30]

After Israel's 1967 occupation of the West Bank, the Gaza Strip, and East Jerusalem, the remainder of the Palestinian population in historic Palestine came under direct Israeli rule, effectively ending partition. Israel began colonizing the land with the intention of making withdrawal impossible and annexation a fait accompli. The problem from the Israeli perspective was how to keep the largest amount of newly acquired territory but not the Palestinians living on it. Palestinians from the Occupied Territories could not be granted the rights of citizens, even to the qualified extent enjoyed by Palestinians in Israel, because that would negate the Israeli Jewish majority. Because of Israel's overriding interest in territory and water resources, Palestinians could not be granted real sovereignty in their own state.

For decades, Israel was able to defer confronting this dilemma. During the first phase of the occupation, from 1967 through the first Intifada, which began in 1987, Israel attempted to suppress Palestinian national aspirations from within through the repressive apparatus of the occupation and from without through successive invasions of Lebanon and the occupation of southern Lebanon from 1978 to 2000. The second phase, which began with the 1993 Oslo Accords, has come to be an endless "peace process" used as an alibi for procrastination and the co-optation of former national- ist Palestinian elites to run the Palestinian Authority, whose main task has been to suppress Palestinian resistance while Israel continues to colonize the land. After the failure of the Clinton administration–sponsored 2000 Camp David summit, Israel briefly flirted with "unilateral disengagement"—the abandonment and isolation of heavily populated Palestinian areas. Israel's 2005 removal of settlers from the Gaza Strip and the hermetic closure of the territory was an experiment Israeli leaders intended to repeat with Pales- tinian cities in the West Bank, but continued resistance from Gaza discred- ited the model.[31] Without other options, Israel reverted to the Oslo formula of endless negotiations and reliance on the Palestinian Authority to combat resistance.

But further postponement has become extremely difficult for several rea- sons: the lack of credibility of the peace process after almost two decades without progress; the discrediting of the Palestinian Authority as a state- building project and its effective exposure as an arm of Israeli occupation; the rise of new forms of Palestinian and regional armed and political re- sistance; the growing perception in the United States that continued con- flict is a liability to broader U.S. goals in the Middle East; and increasing international mobilization in response to Israeli actions, particularly the global boycott, divestment, and sanctions campaign modeled on the anti- apartheid movement of the 1980s. Adding to the urgency has been aware- ness that inexorable demographic shifts mean that Israeli Jews face the fu- ture as a minority in Palestine/Israel.

The question confronting Zionism at the beginning of the twenty-first century is how Jews can maintain their political, cultural, and economic su- premacy in Palestine/Israel, while retaining their status and self-perception as members of the club of enlightened liberal democracies. Alarmingly, in- creasing numbers of Israeli Jews are comfortable choosing ethnic supremacy over democracy, as the rise of unabashedly racist parties including Foreign Minister Avigdor Lieberman's Yisrael Beitenu attests. A dwindling number hopes that some form of repartition to restore a Jewish majority within fixed borders—the elusive two-state solution—can still provide a way out. Then Israeli prime minister Ehud Olmert summed up prevailing anxieties in 2007 when he warned, "If the day comes when the two-state solution collapses, and we face a South African-style struggle for equal voting rights . . . as soon as that happens, the State of Israel is finished."[32] It is in this context that Is-raeli governments have continued to actively colonize the West Bank, es-pecially East Jerusalem, while purporting to participate in U.S.-sponsored peace negotiations shepherded by Mitchell that, given this colonization, ap-peared stillborn.

Decolonization and Equality, Not Ethnic Sovereignty

Urgent calls for a two-state solution have been increasingly defended not because such an outcome would restore Palestinian rights, but explicitly because it would allow Israeli Jews to maintain their ethnic privileges in "a Jewish and democratic state."[33] These calls are increasingly accompanied by warnings that the window for achieving a two-state solution is closing, if it was ever open at all. As Joseph Massad has observed, the essence of the two-state solution and peace process so far has been to demand that one section of the Palestinian people—the diaspora, refugees, and Palestinian citizens of Israel—forfeit all its rights, so that another—natives of the West Bank and Gaza Strip—receive limited self-rule in a Bantustan-like state.[34] In ef-fect, Palestinians are required to choose *among* their internationally recog-nized human rights and who among their population will get them rather than seek all of them, in order to sustain Israel's dubious claim that it has a "right to exist as a Jewish State."

A useful lens through which to examine the legitimacy of Israel's claim is the legal maxim that there is no right without a remedy.[35] If Israel has a "right to exist as a Jewish state," then what is the remedy if Palestinians living under its control "violate" this right by having too many of the wrong kind of ba-bies, undermining a Jewish majority? Can Israel expel non-Jews, fine them, strip them of citizenship, or limit the number of children they are allowed to have? While these suggestions may sound outrageous, over the past six years Israel has adopted marriage restriction laws designed specifically and exclu-sively to limit whom the Palestinian citizens of Israel can marry.[36] In 2009, the Yisrael Beitenu party led by Avigdor Lieberman sponsored or supported several bills aimed at further curtailing the rights of non-Jews. One requires all citizens, including Palestinian Muslims and Christians, to swear alle-giance to Israel as a Jewish state. Another proposes to punish anyone who commemorates the Nakba (the name Palestinians give to their forced dis-possession in the months before and after the state of Israel was established in 1948) with up to three years in prison.[37] Like the existing restrictive marriage laws and subsequent proposals, it is impossible to think of a "remedy" that does not do outrageous violence to universal human rights principles and international law. No state, therefore, can demand a "right" to discriminate on ethnic, religious, or racial grounds.

This does not necessarily mean that a two-state solution can never be just, but it would have to look very different from what is contemplated because it would have to be founded on equality. Ireland provides a model of an attempt do this in practice. The partition of Ireland indeed created a "two-state solution," but it did not bring peace because one of those states had an institutionalized commitment defended by the British to unionist Protestant supremacy. Once the British dropped this commitment, space opened for new forms of politics. A breakthrough moment came in 1992 when the UK secretary of state for Northern Ireland gave a landmark speech conceding that "provided it is advocated constitutionally, there can be no proper reason for excluding any political objective from discussion. Certainly not the objective of a united Ireland."[38] There remain two separate jurisdictions on the island, but the Belfast Agreement provides a framework for legitimacy, equality, and power sharing.

The Belfast Agreement

The Belfast Agreement was reached after two years of negotiations among Northern Ireland's main nationalist and unionist political parties and the British and Irish governments. It was overwhelmingly endorsed in simultaneous referendums in the south and north of Ireland, though in the north support was much stronger among nationalists than unionists. It contains several interlocking agreements. The first section deals with constitutional issues, and subsequent sections establish governance institutions and frameworks for guaranteeing human rights. These institutions embody three "strands": a power-sharing agreement for Northern Ireland; a North-South council; and a British-Irish, or East-West, council. The Agreement notably does not resolve whether the contested six counties should remain part of the United Kingdom or rejoin a united Ireland, but it establishes principles and mechanisms for determining where sovereignty should lie and what would happen if it changes. It guarantees that whoever governs what is now Northern Ireland must always do so based on equality and universal human rights principles. The Agreement states,

The power of the sovereign government with jurisdiction there shall be exercised with rigorous impartiality on behalf of all the people in the diversity of their identities and traditions and shall be founded on the principles of full respect for, and equality of, civil, political, social, and cultural rights, of freedom from discrimination for all citizens, and of parity of esteem and of just and equal treatment for the identity, ethos, and aspirations of both communities.[39]

Public bodies and officials in Northern Ireland are under a "statutory obligation to promote equality" among individuals and communities, and safeguards enacted in British and Irish law are designed to ensure that practices conform to European and international human rights standards. A Northern Ireland bill of rights, contemplated in the Agreement, has yet to be enacted.[40] The Belfast Agreement preserves an existing "two-state solution" in Ireland unless and until people in both jurisdictions choose any other arrangement. But in the meantime, it requires one of the states to transform into an inclusive democracy rather than an ethnic enclave: there can never again be a "Protestant state for a Protestant people." (The Agreement also required the Republic of Ireland to strengthen its own human rights guarantees. Although the Republic always had Protestant citizens who became fully integrated—its first and fourth presidents were Protestants[41]— unionists in Northern Ireland traditionally criticized the Republic for allowing the Catholic Church too influential a role.)

The precedent established here for Palestine/Israel is that in a two-state solution, should one ever come about, Israel could not continue to discriminate against its Palestinian citizens or against Palestinian refugees on the grounds that a Palestinian state exists elsewhere. Israel would have to undergo a transformation similar to the one under way in Northern Ireland, with inclusive and robust mechanisms to monitor and enforce equal rights, redistribute resources equitably, and adopt neutral symbols acceptable to all communities. A one-state solution would entail exactly the same challenges on a larger territory.

Constitutional Issues: The National Question—Asked But Not Answered

Under the Agreement, nationalists conceded that any change in the status of Northern Ireland would have to be approved by a majority of the people living there. This represented a major concession because nationalists regarded the unionist majority within Northern Ireland as the product of an illegitimate partition. Nationalists considered only the island as a whole as the valid unit for self-determination, and argued that the choice for independence as a unitary state had been clearly made in the 1918 election. For their part, unionists accepted that if a majority voted for a united Ireland in a referendum, the result would be binding on them and on the Irish and British governments. No side was required to renounce its political program— for a united Ireland or for maintaining the union with Britain—but all parties committed themselves to exclusively peaceful and democratic means.

This formula was ambiguous enough that each side could claim victory, or at least say it was not defeated. Pro-Agreement nationalists argue that the Agreement is a means toward an eventual united Ireland. At partition Catholics were a third of the population in Northern Ireland. By 2001 they were 44 percent, although since then the Catholic birth rate has slowed considerably. Demographic shifts are a factor in nationalist confidence although they do not guarantee a nationalist majority in the foreseeable future. Nationalists argue that the North-South bodies established by the Agreement provide the basis for de facto all-Ireland integration, mitigating what Sinn Fein president Gerry Adams has called "the evil of partition" until formal unity is achieved.[42] Already there is freedom of movement, residency, and cross-border employment (something guaranteed in any case under European Union rules) between the two jurisdictions and the right to full citizenship in either state. Unionists can argue that the Agreement preserves the union with Britain for the foreseeable future, and has forced republicans to renounce armed struggle and disarm.

The Belfast Agreement affirms that no state arrangement is legitimate in and of itself unless it can gain the freely given consent of the people who would live under it. Notably, the Agreement does not recognize any separate right to self-determination for unionists qua unionists or Protestants qua Protestants that would be analogous to a specifically Jewish right to self-determination within historic Palestine. Unionists enjoy the right to participate in self-determination, along with nationalists, as legitimate residents of the territory.[43]

Applying these principle to Palestine/Israel would require considering a range of outcomes including a two-state solution or a one-state solution as long as they are founded on consent and equality within and between all jurisdictions. Equality, naturally, would mean respecting and implementing the right of return for Palestinian refugees wishing to return home, who are currently prevented from doing so by Israel solely on the discriminatory grounds that they are not Jews.

Rights without Borders

A significant and innovative aspect of the Belfast Agreement is that it separates state sovereignty from citizens' and communities' rights in two ways. First, as we have seen, it guarantees equality for individuals and "parity of esteem" for communities regardless of the state sovereign. Second, it vests citizenship inalienably in the individual irrespective of changes to state borders. The Agreement affirms that

> the birthright of all the people of Northern Ireland to identify themselves and be accepted as Irish or British, or both, as they may so choose, and accordingly confirms that their right to hold both British and Irish citizenship is accepted by both Governments and would not be affected by any future change in the status of Northern Ireland.

The principle that citizenship status attaches to the individual based on her own choice has an important application in Palestine/Israel, where changes in borders are still threatened in order to gerrymander an artificial Jewish majority. Avigdor Lieberman, for example, advocated that the 1.5 million Palestinian citizens of Israel be stripped of their citizenship and areas where they are heavily concentrated be attached to a Palestinian entity in order to "guarantee a Jewish majority in Israel."[44]

The Agreement thus offers a clear precedent for any outcome that establishes more than one state in Palestine/Israel: no entity should be allowed to use border changes in order to deprive people of citizenship for the purpose of demographic gerrymandering.

Governance

Governance structures detailed in the Belfast Agreement also offer an interesting example, if not a blueprint, for Palestine/Israel. An elected power-sharing assembly and executive (cabinet) for Northern Ireland form the first strand of governance under the Belfast Agreement. The assembly elects a first minister and deputy first minister through a system, the practical result of which is that one is unionist and the other nationalist. Seats in the executive are allocated by proportional representation so that all parties winning a certain threshold of votes are guaranteed positions. For certain key decisions requiring "cross-community support," assembly members must designate themselves as "unionist," "nationalist," or "other," and the decision must pass by "parallel consent" (a majority in each community), or a 60 percent supermajority of all members present. Many nationalists—especially republicans—were traditionally wary of an assembly because of the abuses of the earlier Stormont regime and because participation suggested recognition of the legitimacy and permanence of Northern Ireland. The safeguards against abuse built into the current assembly as well as the agreement on constitutional issues mitigated those concerns.

A North/South council made up of ministers from the Republic of Ireland and the Northern Ireland executive oversees cooperation in substantive areas including transport, health, environment, education, agriculture, tourism, and economic development. The all-Ireland element, the second strand, was essential to gain nationalist and republican support although unionists attempted to limit its scope in keeping with their traditional hostility to any Irish government involvement in northern affairs. The third strand established an East/West, or British/Irish, council, bringing together representatives of the two national governments and the devolved governments of Northern Ireland, Scotland, Wales, the Isle of Man, and the Channel Islands, an arrangement that unionists can argue dilutes the significance of the north-south bodies valued by nationalists. In practice, the second and third strands have assumed much less importance than the first—the assembly and power-sharing executive.

Implementation and Criticism

As difficult as it was to make the Agreement, implementing it has by all accounts been even harder. Between 1998 and 2007, the assembly and executive functioned intermittently and with frequent crises prompting their suspension by the British government. The main source of contention for unionists was "decommissioning"—the demand that the IRA disarm prior to the entry of the nationalist party Sinn Fein into the executive. For nationalists the main obstacle was demilitarization and reform of the police service to rid it of its sectarian composition, symbols, and practices. In the 2003 assembly election, Ian Paisley's Democratic Unionist Party (DUP)—which had boycotted the negotiations—displaced the Ulster Unionist Party

(UUP) as the largest unionist party. Paisley, long notorious for overtly anti-Catholic demagoguery, incitement, and repeated vows "never" to go into government with Sinn Fein "murderers," became the leader of unionism. The DUP's rise was seen as symptomatic of the generalized loss of unionist support for the Agreement. In the same election Sinn Fein became the largest nationalist party, displacing the Social Democratic and Labor Party (SDLP), whose leader John Hume had shared the Nobel Peace Prize with UUP leader David Trimble.

Confounding many expectations, Sinn Fein and the DUP went into government together, leading the power-sharing executive from May 2007. The relationship between Paisley—who retired in May 2008—as first minister, and Sinn Fein deputy first minister Martin McGuinness, a former IRA commander, was apparently so good-natured that the media dubbed them the "Chuckle Brothers," after a well-known comedy duo. An executive led by DUP and Sinn Fein, representing the "extremes" of both communities, was once as outlandish as a Hamas-Likud-led executive in a single Palestinian-Israeli state would seem today. If repartition of historic Palestine into two states does indeed prove impossible, then power-sharing built on a constitutional foundation of equal rights and nondiscrimination is a model being demonstrated in Northern Ireland that is seemingly able to accommodate political movements whose goals and worldviews would otherwise appear to be mutually exclusive.

Polemical and academic debates rage about whether the power-sharing structure adopted for Northern Ireland entrenches or provides a framework that ultimately transcends existing inequalities, communal divisions, and sectarian attitudes and modes of behavior.[45] It is conceivable, as some critics assert, that the Agreement simply encourages a "carve-up" of resources between two ethno-national blocs while doing nothing to transcend divisions. It is also possible that the Agreement reflects only the present balance of power—and stalemate—between the two communities and could collapse if the balance shifted decisively in one direction or another. Others assert that a strong equality framework, if implemented, may over time lessen the salience of national allegiances and ethnic solidarities. The new institutions may, as Beatrix Campbell has suggested, allow the sectarian discourse, if not to be eliminated, then at least "to be mediated through the constitutional duty to practice equality and social justice."[46] Consultations aimed at informing government policy indicate considerable public support for achieving a less segregated society, but there are divergent views as to how, and to what extent this can or should be pursued.[47]

For the visitor to Belfast, there are a number of striking features that suggest that although the Agreement has exceeded many expectations of what was thought to be possible, its long-term success is not a foregone conclusion and will require considerable effort to sustain. Almost anyone old enough to remember the Troubles is quick to affirm that the situation a decade after the Agreement is incomparably better than it was before. Employment antidiscrimination legislation is strictly enforced. The so-called "ring of steel" security barriers have been removed from Belfast city center, and cross-border roads have all been opened. Yet in other places "peace walls"—hardened barriers between nationalist and unionist communities—have multiplied and invisible barriers are everywhere.[48] There are still occasional sectarian murders.[49] Few children attend integrated schools or socialize with peers from the "other" community, although on the positive side there is some evidence that the most bigoted attitudes evident in the past are not being widely reproduced among children born since the Agreement.[50] Despite advances in education and employment for an enlarged Catholic middle class, the map of poverty in Northern Ireland still overlaps strikingly with the map of Catholic-dominated wards.

Some pro-Agreement republican activists see growing disaffection in working-class areas fueling support for so-called "dissidents," a small minority of whom advocate a return to armed action. Republicans who gave their support to the reformed Police Service of Northern Ireland (PSNI), which replaced the hated Royal Ulster Constabulary (RUC), increasingly found themselves accused of abandoning key republican goals and agreeing to "administer British rule." The problem, these activists have said, is that reforms were slow to produce changes on the ground that could overcome the nationalists' mistrust toward state forces built over decades.[51] (There is little electoral evidence that dissident republicanism has dented support for Sinn Fein. Although dissident groups did not contest the May 2010 United Kingdom general election, Sinn Fein nonetheless saw its vote increase overall, narrowly overtaking the DUP as the party with the largest share of the vote in Northern Ireland.[52] Similarly, the decisions in 2009 by the main loyalist paramilitary organizations, the Ulster Volunteer Force and Ulster Defence Association, to disarm suggest that a return to widespread violence remains a remote possibility.) A notable turning point was the February 2010 Sinn Fein–DUP agreement allowing the devolution of policing and justice powers from London to Belfast, avoiding a collapse in the power-sharing executive and completing what was widely seen as the last major element of power sharing.

The infusion of the Belfast Agreement with an "equality agenda" was not the inevitable product of traditional nationalist/republican politics focused on ending partition, nor the priority of the UK and Irish governments. Many unionists still view the word "equality" as a code word for republican political goals. The equality agenda reflected how people across divides came to see a solution to the conflict. It had its roots in the civil rights movement as well as years of grassroots and women's organizing in working-class communities. This work gradually politicized a new generation of republicans to place the demand for equality at the center of their struggle. Moreover, the focus on equality opened a space for politics that the exclusive focus on self-determination and borders would not allow: representatives of working-class Protestant communities, including loyalist ex-combatants and prisoners, were able to view the equality agenda as a more promising means to secure their futures and improve their communities.

The late David Ervine, a former combatant and prisoner and leader of the small Progressive Unionist Party (PUP), spoke for working-class loyalists who rejected reflexive ethnic solidarity with the unionist middle classes who they felt had exploited them as foot soldiers. Without the legitimacy provided by the support of loyalists like Ervine, it is doubtful the Agreement would have been reached.[53] Though vocal, pro-Agreement loyalists were always few in number and unable to build on their role brokering the Agreement.

The experience in Northern Ireland indicates that unequal power relationships produced by settler-colonialism and ratified by partition are durable and are likely to generate resistance as long as they exist. Ending a conflict requires a sustained and deliberate effort to dismantle existing relationships and replace them with ones that are more equal and just—in other words, effective decolonization. It is in delivering political, social, economic, and cultural equality for those who have been most excluded, including working-class unionists, and not merely assuring the formal functioning of power-sharing, that the new Northern Ireland institutions still face their greatest opportunities and challenges and on which their long-term viability is likely to rest. It is the totality of this experience, not just the constitutional and political elements—as important as they may be—that are likely to provide rich lessons for Palestine/Israel.

Lessons for the "Peace Process"

So far this discussion has focused on substantive principles and institutions established in Northern Ireland that could be adapted for Palestine/Israel. There are also lessons for the process, that is, how to get there.

Whom to Include

The most obvious lesson is about whom to include and under what terms. An agreement in Northern Ireland was impossible as long as Sinn Fein, a party with a considerable mandate from nationalists, was excluded from negotiations. It could not join negotiations as long as unreasonable preconditions for its participation were imposed by unionists and the British. Here the obvious parallel is Hamas and other Palestinians resistance organizations, whose exclusion because of their refusal to submit to Israeli and Quartet preconditions have long doomed any possibility of a political agreement over the future of Palestine/Israel.

Within days of Hamas's January 2006 victory in elections held in the Israeli-occupied West Bank and Gaza Strip, the Quartet vowed not to provide any assistance or recognition to any Palestinian Authority government that did not commit "to the principles of nonviolence, recognition of Israel, and acceptance of previous agreements and obligations, including the Roadmap."[54] Israel and its Western supporters maintained a stringent boycott on political contact with Hamas, with the effect that the democratically elected representatives of Palestinians under occupation have been totally excluded from the Quartet-sponsored political process. Instead, Western support has been thrown exclusively to Fatah leader and Palestinian Authority president Mahmoud Abbas. As noted earlier, this intervention exacerbated Palestinian political differences to the point of fomenting civil war in 2006–2007.

This misguided policy had a precedent in the long-standing British ban on contacts with Sinn Fein (though in fact there was a long history of secret contact).[55] American intervention helped to ensure that public political contacts began before there was an IRA ceasefire. Most controversially, in 1994, President Bill Clinton—against strenuous protests by the British government of Blair's predecessor John Major—issued a visa to Sinn Fein president Gerry Adams. George Mitchell was one of several senators who signed a letter urging Clinton to grant the visa, on the grounds that it would "enhance Adams' stature" and "enable him to persuade the IRA to declare a cease-fire and permit Sinn Fein to enter into inclusive political negotiations."[56]

Once negotiations began, the British still invested most of their efforts in securing agreement and then power sharing between "moderates"—the SDLP on the nationalist side and the UUP on the unionist side—in the hope that this would undermine those on the margins, including Sinn Fein and the DUP. British chief negotiator Jonathan Powell has conceded that the strategy of "building out from the center" failed and in the end "it is only the extremes who can build a durable peace because there is no one left to outflank them."[57] Ultimately it was Sinn Fein and the DUP that had the credibility in their respective constituencies to make the power-sharing administration function when they took office in May 2007.

A related factor was the British attitude toward different segments of the nationalist movement. Powell has acknowledged that British policy had long been to "pursue a policy of divide and rule" among nationalists.[58] The Blair government eventually understood that it had an interest in nationalists remaining united if it wanted a deal that had credibility. This provides a remarkable contrast with Blair's later role as Quartet envoy carrying out policies that originated in Washington and reinforced division among Palestinian factions. None of this suggests that including the "extremes" predetermines that they would be the ones to achieve peace in Palestine/Israel, but only that efforts to do so excluding them will definitely fail.

Of course Hamas alone, even with its electoral mandate, cannot represent the Palestinian people by itself any more than a Western-backed Palestinian Authority that excludes it can. Even if the West accepted a Palestinian Authority "national unity government" including Hamas, that too would not represent the Palestinian people, but only residents of the West Bank and Gaza Strip. Hamas can and must be part of a broad, inclusive leadership that includes representatives of the majority of Palestinians—those in the diaspora and perhaps even in Israel. Whether such representation could be achieved through a reformed, reconstituted PLO or some other structure is an open question, but it can never happen as long as the external interference in Palestinian politics, the imposition of lopsided preconditions, and the denial of democratic mandates persists.

No Preconditions

Drawing lessons from Northern Ireland for other peace processes, Powell also asserted that "it is always an error to set a precondition to a negotiation."[59] This message was reinforced in a public letter by other British and Irish negotiators, including former SDLP leader John Hume, after the December 2008 Israeli attack on Gaza:

> Whether we like it or not, Hamas will not go away. Since its victory in democratic elections in 2006, Hamas has sustained its support in Palestinian society despite attempts to destroy it through economic blockades, political boycotts, and military incursions. This approach is not working; a new strategy must be found. Yes, Hamas must recognize Israel as part of a permanent solution, but it is a diplomatic process and not ostracization that will lead them there. The Quartet conditions imposed on Hamas set an unworkable threshold from which to commence negotiations.[60]

It is not necessary to share the authors' commitment to a two-state solution to accept their conclusion "that engaging Hamas does not amount to condoning terrorism or attacks on civilians. In fact, it is a precondition for security and for brokering a workable agreement."

The Quartet preconditions, however—nonviolence, recognizing Israel, and commitment to signed agreements—are obstacles, especially when imposed only on Palestinians. Israel has never been asked to commit to nonviolence, recognize Palestine, or commit to signed agreements. As we have seen, Israel's more recent demands for recognition, specifically as a "Jewish state," violate universal principles as well as the principle of consent embodied in the Belfast Agreement. Recognition of Israel but only as, say, a decolonized, nonracist, and democratic state of all its citizens is not an unreasonable demand, but would surely be—as the negotiators' letter states—an outcome of negotiations and not a condition for them. From a Palestinian perspective there are sound reasons to withhold any such recognition until Palestinian rights and interests are secured, something that can never be the case as long as Israel defines itself as a "Jewish state" with the right to discriminate against Palestinians.

Palestinians have long viewed demands to recognize Israel as a demand to legitimize and acquiesce to the dispossession and partition that occurred in 1948. Nevertheless, in 1993, in an official exchange of letters, PLO chairman Yasser Arafat wrote to then Israeli prime minister Yitzhak Rabin that the "PLO recognizes the right of the State of Israel to exist in peace and security."[61] This has never been withdrawn by the PLO, but it did not result in any practical benefit to Palestinians or change of behavior on the part of Israel. In return for this concession, Israel has never recognized Palestinian political goals or even rights enshrined in international law and UN resolutions. Hamas officials regularly cite this experience to justify their own refusal to recognize Israel. Palestinians also commonly argue that it is absurd for them, as a stateless people living as refugees, under Israeli military occupation, or as second-class citizens in Israel, to be asked to recognize the state that is patently responsible for this condition and that denies responsibility for their status. Israel has never declared its borders and has continued to expand its boundaries through confiscation and colonization of Palestinian-owned land.

Even Hamas has understood the significance of the Northern Ireland precedent. As Ahmed Yousef, an advisor to Ismail Haniyeh, the Hamas prime minister elected in 2006, wrote,

> Irish Republicans continue to aspire to a united Ireland free of British rule, but rely upon peaceful methods. Had the IRA been forced to renounce its vision of reuniting Ireland before negotiations could occur, peace would never have prevailed. Why should more be demanded of the Palestinians, particularly when the spirit of our people will never permit it?[62]

Thus, the precondition that Palestinians recognize Israel has served no purpose but to permanently block any meaningful negotiations.

Nonviolence

Notwithstanding secret contacts with Sinn Fein and even the IRA, the British position had long been that there would never be political talks until the IRA abandoned violence.[63] American intervention helped soften this position, but once the IRA declared a ceasefire in 1994, the British still insisted on "prior decommissioning"—disarmament of IRA weapons—before Sinn Fein could take part in political negotiations. As chair of a three-man international committee, Mitchell helped the British get out of this corner. What came to be known as the Mitchell Principles required all parties, including Sinn Fein and unionist parties affiliated with loyalist militias, to sign on to nonviolence principles as a condition for participation in negotiations. But crucially, disarmament was to be carried out "parallel" to negotiations because, as Mitchell recognized, "prior decommissioning was simply not a practical solution."[64]

The Mitchell Principles did not bind the RUC and the British Army, which, from the nationalist perspective, were just as much combatants as the IRA. In implementing the Belfast Agreement, however, the Blair government conceded the parallel by coordinating IRA decommissioning with British Army withdrawals, "security normalization," and the dismantling of military installations in nationalist areas. [65]

There is no reason the Mitchell Principles could not be expanded to encompass states whose armed forces are recognized to be combatants. Indeed, Mitchell already did something similar when at the behest of President Clinton he chaired a fact-finding mission into the causes of Palestinian-Israeli violence in 2000. The report recommended that Israel and Palestinians "should immediately implement an unconditional cessation of violence" as a prelude to negotiations. While Palestinians were urged to act against "terrorists," Israel was simultaneously expected to end its own violence, including the lethal use of force against civilians. The report urged "[Israeli] security forces and settlers [to] refrain from the destruction of homes and roads, as well as trees and other agricultural property in Palestinian areas," and said that Israel should "freeze all settlement activity, including the 'natural growth' of existing settlements."[66]

The Mitchell Report recognized Israeli violence, including ongoing colonization and harassment by settlers, as constitutive of the conflict. Thus, it is more realistic and fair than the position of the Bush and Obama administrations and the Quartet, which have presented Palestinian violence as purely aggressive, senseless "terrorism," while often unprovoked and astronomically greater Israeli violence—including the war crimes and crimes against humanity detailed in the UN-commissioned Goldstone Report—are held to be legitimate and necessary if occasionally "excessive." From the perspective of international law, the Mitchell Report can be criticized for suggesting that an occupying power and an occupied population have equivalent responsibilities. But it is not necessary to agree that Palestinian violence is legitimate resistance or that Israeli violence is legitimate self-defense to accept a mutual and reciprocal cessation of violence as a prelude to political negotiations. In contrast, the Quartet position that Palestinians must forswear violence even while they are under occupation, colonization, and attack by Israel is indistinguishable from a demand for an unconditional surrender.

By offering Israel a long-term ceasefire, or *hudna*, Hamas leaders demonstrated their acceptance of a Mitchell Principles–like approach and reaffirmed it after Obama took office—though with no positive response.[67] As Hamas advisor Ahmed Yousef explained, the *hudna* "extends beyond the Western concept of a cease-fire and obliges the parties to use the period to seek a permanent, nonviolent resolution to their differences." The precedent he cited as a model was, again, the IRA ceasefire.[68] That was sufficient to start the arduous peace talks that ended in the Belfast Agreement. Hamas's *hudna,* if Israel ever accepted it, should be enough as well.

In its first year, the Obama administration appeared to make some modest shifts in tactics without altering the overall American approach. The administration demanded more forcefully than any of its predecessors a complete halt to Israeli settlement construction in the occupied West Bank, but repeatedly backed off pressuring the Palestinian Authority to resume negotiations while settlement construction continued. At the same time, President Obama committed the United States to assuring that "Israel's security as an independent Jewish state is maintained"—thus endorsing a profoundly undemocratic demand—and declared that the two-state solution was the only possible outcome.[69] The administration repeatedly reaffirmed the Quartet preconditions for dealing with Hamas and continued the Bush administration policy of providing exclusive support to the Abbas-led Palestinian Authority.

It has been said that the definition of insanity is doing the same thing over and over and expecting different results As time wore on and the initial optimism of his appointment faded, it seemed that Mitchell was unable to use the lessons learned in Belfast to bring to Jerusalem a more realistic and promising approach.

Notes

1. Palestinian Centre for Human Rights, "Confirmed Figures Reveal the True Extent of the Destruction Inflicted upon the Gaza Strip; Israel's Offensive Resulted in 1,417 Dead, Including 926 Civilians, 255 Police Officers, and 236 Fighters," 12 March 2009, http://pchrgaza.org/files/PressR/English/2008/36–2009.html.

2. Patrick Cockburn, "In Israel, Detachment from Reality is Now the Norm," *Independent* (London), 22 January 2009, accessed 10 May 2010, http://www

.independent.co.uk/opinion/commentators/patrick-cockburn-in-israel
-detachment-from-reality-is-now-the-norm-1488583.html.

3. For an insightful analysis of the political responses to the March 2009 killings, see Robin Wilson, "Northern Ireland: Guns, Words and Publics," OpenDemocracy.net, 16 March 2009, accessed 10 May 2010, http://www.opendemocracy.net/node/47537/pdf.

4. It is also commonly referred to as the "Good Friday Agreement." For Mitchell's account of the Northern Ireland peace process, see his memoir *Making Peace* (Berkeley: University of California Press, 2000). Mitchell was appointed as the first U.S. special envoy for Northern Ireland by President Bill Clinton in 1995. He subsequently chaired an international commission on disarmament of paramilitary groups and the negotiations that led in 1998 to the Belfast Agreement.

5. Jonathan Powell, *Great Hatred, Little Room* (London: Bodley Head, 2008), 147.

6. Aaron David Miller, "Israel's Lawyer," *Washington Post*, 23 May 2005.

7. For a detailed account of U.S. efforts to undermine Hamas, see David Rose, "The Gaza Bombshell," *Vanity Fair*, April 2008, http://www.vanityfair.com/politics/features/2008/04/gaza200804. For a thorough account of how international aid to the Palestinians has indirectly subsidized and enabled Israeli colonization and occupation, see Anne Le More, *International Assistance to the Palestinians after Oslo: Political Guilt, Wasted Money* (New York: Routledge, 2008).

8. General Dayton laid out the goals and methods of his mission in extraordinary detail in a speech to the Washington Institute for Near East Policy on 7 May 2009. "U.S. Security Coordinator Keith Dayton, Address Detailing the Mission and Accomplishments of the Office of the U.S. Security Coordinator, Israel and the Palestinian Authority, 7 May 2009 (Excerpts)," *Journal of Palestine Studies* 8, no. 4 (Summer 2009): 223–229.

9. Joe Cleary, *Literature, Partition and the Nation State; Culture and Conflict in Ireland, Israel and Palestine* (Cambridge: Cambridge University Press, 2002), especially the introduction and chapters 1 and 2; Gershon Shafir, "Zionism and Colonialism: A Comparative Approach," in *The Israel/Palestine Question*, ed. Ilan Pappé (New York: Routledge, 1999), 81–96..

10. Powell, *Great Hatred, Little Room*, 50.

11. Michael MacDonald, *Children of Wrath: Political Violence in Northern Ireland* (Cambridge: Polity Press, 1986), 18.

12. MacDonald, *Children of Wrath*, 54. For other analyses of the situation in Northern Ireland as being the product of settler-colonialism, see John McGarry and Brendan O'Leary, *Explaining Northern Ireland* (Oxford: Blackwell, 1995), 330–336; and Ian Lustick, *Unsettled States, Disputed Lands* (Ithaca, NY: Cornell University Press, 1993).

13. In the Northern Ireland context "nationalist" refers to the belief that Northern Ireland should be part of a united all-Ireland republic. Historically, the vast majority of nationalists have been Catholics who identify culturally as Irish. "Nationalist" is often used as a general descriptor for this community. Within nationalism, "republican" refers to a particular strand of nationalism that has favored or tolerated armed struggle to achieve unification, and which has had a particular alle-

giance to the Irish Republic declared in 1916. "Unionist" refers to the community—historically overwhelmingly Protestant—that identifies culturally as British and prefers to maintain a link with the United Kingdom. "Loyalist" refers to a branch of unionism that has been traditionally allied with paramilitary organizations and activity.

14. MacDonald, *Children of Wrath*, 61.

15. Joseph Ruane and Jennifer Todd, *The Dynamics of Conflict in Northern Ireland* (Cambridge: Cambridge University Press, 1996), 178–184.

16. The formula "a Protestant state for a Protestant people" is widely attributed to Craig and became an iconic description of Northern Ireland's political regime both for supporters and for detractors. It is in fact a misquotation. Craig's actual words were, "In the South they boasted of a Catholic State. They still boast of Southern Ireland being a Catholic State. All I boast of is that we are a Protestant Parliament and a Protestant State." Official Report of the Parliament of Northern Ireland, vol. 16 (1933, 1934), 1095–1096, accessed 9 May 2010, http://www.ahds.ac.uk/stormont//index.html.

17. MacDonald, "The Troubles," chap. 4 in *Children of Wrath; Cleary, Literature, Partition and the Nation State*, 41.

18. John Newsinger, *British Counterinsurgency: From Palestine to Northern Ireland* (New York: Palgrave Macmillan, 2002), 151; and University of Ulster Conflict Archive on the Internet (CAIN), http://cain.ulster.ac.uk/.

19. See Newsinger, *British Counterinsurgency*, for a detailed account of British counterinsurgency tactics.

20. On collusion, see Beatrix Campbell, *Agreement! The State, Conflict and Change in Northern Ireland* (London: Lawrence and Wishart, 2008), 220–275.

21. MacDonald, "The Troubles.."

22. McGarry and O'Leary, *Explaining Northern Ireland.*

23. Terence O'Neill, quoted in Joseph Lee, *Ireland, 1912–1985* (Cambridge: Cambridge University Press, 1989), 426.

24. For discussions of culturalist discourses in Northern Ireland compared with those in Palestine/Israel, see Cleary, "Estranged States: National Literatures, Modernity and Tradition, and the Elaboration of Partitionist Identities," chap. 2 in *Literature, Partition and the Nation State.*

25. Like all settler-colonial projects, Zionism proclaimed its uniqueness, though in its ideology and methods it was very similar to other such endeavors. Gabriel Piterberg, *The Returns of Zionism: Myths, Politics and Scholarship in Israel* (New York: Verso, 2008), especially chap. 2.

26. Nur Masalha, *Expulsion of the Palestinians: The Concept of Transfer in Zionist Political Thought, 1882–1948* (Washington, DC: Institute for Palestine Studies, 1992).

27. Ilan Pappé, *The Ethnic Cleansing of Palestine* (London: Oneworld, 2006).

28. For a discussion of the political orientations and responses of Palestinians inside Israel, see Nadim Rouhana, *Palestinian Citizens in an Ethnic Jewish State* (New Haven, CT: Yale University Press, 1997), especially chaps. 3, 4, 5, and 6; and Pappé, *The Forgotten Palestinians* (New Haven, CT: Yale University Press, 2011).

29. "The Future Vision of the Palestinian Arabs in Israel," National Committee for the Heads of the Arab Local Authorities in Israel, December 2006, http://www.adalah.org/newsletter/eng/dec06/tasawor-mostaqbali.pdf; "The Democratic Constitution," Adalah—The Legal Center for Arab Minority Rights in Israel, http://www.adalah.org/eng/constitution.php; "An Equal Constitution for All? On a Constitution and Collective Rights for Arab Citizens in Israel," Mossawa Center—The Advocacy Center for Arab Citizens in Israel, http://www.mossawacenter.org/files/files/File/An%20Equal%20Constitution%20For%20All.pdf; "The Haifa Declaration," http://www.mada-research.org/archive/haifaenglish.pdf.

30. Yoav Stern, "Arab Leaders Air Public Relations Campaign against Shin Bet," *Haaretz*, 6 April 2007, http://www.haaretz.com/hasen/spages/846247.html.

31. I have discussed this at length in the second chapter of my book, *One Country: A Bold Proposal to End the Israeli-Palestinian Impasse* (New York: Metropolitan Books, 2007).

32. Barak Ravid, David Landau, Aluf Benn, and Shmuel Rosner, "Olmert to Haaretz: Two-state Solution, or Israel is Done for," *Haaretz*, 30 November 2007, http://www.haaretz.com/hasen/spages/929439.html.

33. An example of just such a proposal was submitted to President Obama by a group of elder statesmen including former national security advisors Brent Scowcroft and Zbigniew Brzezinski and former senator Chuck Hagel. It sought to assure Israel's future as a "democratic Jewish state" by imposing, among other things, "a solution to the refugee problem consistent with the two-state solution that does not entail a general right of return." Clearly this would suit Israel but it is difficult to see how it would meet the needs of Palestinian refugees. Palestinians would not even receive a fully sovereign state, but a demilitarized Kosovo-like NATO dependency riddled with annexed Israeli settlements and occupied by a "multinational force" that would include Israeli soldiers. "A Last Chance for a Two-State Israel-Palestine Agreement: A Bipartisan Statement on U.S. Middle East Peacemaking," U.S./Middle East Project, March 2009. For my critique of a similar peace plan put forward by Brzezinski and former U.S. congressman Stephen Solarz, see "Breaking the Middle East impasse," *The Hill*, 29 April 2010, accessed 9 May 2010, http://thehill.com/opinion/op-ed/95055-breaking-the-middle-east-impasse.

34. Joseph Massad, "The Binational State and the Reunification of the Palestinian People," *Global Dialogue* 4, no. 3 (Summer 2002): 123–129.

35. In a famous case in England in 1703, Lord Chief Justice John Holt wrote, "If the plaintiff has a right, he must of necessity have a means to vindicate and maintain it, and a remedy if he is injured in the exercise or enjoyment of it, and, indeed it is a vain thing to imagine a right without a remedy; for want of right and want of remedy are reciprocal." Ashby v. White (1703) 92 ER 126.

36. Amnesty International, "Israel/Occupied Territories: New Report Demands Repeal of Discriminatory Citizenship Law," 13 July 2004, accessed 6 June 2009, http://www.amnesty.org.uk/news_details.asp?NewsID=1548.

37. See, for example, "Israel Moves Closer to Banning Mourning of Its Independence," *Haaretz*, 24 May 2009, accessed 5 June 2009, http://www.haaretz.com/hasen/spages/1087792.html.

38. Cited in Powell, *Great Hatred, Little Room*, 71.

39. See text of the Belfast Agreement, http://cain.ulst.ac.uk/events/peace/docs/agreement.htm.

40. See the website BORINI ("Bill of Rights in Northern Ireland"), http://www.borini.info.

41. They were Douglas Hyde (1938–1945) and Erskine Childers (1973–1974).

42. Gerry Adams, *A Farther Shore* (New York: Random House, 2005), 29.

43. For a more detailed discussion of self-determination for legitimate residents as opposed to national groups, see Tomis Kapitan, "Self-Determination," in *The Israeli-Palestinian Conflict: Philosophical Essays on Self-Determination, Terrorism and the One-State Solution,* eds. Tomis Kapitan and Raja Halwani (New York: Palgrave Macmillan, 2008), 13–71.

44. Ronny Sofer, "Lieberman Demands Population Exchange," *Yediot Aharonot,* 28 October 2007, accessed 23 May 2009, http://www.ynetnews.com/Ext/Comp/ArticleLayout/CdaArticlePrintPreview/1,2506,L-3464689,00.html.

45. The academic debate has been conducted primarily over a form of power sharing called "consociationalism," which proponents argue describes the Belfast Agreement. For a description of consociationalism and current debates, see John McGarry and Brendan O'Leary, "Consociational Theory and Peace Agreements in Pluri-National Places: Northern Ireland and Other Cases," in *The Failure of the Middle East Peace Process?,* ed. Guy Ben-Porat (New York: Palgrave Macmillan, 2008), 70; John McGarry and Brendan O'Leary, "Consociational Theory, Northern Ireland's Conflict, and its Agreement. Part 1: What Consociationalists Can Learn from Northern Ireland," *Government and Opposition* 41, no. 1 (2006):43–63; John McGarry and Brendan O'Leary, "Consociational Theory, Northern Ireland's Conflict, and its Agreement. Part 2:What Critics of Consociation Can Learn from Northern Ireland," *Government and Opposition* 41, no. 2 (2006): 249–277. For critiques of consociationalism in general and the Belfast Agreement in particular, see Rupert Taylor, "Ending Apartheid: The Relevance of Consociationalism," in *The Failure of the Middle East Peace Process?,* ed. Guy Ben-Porat (New York: Palgrave Macmillan, 2008), 97–110; Rupert Taylor, "The Belfast Agreement and the Politics of Consociationalism: A Critique," *Political Quarterly* 77, no. 2 (April–June 2006): 217–226; Paul Dixon, "Why the Good Friday Agreement in Northern Ireland is not Consociational," *Political Quarterly* 76, no. 3 (2005): 357–367; Ian Lustick, "Lijphart, Lakatos, and Consociationalism," *World Politics* 50, no. 1 (1997).

46. Campbell,*Agreement!,* 12.

47. See, for example, the various consultation documents and reports produced by the "Shared Future" initiative, http://www.asharedfutureni.gov.uk.

48. "Security and Segregation: Interface Barriers in Belfast," *Shared Space: A Research Journal on Peace, Conflict and Community Relations in Northern Ireland,* Community Relations Council, June 2008, http://www.nicrc.org.uk/filestore/documents/shared-space-neil-jarmon.pdf.

49. For example, in May 2009 four Protestant men were convicted and jailed for the 2006 sectarian murder of a fifteen-year-old Catholic boy, Michael McIlveen. In May 2009, Kevin McDaid, a Catholic community worker married to a Protestant woman, was beaten to death outside his home in what police said was a sectarian attack by a loyalist.

50. Ali Abunimah, "Does Peace Always Mean Burying Differences?," *Prevention Action,* 21 August 2007, accessed 24 May 2009, http://www.preventionaction.org/comment/does-peace-always-mean-burying-differences.

51. The impressions I am reporting are based on a one-week visit to Belfast in April 2009, during which I met with community and political activists from nationalist/republican and unionist/loyalist backgrounds, including former prisoners and combatants, as well as several people who had been involved in negotiations with paramilitary organizations. As of this writing there are few recent published scholarly sources on dissident republicans.

52. Sinn Fein: 25.5 percent (+1.2); Democratic Unionist Party (DUP): 25.0 percent (-8.7); Social Democratic and Labour Party (SDLP): 16.5 percent (-1); Alliance Party: 6.3 percent (+2.4); Ulster Conservatives and Unionists—New Force (formerly Ulster Unionist Party): 15.2 percent (-2.6); others: 13.5 percent. BBC Election 2010 website, accessed 10 May 2010, http://news.bbc.co.uk/2/shared/election2010/results/region/6.stm.

53. For an account of the grassroots political movements that shaped the Agreement, see Campbell, *Agreement!* On the role of Protestant working-class representatives, see George Mitchell, "A Different Route," chap. 4 in *Making Peace.*

54. Quartet statement, 30 January 2006, http://www.un.org/news/dh/infocus/middle_east/quartet-30jan2006.htm.

55. Adams, *A Farther Shore,* especially 98–99; Powell, "The Talking Starts," chap. 3 in *Great Hatred, Little Room.*

56. Mitchell, *Making Peace,* 113.

57. Powell, *Great Hatred, Little Room,* 236, 312.

58. Powell, *Great Hatred, Little Room,* 25.

59. Powell, *Great Hatred, Little Room,* 317.

60. "Peace Will be Achieved Only by Talking to Hamas," *Times* (London), 26 February 2009, http://www.ekopolitik.org/en/news.aspx?id=3842&pid=1830.

61. Letter from Yasser Arafat to Prime Minister Yitzhak Rabin, 9 September 1993, http://www.mfa.gov.il/MFA/Peace+Process/Guide+to+the+Peace+Process/Israel-PLO+Recognition+-+Exchange+of+Letters+betwe.htm.

62. Ahmed Yousef, "Pause for Peace," *New York Times,* 1 November 2006.

63. Adams, *A Farther Shore,* especially 98–99; Powell, "The Talking Starts."

64. Mitchell, *Making Peace,* 35–36.

65. Powell, *Great Hatred, Little Room,* 162–163.

66. "Sharm El-Sheikh Fact-Finding Committee Report" ("Mitchell Report"), 30 April 2001, http://www.globalpolicy.org/security/issues/israel-palestine/document/mitchell043001.pdf.

67. Ali Abunimah, "Hamas' Choice: Recognition or Resistance in the Age of Obama,"
Electronic Intifada, 6 July 2009, accessed 10 May 2010, http://electronicintifada.net/v2/article10647.shtml.

68. Yousef, "Pause for Peace."

69. He declared this at a press conference in Washington, DC, with Israeli Prime Minister Benjamin Netanyahu, 18 May 2009. See also Obama's speech to the Muslim world made in Cairo on 4 June 2009.

12. One State

The Realistic Solution

SAREE MAKDISI

Avigdor Lieberman, the Israeli foreign minister, declared in April 2009 that Israel is not bound by the commitments it entered into at the Annapolis summit in November 2007.[1] He was followed by Benjamin Netanyahu, the then freshly minted prime minister, in a policy speech in June of the same year, which categorically ruled out the possibility of the creation of a genuinely independent Palestinian state.[2] These declarations came as close as we are likely to get to an official announcement of the end of the two-state solution to the Zionist conflict with the Palestinians. And in essentially renouncing the two-state solution, the Israeli government effectively committed itself to the only other realistic alternative—a one-state solution. Of course, the one state that Lieberman and Netanyahu have in mind is not a state of equal citizens, but rather a state in which the Jewish inhabitants of historic Palestine would continue to enjoy rights and privileges denied to—and founded at the expense of—the land's non-Jewish (that is, Palestinian) inhabitants. Far from being something radically new, this represents the continuation of a status quo already in place for several decades, in which Jewish inhabitants of the land (and new Jewish immigrants, like Lieberman himself) have been coming and going freely, while Palestinians in the Occupied Territories and in Israel itself—not to mention those who have lived in involuntary exile for six decades—have been subjected to draconian forms of control, blockade, confinement, and worse, for no other reason than that they are not Jewish.[3]

There were many expressions of dismay in response to Lieberman's declaration: the *New York Times* called it "blunt and belligerent";[4] the former foreign minister Tzipi Livni said that in twenty minutes Lieberman undid fifteen years of patient diplomacy;[5] and the U.S. State Department said that despite his remarks it still hoped for a two-state solution.[6] Only the official Palestinian negotiator Saeb Erekat seemed (almost comically) out of sync with the world reaction, when he asked after Lieberman's speech, "I'd really like to know, are we going to see a settlement freeze?"[7]

If the answer to that question was not already obvious in what Lieberman said, it would be driven home once and for all in Netanyahu's first major policy speech, in June 2009. That speech also outlined more clearly than ever the profoundly racialized contours of the Zionist conflict with the Palestinians—with which any approach to the conflict must contend.[8] Although the reception of Netanyahu's speech in most of the U.S. and UK media made it seem as though he had accepted the creation of an independent Palestinian state, he actually did no such thing. For an amorphous and permanently disarmed entity lacking a definite territory, not allowed to control its own borders or airspace, not allowed to enter into treaties with other states, and shorn of any vestige of sovereignty (other than symbolic trappings such as a flag and a national anthem)—which is all that Netanyahu said the Palestinians might, possibly, be allowed to have—meets no conventional, customary, or dictionary definition of the term "state."

It was in fact merely by juxtaposing the word "Palestinian" with the word "state" that Netanyahu earned the praise of much of the Western media as well as the State Department and White House, which called the speech "an important step forward."[9] Only by using the term "state" did Netanyahu's proposal differ from what had been on the negotiating table from the time of the Oslo Accords of 1993–1995. It ought to be clear by now that the official peace process, as it was launched in secret negotiations at Oslo in 1993 and carried on ever since by Ehud Olmert, Livni, and others, has itself been the greatest obstacle to a lasting and genuine peace between Israelis and Palestinians.

Although the Israeli-Palestinian conflict has never seemed further from a just and lasting peace than it is at the moment, what I want to suggest is that a genuine resolution to the conflict is closer at hand than it has ever been, and that, as counterintuitive as this may seem, the terminal breakdown in the official so-called peace process, Israel's post-Christmas 2008 bombardment of Gaza, and the sweeping victory of the right wing in Israel's 2009 elections actually make a real peace all the more likely in the medium to long run, though in the short term there will undoubtedly be more suffering and bloodshed.

For all the rhetoric accompanying the official peace process since 1993, it never intended to bring about a genuine and lasting peace; it actually strengthened and made more permanent the Israeli occupation of Palestinian territory. That was the least of its flaws, however. There were two even greater problems with the so-called peace process. The first was that it restricted itself to talks addressing the future status of the Palestinian territories occupied by Israel in 1967; those territories comprise only about 20 percent of historic Palestine, and only a minority of the Palestinian people actually live in the Occupied Territories (the majority live either in forced exile or as second-class citizens of the state of Israel[10]).

At its best, then, the official peace process addressed only a fraction of the question of Palestine and only a minority of the Palestinian people, ignoring all the rest—and, even in the Occupied Territories themselves, it made the chance of a just and lasting peace all the more remote because its primary accomplishment was the institutionalization of the Israeli occupation (for example, it made permanent the dismemberment of the Palestinian territories into isolated enclaves, and it allowed the doubling of the population of Jewish settlers colonizing the land).[11]

But for all its failures in the Occupied Territories, the official peace process failed all the more completely because from the beginning it deliberately ignored the very core of the Israeli-Palestinian conflict, which is the unavoidable fact that what drives—and has always driven—this conflict is the project to supplant the non-Jewish population of Palestine with a Jewish population.

It is obvious to everyone that just such a supplanting is what has been happening in the Occupied Territories since 1967, where the proliferation of Israeli colonies was intended all along to secure Israel's grip on territory. Even many of Israel's supporters are opposed to Israel's colonization of the West Bank. Much of the criticism of Israel's colonization program, though, is premised on a false distinction between the wars of 1948 and 1967, between the colonization of territories seized by force from its indigenous Palestinian inhabitants in 1967 and the settlement of territory seized by force from its indigenous Palestinian inhabitants in 1948. For Israel's liberal supporters in the United States, there is a world of difference between the conquest of Palestine in 1948 and the conquest of the West Bank, Gaza, and East Jerusalem in 1967. This is also a distinction that is vital to the majority of liberal Israelis, who favor coexistence with the Palestinians and want to end the occupation of the West Bank and Gaza, but at the same time also want to preserve the

Zionist program within Israel's pre-1967 borders. Palestinians see no distinction between 1948 and 1967: for them, they represent one continuing narrative and process of dispossession, that is, one continuous history. To address the consequences of 1967 without addressing those of 1948 can never lead to a just and lasting peace.

The false distinction between 1948 and 1967 takes us to the core of the conflict. Many liberal Zionists and their sympathizers in the United States are opposed to the Israeli settlement of the Occupied Territories not simply because they regard it as wrong in itself, but also because they see it as endangering the increasingly precarious claim to the Jewishness of the Jewish state. This point has been illustrated in clear terms in a series of articles in the Israeli newspaper *Haaretz* by one of the most vocal Israeli opponents of the settlement of the Occupied Territories, Zeev Sternhell.

By making it impossible for Israel to return the Occupied Territories to the Palestinians, Sternhell's argument goes, the settlements will prevent the creation of a separate Palestinian state and will bolster Palestinian demands for an equal sharing of all of historic Palestine, in other words, not only the territories occupied in 1967 but also those occupied in 1948. This argument starkly reveals the limits of Sternhell's liberalism and the contradictions inherent in any attempt to formulate a liberal version of Zionism, for political Zionism, by definition, regards the principle of genuine political equality among Jews and non-Jews in what is, after all, supposed to be the Jewish state, as a mortal threat. Here is how Sternhell himself expresses this point, in a piece that he published in *Haaretz* in October 2008: "If Israeli society is unable to muster the courage necessary to put an end to the settlements, the settlements will put an end to the state of the Jews and will turn it into a binational state."[12] Israel's former prime minister Ehud Olmert made almost exactly the same point on several other occasions. The alternative to at least a partial dismantlement of Israel's settlements in the West Bank, he said, is a binational state, an idea that "ever-growing segments of the international community are adopting."[13]

Olmert made the point even more clearly in a major policy speech that he gave as deputy prime minister in January 2006. "The existence of a Jewish majority in the State of Israel cannot be maintained with the continued control over the Palestinian population in Judea, Samaria, and the Gaza Strip," he said, using Israel's official, Biblical-sounding terminology for the West Bank.[14] "Every hill in Samaria and every valley in Judea is part of our historic homeland," he continued.

We do not forget this, not even for one moment. However, the choice between the desire to allow every Jew to live anywhere in the Land of Israel
[and] the existence of the State of Israel as a Jewish country obligates relinquishing parts of the Land of Israel. This is not a relinquishing of the
Zionist idea, [but] rather the essential realization of the Zionist goal—
ensuring the existence of a Jewish and democratic state in the Land of Israel. In order to ensure the existence of a Jewish national homeland, we
will not be able to continue ruling over the territories in which the majority of the Palestinian population lives. We must create a clear boundary as soon as possible, one which will reflect the demographic reality on
the ground. Israel will maintain control over the security zones, the Jewish settlement blocs, and those places which have supreme national importance to the Jewish people.

The alternative, he said in that speech—and he has made this point several
times before and since[15]—is a single state for Jews and non-Jews, Israelis
and Palestinians.

Indeed, Olmert was already sounding a warning in 2003, saying,

There is no doubt in my mind that very soon the government of Israel
is going to have to address the demographic issue with the utmost seriousness and resolve. This issue above all others will dictate the solution
that we must adopt. We don't have unlimited time. More and more Palestinians are uninterested in a negotiated, two-state solution, because they
want to change the essence of the conflict from an Algerian paradigm
to a South African one. From a struggle against "occupation," in their
parlance, to a struggle for one-man-one-vote. That is, of course, a much
cleaner struggle, a much more popular struggle—and ultimately a much
more powerful one.[16]

Following the Annapolis summit in November 2007, he made the same
warning in an interview with *Haaretz:* "If the day comes when the two-state
solution collapses, and we face a South African style struggle for equal voting rights [also for the Palestinians in the territories], then, as soon as that
happens, the State of Israel is finished."[17]

It is obvious from what Sternhell and Olmert say (and they are merely
examples of a much larger political bloc spanning almost the entire spectrum of Israeli politics) that those who support the project to create and
maintain an exclusively Jewish state regard as anathema the notion of a state

that treats all its citizens, Jews and non-Jews alike, as equals. What I want to argue is that this position is, and has always been, the primary obstacle to peace between Israelis and Palestinians, and that, insofar as the official peace process and the notion of a two-state solution that it held forth as the ideal outcome of the conflict express this underlying political position, the official peace process could never have led to peace. Peace, a genuine, comprehensive and lasting peace, with justice for both peoples, not just one, requires an altogether different approach to the problem. A genuine peace requires a state that treats all of its citizens equally: a single democratic, secular, and multicultural state in all of historic Palestine (that is, Israel plus the Occupied Territories) in which Jews, Muslims, Christians, and, indeed, the adherents of other faiths or of no faith at all will be regarded as equals, a state in which the politics of religion will be replaced by a politics of citizenship.

There is, in any case, no longer a two-state solution to the question of Palestine. One state controls all of historic Palestine—that is, all of the territory between the Mediterranean and the Jordan River—and it has done so for more than four decades, or two-thirds of Israel's existence as a state. The only question now is how much longer that state can go on discriminating between the Jewish and non-Jewish residents of the territory that it controls—and how long it will be before a totally reconstituted, genuinely democratic, secular, and multicultural state takes the place of the presently existing ethno-religious state of Israel, to offer Jewish Israelis and Muslim and Christian Palestinians alike a future free of discrimination, occupation, fear, and violence. The question, in other words, is not *whether* there will be a one-state solution, but *when,* and how much needless suffering there will be in the meantime, until those who are committed to the project of creating and maintaining a religiously exclusivist state in what has always been a culturally and religiously heterogeneous land finally relent and accept the inevitable: that they have failed.

This last point is especially important to bear in mind because the conflict between Zionism and the Palestinians is—and has always been—driven by the notion that hundreds of years of cultural heterogeneity and plurality in Palestine can be negated and replaced by a state with a single cultural and religious identity. It was recognized very early on that the indigenous population of a land that began the twentieth century with an overwhelmingly non-Jewish population (93 percent) would resist their country's transformation into an exclusively Jewish state (to be populated largely with Jews from Europe, for the native Jewish Palestinian population were no more consulted by Zionists meeting in Vienna and Basel than their Muslim and Christian compatriots were).

This point was obvious to Edwin Montagu, the only Jewish member of the British cabinet when the British Empire committed itself to Zionism by issuing the Balfour Declaration in 1917. Adamantly opposed to what he recognized as the inherent injustice of Zionism, Montagu warned prophetically that having Muslim and Christian Palestinians "make room" for Jewish immigrants would result in their expulsion, so that wherever they went they would "be regarded as foreigners, just in the same way as Jews [would] hereafter be treated as foreigners in every country but Palestine."[18] The same point was equally obvious to the King-Crane Commission dispatched to Palestine by President Woodrow Wilson in 1919 to assess, among other things, the viability of the Zionist project. "Decisions, requiring armies to carry out, are sometimes necessary," they warned, "but they are surely not to be gratuitously taken in the interests of a serious injustice."[19] And it was obvious to Zionist ideologues such as Vladimir Jabotinsky. "Any native people—it's all the same whether they are civilized or savage—views their country as their national home, of which they will always be the complete masters," he wrote in a 1923 essay entitled "The Iron Wall."[20]

> Compromisers in our midst attempt to convince us that the Arabs are some kind of fools who can be tricked by a softened formulation of our goals, or a tribe of money grubbers who will abandon their birth right to Palestine for cultural and economic gains. I flatly reject this assessment of the Palestinian Arabs. Culturally they are 500 years behind us, spiritually they do not have our endurance or our strength of will, but this exhausts all of the internal differences. We can talk as much as we want about our good intentions; but they understand as well as we what is not good for them. They look upon Palestine with the same instinctive love and true fervor that any Aztec looked upon his Mexico or any Sioux looked upon his prairie.

Jabotinsky's point was quite simple. If, he argues, "every indigenous people will resist alien settlers as long as they see any hope of ridding themselves of the danger of foreign settlement," the point is not that the Zionists should abandon their project to transform Palestine into a Jewish state, but rather that the project can only be effected by the uncompromising subjugation of the will of the Palestinians:

> Zionist colonization, even the most restricted, must either be terminated or carried out in defiance of the will of the native population. This colonization can, therefore, continue and develop only under the protection of a force independent of the local population—an iron wall which the native population cannot break through. This is, *in toto,* our policy toward the Arabs. To formulate it any other way would only be hypocrisy.

Looking back at it now, Jabotinsky's candor is certainly a refreshing change from the endless equivocation and dissimulation of those who followed him. And his argument makes it perfectly clear why this conflict will end only when Zionism's exclusivist claims to the land are abandoned, that is, when Zionism itself is abandoned as an ideology trapped in the nineteenth century, an ideology whose time has passed.

Since Jabotinsky wrote that essay in the 1920s, of course, the situation on the ground has changed entirely. Some three quarters of a million Palestinians were forcibly removed from their homes during the creation of Israel and concomitant destruction of Palestine in 1948, a mass expulsion that was necessary in order for a Jewish state to be created in the first place (even with extensive Jewish immigration from Europe before, during, and after the Nazi Holocaust, Jews constituted barely a third of the population of Palestine as late as 1948). "There are circumstances in history that justify ethnic cleansing," says the Israeli historian Benny Morris.[21]

> A Jewish state would not have come into being without the uprooting of 700,000 Palestinians. Therefore it was necessary to uproot them. There was no choice but to expel that population. It was necessary to cleanse the hinterland and cleanse the border areas and cleanse the main roads. It was necessary to cleanse the villages from which our convoys and our settlements were being fired on.

When the 1948 war ended, Israel was in control of almost 80 percent of Palestine, far more than had been allotted to it in the UN's 1947 Partition Plan, on the basis of which it had declared independence and—more importantly—had been admitted as a member of the United Nations. Israel was also admitted to the UN on the basis of General Assembly Resolution 194 of December 1948, which was explicitly recapitulated by General Assembly Resolution 273. This resolution admitted it to membership and stated unequivocally the legal and moral right of return of those Palestinians who had been expelled from their homes during the destruction of Palestine, an event to which Palestinians refer as the *nakba,* or catastrophe.[22] Israel continues to deny their right of return to this day. Not only does it deny the right, it gets angry when this history of expulsion is raised and even when the word *nakba* is invoked. Israel complained formally to the UN when the secretary-general used the word in May 2008, for example,[23] and the Israeli foreign minister went so far as to say that if the Palestinians want peace they will have to purge the word *nakba* from their vocabulary.[24] Clearly, the slogan "never forget" applies only to some people and to certain catastrophes; others are forbidden even to remember.

In 1967, Israel captured what had remained of Palestine after 1948, namely, the West Bank, Gaza Strip, and East Jerusalem. It has since extensively colonized the Occupied Territories with its own population, in stark violation of international law. It subjects the two populations of the Occupied Territories—Jewish and non-Jewish—to two distinct legal and administrative systems, one for Jews, one for non-Jews, privileging the former over the latter.[25]

Palestinians in the Occupied Territories, for example, are subject to a harsh form of military law; the Jewish colonists there are subject to Israeli civil law, even though they live beyond the borders of their state. And there are literally two different transportation systems for the two populations. Jewish settlers use wide, well-lit, well-paved roads that bypass Palestinian communities; they are not subject to the hundreds of roadblocks and checkpoints or the arduous pass-and-permit system that the Israeli Army imposes on the indigenous Palestinian population. Israel continues to approve the illegal construction of homes in Jewish settlements throughout the Occupied Territories, while systematically denying construction permits to Palestinians and demolishing their homes when they build anyway. Israel is the only state on earth that deliberately demolishes family homes not under extraordinary circumstances, but as a matter of routine, everyday policy. To realize the severity of the difference in treatment meted out to the two populations, one need only consider that the entire Palestinian population in the West Bank is subject to a comprehensive twenty-four-hour curfew on every Jewish holiday, whereas the settler population is free to come and go as usual on those days.

Palestinians who live inside Israel within its pre-1967 borders face legal obstacles as non-Jews in the Jewish state; because they are not Jewish, they may be granted a restricted form of *citizenship,* but they are not considered *nationals* of the state.[26] The nation to which the state of Israel corresponds is the Jewish people, not the people who actually live within the borders of the state. Juridically speaking, Israel does not recognize such a thing as a specifically Israeli national identity; in terms of nationality, in other words, the state makes no distinction between Jews and Israelis. As the Israeli High Court ruled in the early 1970s, "There is no Israeli nation separate from the Jewish people."[27]

This astonishing distinction between *citizenship* and *nationality* is unique to Israel: because they are considered *nationals* of the state, Jewish *non-citizens* actually enjoy rights and privileges that Israel denies to Palestinian *citizens* of the state, who are not considered *nationals* and who are therefore disqualified from the privileges Israel reserves exclusively for Jews, whether they are citizens of the state or not. Israel is a Jewish state, then, not because all of its population is Jewish (it's not), but because it claims to represent all Jews everywhere, who enjoy rights and privileges—beginning with the right of return—that are systematically denied to the non-Jewish Palestinian population of the state of Israel (let alone that of the Occupied Territories).

And that is how things stand today: there is one land inhabited by two populations who are numerically more or less at parity, but are treated with distinct inequality, with Jews systematically, legally, institutionally privileged over non-Jews. Can anyone really imagine some kind of just peace compatible with this extraordinary level of discrimination and even uncloaked racism? Can anyone really accept that there is no alternative to this?

There are three simple premises behind the one-state solution: first, that both populations are there to stay; second, that those Palestinians expelled from their homes in 1948 and their descendants have the moral and legal right to return and be compensated for their loss; and third, that the land must be shared equally by all citizens of a state to be reconstituted along lines that do not discriminate among people on the basis of religious or ethnic affiliation.

These premises are quite squarely at odds with those of the so-called peace process inaugurated at Oslo in the mid-1990s, the primary aim of which was, as I have said, to preserve Israel's claim to Jewishness while designating certain territorial reservoirs as—essentially—holding pens for the land's non-Jewish population, holding pens that might artificially be sutured together via a network of bridges and tunnels and, as Netanyahu suggested in his June 2009 speech, might even perhaps be called a Palestinian "state," but which would in fact be little more than a set of discrete reservations created by a logic that American Indians or the aboriginal peoples of Australia would recognize at a single glance. The one purpose of such a Palestinian "state" is to preserve Israel's claim to Jewishness simply by artificially deleting as many non-Jews as possible from the state's accounting books. The notion of two states, in other words, is premised—at Israel's insistence—on the ethnic and religious separation, drive for homogeneity, and fear of infiltration and even miscegenation that are essential to Zionism. The premise of the one state, by contrast, is based on sharing, mixture, plurality, and equality: concepts that are, and have always been, anathema to Zionism.

The idea of one democratic and secular state as the only just solution to the Israeli-Palestinian conflict is sometimes dismissed as unrealistic and unworkable (just as the two-state solution was dismissed out of hand when the Palestinians first proposed it in 1988 when they declared the independence of a state in the West Bank, Gaza, and East Jerusalem). But this is one of those cases where the utopian option is the only realistic one, while the apparently realistic one has become little more than a fantasy.

According to a report published in July 2007 by the United Nations Office for the Coordination of Humanitarian Affairs (UN OCHA), almost 40 percent of the West Bank is now taken up by Israeli infrastructure (roads, colonies, army bases, etc.) to which indigenous Palestinians are largely denied access.[28] The pace of Jewish colonization in the West Bank and East Jerusalem—colonization that has taken place on the illegally expropriated private property of Palestinian families or, equally illegally, on land that was declared state property by the Israeli Army—has not significantly slackened for one moment in the past four decades, even though Israel's colonial enterprise has been repeatedly condemned as a violation of international law by the United Nations General Assembly and Security Council as well as the International Court of Justice in the Hague.[29] The number of Jewish colonists in the Occupied Territories doubled during the period of the Oslo negotiations (1993–2000), for example, and it has quadrupled since peace negotiations began at Madrid in 1991.[30] Since the supposed renewal of the so-called peace process at the Annapolis summit hastily arranged by President George W. Bush in November 2007, Israel has announced the construction of thousands of new housing units exclusively for Jews in the West Bank and East Jerusalem.

There are today almost half a million Jewish colonists in the Occupied Territories; the UN has warned that their population has been increasing at a rate three times greater than the population of Israel itself, and is set to double to almost one million in another decade.[31] Many settlers are heavily armed religious zealots who take seriously the idea that they are God's chosen people and that they are therefore uniquely entitled to the land.

According to the UN OCHA, the remainder of the West Bank, which is supposed to provide the main component of a Palestinian state, has been broken up into dozens of isolated fragments, separated from each other and the outside world by Israeli walls, ditches, tunnels, roads, borders, roadblocks, and checkpoints. Despite the restoration of an American- and Israeli-backed Palestinian Authority in the West Bank in the summer of 2007 and the subsequent and repeated promises of the Israelis to relax their grip on that territory (while continuing to strangle Gaza), the Israelis have in fact tightened it further. According to the UN, there were, for example, 528 Israeli military roadblocks and checkpoints in the West Bank in September 2006; that number grew to 563 in September 2007 during the buildup to Annapolis. to 580 in February of 2008, to 612 in the summer of 2008, and to 630 by September 2008.[32] In the fall of 2008, according to the UN, three quarters of the main roads leading into the largest Palestinian towns in the West Bank were either blocked or controlled by an Israeli Army checkpoint.

The Gaza Strip is in fact the prototype of the kind of Palestinian state the Israelis have in mind. The traumatic increase in violence visited upon the hapless residents of Gaza in December 2008 and January 2009 marks only a recent stage of years of isolation, closure, and bombardment by Israeli forces. The 1.5 million residents of Gaza have been entirely cut off from the outside world since 2005, when, according to John Dugard, the UN's special rapporteur on human rights, Israel turned Gaza into an open-air prison and threw away the key.[33] Reduced to what another UN official, John Ging, referred to as a "subhuman existence,"[34] the people of Gaza have been largely cut off from fresh supplies of food and medicine. Eighty percent of them—1.2 million men, women, and children—now depend for their day-to-day survival (such as it is) on meager and nutritionally insufficient aid handouts from UN agencies, and Israel has even limited the delivery of emergency food aid to far less than the minimum needed (the Israeli Army's ban on pasta shipments to Gaza is only one example of this).[35] At times, Israel has cut this aid off altogether.[36] Gazans also lack reliable supplies of fuel and electricity, and their crops are dying because, even before the recent bombardment, what little water there is was being diverted for human consumption. Now there is not enough water for people, let alone crops.[37]

There is one thing, however, that the people of Gaza have far too much of: raw sewage. Without sufficient supplies of fuel and electricity (Israel allows in a fraction of the diesel fuel needed, and, with the blessing of its own High Court, has also been cutting electricity supplies to the population for whom international law holds it responsible as the occupying power), Gaza is unable to treat sewage, and has had no other option than to start dumping it into the sea—at one point it was reported as up to sixty million liters a day.[38]

All this is the deliberate and premeditated result of Israeli policy. "When 2.5 million people live in a closed-off Gaza, it's going to be a human catastrophe," predicted the University of Haifa geographer Arnon Sofer, the intellectual architect of the isolation of Gaza, in 2004.[39] "Those people will become even bigger animals than they are today, with the aid of an insane fundamentalist Islam," he added. "The pressure on the border is going to be awful. It's going to be a terrible war. So, if we want to remain alive, we will have to kill and kill and kill. All day, every day." Sofer admits of only one worry with all the killing, which will, he says—absolutely correctly—be the necessary outcome of a policy that he himself helped to invent. "The only thing that concerns me," he says, "is how to ensure that the boys and men who are going to have to do the killing will be able to return home to their families and be normal human beings." But in the end the point of all this is not just killing for the sake of killing. "Unilateral separation doesn't guarantee 'peace,'" Sofer says. "It guarantees a Zionist-Jewish state with an overwhelming majority of Jews."

If one supports the existence of a Jewish state in a largely non-Jewish land, this kind of violence is what has always—and will always—attend it, and, if one is as honest as Sofer (or Jabotinsky) one must support such violence as well. But if the drive to create and maintain such a state is what has led to this catastrophic situation, it ought to be clearer than ever that only the abandonment of this notion of statehood can lead to a just and lasting peace. The necessary antidote, then, is a state that treats all of its citizens equally and does not have to worry about the ratio of this to that segment of the population. Such a state would end the system of apartheid in the territories militarily occupied by Israel since 1967. It would end the somewhat more subtle form of apartheid practiced in Israel itself. And it would end the legalized institutionalization of Jewish supremacism on which the state of Israel is founded.

One possible—and I would say inspiring—blueprint for such a state already exists; it was published in March 2007 by the Israeli-Palestinian human rights group Adalah in the form of a draft "Democratic Constitution" for a secular and multicultural state.[40] Having lived under military rule for the first two decades of their experience as a minority, Israeli Palestinians had once been quiescent and reluctant to challenge their classification by the Jewish state as deracinated "Arabs" rather than members of the Palestinian people. Israel could once count on their silence while dealing with the national aspirations of the Palestinians living under its occupation. That is no longer the case.

The Democratic Constitution was intended to fill a gap left by contemporary constitutional debates in Israel, which, according to Adalah, "have been preoccupied with the question of, 'Who is a Jew?' [a regularly rehearsed debate in Israel] and have neglected the primary constitutional question of, 'Who is a Citizen?'" The document is founded on the principles enshrined in the Universal Declaration of Human Rights, notably the idea that all human beings are equal and that no nation or people possesses rights that can cancel out those of another. It affirms the fact that "the Palestinian Arab citizens of Israel have lived in their homeland for innumerable generations," are "an inseparable part of the Palestinian people," and have "not relinquished their national identity" but had their political status "changed against their will" when they became "a minority in their homeland" in 1948. It insists that the point of departure for peace and reconciliation between Israel and the Palestinian people—and the entire Arab nation—must be for Israel to recognize "its responsibility for the injustices of the Nakba and the Occupation; recognize the right of return of the Palestinian refugees based on UN Resolution 194; recognize the right of the Palestinian people to self-determination; and withdraw from all of the territories occupied in 1967." But the document's principal aim is to propose a constitution for a state "that does not control or occupy another people and that is based on full equality between all of its residents and between all of the different groups within it," a state in which "Jewish and Arab citizens shall respect each other's rights to live in peace, dignity, and equality, and will be united in recognizing and respecting the differences between them, as well as the differences that exist between all the groups in a democratic, bilingual, and multicultural state."

The publication of Adalah's Democratic Constitution—which was bitterly denounced from across the Jewish Israeli political spectrum—happened to coincide with the publication of a report by the UN's Committee on the Elimination of Racial Discrimination (CERD).[41] The CERD report challenged Israel to explain how its sense of itself as a Jewish state "does not result, in any systematic distinction, exclusion, restriction, or preference based on race, color, descent, or national or ethnic origin in the enjoyment of human rights," which would constitute a violation of the International Convention on the Elimination of All Forms of Racial Discrimination. The CERD report refers specifically to Israel's revised citizenship law (which denies the right of a Palestinian citizen of the state to marry a Palestinian from the Occupied Territories); to the unequal provision of state services; to structural inequalities between Arab and Jewish "sectors" of the Israeli economy; to the differential accessibility of land; to the "unrecognized villages"; and to many other issues. It respectfully recommends that Israel eliminate all forms of discrimination within the state.

As it is presently constituted, however, Israel could not possibly do that, because those forms of discrimination are inherent in its claim to be a Jewish state despite its large and growing non-Jewish population. Although Adalah's proposal is explicitly intended as a constitution for the state of Israel within its pre-1967 borders, if all of its principles of equality and justice were to be applied, Israel would no longer be, or claim to be, a Jewish state. And there would be no need for two separate states at all. Adalah's Democratic Constitution thus serves implicitly as a draft constitution for one democratic and secular state in all of historic Palestine, a state in which Jews and Palestinian Arabs could live together as equal citizens.

This vision of a genuinely multicultural democracy is quickly gaining the support of more and more Palestinians inside Israel, in the Occupied Territories, and in exile. There have been two major "one-state declarations" published, in London and in Madrid, and others will be following. Such declarations enjoy the support of a small number of Israelis as well. But there is no question that committed Zionists from across the political spectrum will resist the move toward the one-state solution in the way that privileged groups have historically resisted the erosion of their privileges. The resistance, even the violent resistance, of privileged groups did not stop South Africa from abandoning apartheid; the United States from abandoning Jim Crow laws or the institution of slavery itself; or, for that matter, the British aristocracy from relinquishing its privileges in the great Reform bills of the nineteenth century. And so it is those who seek to protect the privileges of the Jewish community in Israel/Palestine today who know perfectly well that they are running out of time, and that the world will not—or at least should not—tolerate the kinds of discrimination practiced in Israel and the Occupied Territories for much longer.

Echoing the statement by Ehud Olmert quoted earlier, the Israeli analyst Gershon Baskin writes,

> The clock is ticking rapidly on the very viability of the two-state solution. The correct reading of the preceding sentence should be that the clock is rapidly running out on the viability and the feasibility of the Zionist enterprise. Without fulfilling the two-state solution, there will be no Jewish State of Israel. The ticking clock is not solely because of the physical realities on the ground in the West Bank and Gaza, which impede the possibility of creating a Palestinian state there. The main factor accelerating the clock is the rapid movement of Palestinian intellectuals away from the idea of a separate Palestinian state in the West Bank and Gaza. It was the Palestinian intellectuals who led their national movement to support this solution from the 1970s onward, and it is today the Palestinian intellectuals who are the driving force toward adoption of the South Africa model for Palestine. Should the Palestinian masses reject the solution of two states in favor of one democratic state from the [Jordan] river to the [Mediterranean] sea, it is only a matter of time before the entire international community comes to their support, and then the end of the Zionist dream is in sight. If the Palestinian masses adopt the one-state democratic solution, Israel cannot win that battle.[42]

The one-state solution is not something that has to be worked out in advance with a series of "interim agreements" negotiated by armies of committees and subcommittees over a period of decades. It is the present reality. The one-state solution was put into effect in 1967: there is one government ruling differentially over two groups of people living on one land, granting to one group what it denies to the other. All that we need is to reconstitute that state as a state of equal citizens.

The antithesis to the institutionalized injustice of Zionism, then, has been carried along within Zionism itself in its drive to unify all of historic Palestine, a mission it accomplished four decades ago. Mutual and democratic cooperation between Palestinians and Israelis is not only feasible, it offers the only real hope for peace in the long run. The idea that people should be forcibly separated from each other according to their religious preferences has no place in the twenty-first century. And if such an approach—separation based on religion—is a guaranteed recipe for endless conflict, only its opposite—secular and democratic cooperation between people—offers a chance for genuine peace.

Notes

1. "Lieberman: Israel is Changing its Policies on Peace," *Reuters,* 17 April 2009.

2. See the full text of Netanyahu's 13 June speech at Bar Ilan University, http://www.haaretz.com/hasen/spages/1092810.html.

3. The forms of institutionalized discrimination practiced against Palestinian citizens of Israel, and the much more severe forms of curtailment imposed by Israel on the Palestinian inhabitants of the Occupied Territories, are covered in detail in Saree Makdisi, *Palestine Inside Out: An Everyday Occupation* (New York: Norton, 2008). Also see "Concluding Observations of the [UN] Committee on the Elimination of Racial Discrimination," International Convention on the Elimination of All Forms of Racial Discrimination, March 2007; Al Haq and other human rights NGOs in Israel/Palestine, "Parallel Report Jointly Submitted to the UN Committee on the Elimination of All Forms of Racial Discrimination, 69th Session," Geneva, July 2006; "NGO Report: Suggested Issues for Consideration Regarding Israel's Combined 10th, 11th, 12th, and 13th Periodic Report to the UN Committee on the Elimination of Racial Discrimination," 15 December 2005.

4. Isobel Kershner, "New Israeli Foreign Minister Bluntly Dismisses U.S. Peace Effort," *New York Times,* 2 April 2009.

5. "Livni: Lieberman Ruined Years of Peace Efforts in Just 20 Minutes," *Haaretz,* 3 April 2009.

6. See Charles Levinson, "Israeli Official Snubs Commitment on Palestinian Statehood," *Wall Street Journal,* 2 April 2009.

7. Quoted in Kershner, "New Israeli Foreign Minister."

8. See David Theo Goldberg, "Targets of Opportunity (On Racial Palestinianization)," chap. 4 in *The Threat of Race* (Oxford: Blackwell, 2008).

9. "Netanyahu Speech 'An Important Step Forward': White House," *AFP,* 14 June 2009.

10. There are around ten and a half million Palestinians today. Around four million live in the Occupied Territories, around five million live in exile, and a further one and a half million live in Israel. For details, see, e.g., Ingrid Jaradat Gassner, "Palestinian Refugees Living in the Diaspora," March 2008, http://thisweekinpalestine.com/details.php?id=2402&ed=151&edid=151.

11. On the number of Jewish colonists in the Occupied Territories, see the statistics published by, among others, the Foundation for Middle East Peace, http://www.fmep.org; Peace Now, http://www.peacenow.org.il; and B'Tselem, http://www.btslem.org.

12. Zeev Sternhell, "Colonial Zionism," *Haaretz,* 23 October 2008. Note that the title of this article is "Colonial Zionism," as though there were some other kind of Zionism, which is, historically speaking, a fantastic proposition.

13. See Shahar Ilan and Barak Ravid, "Olmert Warns of Binational State if No Peace Deal Reached," *Haaretz,* 16 September 2008.

14. Ehud Olmert, speech to Sixth Herzliya Conference, 24 January 2006.

15. For example, he made this point in September 2008. See Ilan and Ravid, "Olmert Warns of Binational State."

16. David Landau, "Maximum Jews, Minimum Palestinians," *Haaretz,* 13 November 2003.

17. Cf. Aluf Benn, "Olmert to Haaretz: Two State Solution, or Israel is Done For," *Haaretz,* 29 November 2007.

18. See the memorandum submitted by Montagu to the British Cabinet in 1917, UK National Archives, CAB 24/24.

19. See "Recommendations of the King-Crane Commission," available on the United Nations website, http://unispal.un.org/.

20. See Vladimir Jabotinsky, "The Iron Wall," in Lenni Brenner, *The Iron Wall: Zionist Revisionism from Jabotinsky to Shamir* (London: Zed Books, 1984), 204.

21. Benny Morris interview with Ari Shavit. See Ari Shavit, "Survival of the Fittest," *Haaretz,* 16 January 2004.

22. See the text of Resolution 273 on the UN website, http://daccessdds.un.org/.

23. Rotem Sela, "Israel Protests UN Chief Ban Ki-Moon's Use of Term 'Nakba,'" *Haaretz,* 16 May 2008.

24. "Livni: Palestinians Can Erase Nakba, Celebrate Independence," *Ynet News,* 15 May 2008.

25. See, among other sources, Human Sciences Research Council, "Occupation, Colonialism, Apartheid? A Re-Assessment of Israel's Practices in the Occupied Palestinian Territories Under International Law," Cape Town, May 2009. Also see Makdisi, *Palestine Inside Out.*

26. See, e.g., Makdisi, *Palestine Inside Out,* 143–50.

27. See, e.g., John Quigley, *The Case for Palestine* (Durham, NC: Duke University Press, 2005), 129.

28. UN Office for the Coordination of Humanitarian Affairs, "The Humanitarian Impact on Palestinians of Israeli Settlements and Infrastructure in the West Bank," July 2007.

29. See International Court of Justice, "Advisory Opinion on the Legal Consequences of the Construction of the Wall in the Occupied Palestinian Territory," 9 July 2004.

30. See note on colonization statistics above.

31. See UN Office for the Coordination of Humanitarian Affairs, "The Humanitarian Impact on Palestinians."

32. Statistics from reports published by the UN Office for the Coordination of Humanitarian Affairs, http://www.ochaopt.org.

33. "UN Human Rights Envoy Says Gaza a Prison for Palestinians," *Reuters,* 27 September 2006.

34. Rory McCarthy, "A Disaster for Everybody," *Guardian* (London), 12 May 2008.

35. Anne Penketh, "The Pasta, Paper and Hearing Aids That Could Threaten Israel's Security," *Independent* (London), 2 March 2009.

36. See the joint NGO publication, "The Gaza Strip: A Humanitarian Implosion," March 2008, http://www.savethechildren.org.uk/sites/default/files/docs/gaza5308_1.pdf.

37. See, e.g., Food and Agriculture Organization of the United Nations, "Agriculture Sector Report: Impact of Gaza Crisis," March 2009, http://unispal.un.org/UNISPAL.NSF/0/4E0F921868AC253785257584004D4C1B.

38. Akiva Eldar, "Gaza Sewage Pumped into Sea over Past Three Months," *Haaretz,* 16 June 2008.

39. Arnon Sofer interview with Ruthie Blum, "It's the Demography, Stupid," *Jerusalem Post,* 21 May 2004.

40. See Adalah, "The Democratic Constitution," http://www.adalah.org/eng/constitution.php.

41. See "Concluding Observations of the Committee on the Elimination of Racial Discrimination (CERD)," March 2007, http://www.universalhumanrightsindex.org/documents/824/1165/document/en/pdf/text.pdf.

42. Gershon Baskin, "An Imaginary Announcement," *Jerusalem Post,* 19 March 2007.

Contributors

Ali Abunimah is a freelance journalist and author of *One Country: A Bold Proposal to End the Israeli-Palestinian Impasse.* He has published and lectured widely on the question of Palestine and is co-founder of the Electronic Intifada, an award-winning online publication about Palestine and the Palestinian-Israeli conflict.

Susan Musarrat Akram is clinical professor of law at Boston University. She has extensive teaching and litigation experience in immigration, international human rights, and refugee law. She is former director of the Immigration Project at Public Counsel in Los Angeles, the Political Asylum/Immigration Representation Project in Boston, and the American Council for Nationalities Service in Riyadh, Saudi Arabia. She is editor (with Michael Dumper, Michael Lynk, and Iain Scobbie) of *International Law and the Israeli-Palestinian Conflict: A Rights-Based Approach to Middle East Peace.*

Tamim al-Barghouti is a Palestinian-Egyptian poet and political scientist, and author of *Benign Nationalism: Egyptian Nation State Building Under Occupation* and *The Umma and the Dawla: The Nation-State and the Arab Middle East.* He studied politics at Cairo University, the American University in Cairo, and Boston University, where he received his PhD. He has taught at the American University in Cairo, Georgetown University, and the Free University of Berlin, and was a fellow at the Berlin Institute for Advanced Studies' Europe in the Middle East program. He is currently the core team leader of the United Nations' ESCWA project "The Arab World in 2025." Al-Barghouti has also published six volumes of poetry in classical and spoken Arabic, including *Mijana* (1999), *Maqam Iraq* (2005), *fil-Quds* (2008), and *Ya Masr Hanet* (2012). He wrote a weekly column in the *Daily Star* (Lebanon) between 2003 and 2004 and has written a biweekly column in the Egyptian daily *al-Shorouk* since 2010.

Rochelle Davis is associate professor of anthropology at the Center for Contemporary Arab Studies at Georgetown University's Edmund A. Walsh

School of Foreign Service. She is author of *Palestinian Village Histories: Geographies of the Displaced,* winner of the 2011 Albert Hourani Book Award from the Middle East Studies Association.

Noura Erakat is a Palestinian human rights attorney, an Abraham L. Freedman Teaching Fellow at Temple University, and adjunct professor of international human rights law at Georgetown University. She was a co-founder of Arab Women Arising for Justice (AMWAJ) and the U.S. Palestinian Community Network (USPCN). She has published in the *Berkeley Law Journal of Middle Eastern and Islamic Law, Middle East Report,* and other publications, and is a contributing editor of *Jadaliyya*.com.

Leila Farsakh is associate professor of political science at the University of Massachusetts-Boston and author of *Palestinian Labor Migration to Israel: Labor, Land and Occupation.* She has published widely on questions related to Palestinian labor, the Oslo process, and the one-state solution and has worked with international organizations including the Organisation for Economic Co-operation and Development (OECD) and the Palestine Economic Policy Research Institute.

As'ad Ghanem is senior lecturer in the School of Political Science, University of Haifa. He is author of *The Palestinian Arab Minority in Israel: A Political Study* and *The Palestinian Regime: A "Partial Democracy,"* as well as *Palestinian Politics after Arafat: The Predicament of a Failed National Movement, Ethnic Politics in Israel—The Margins and the Ashkinazi Centre,* and (with Mohanad Mustafa) *Palestinians in Israel: Indigenous Group Politics in the Jewish State.*

Michael C. Hudson is director of the Middle East Institute and professor of political science at the National University of Singapore. He is a past president of the Middle East Studies Association and professor emeritus at Georgetown University, where he served as director of the Center for Contemporary Arab Studies for many years. He is author of *Arab Politics: The Search for Legitimacy, The Palestinians: New Directions,* and *The Precarious Republic: Political Modernization in Lebanon,* and editor of *Middle East Dilemma: The Politics and Economics of Arab Integration.*

Islah Jad is associate professor and lecturer on gender issues and politics at the Women's Studies Institute and Cultural Studies Department of Birzeit

University. She has published widely on the role of women in politics, Palestinian women and the relationships among them, Islam, and NGOs. She is a consultant on gender issues to the United Nations Development Programme and coauthor of the UN's Arab Development Report on Women's Empowerment.

Mimi Kirk is research director for the Middle East Institute in Washington, DC. She is editor of *Modern Middle East Authoritarianism: Roots, Ramifications, and Crisis,* with Noureddine Jebnoun and Mehrdad Kia (2013); *Uncovering Iraq: Trajectories of Disintegration and Transformation,* with Chris Toensing (2011); and *Industrialization in the Gulf: A Socioeconomic Revolution,* with Jean-François Seznec (2009). Her writing has appeared in *Middle East Report, Jadaliyya,* the *Atlantic,* and *Foreign Policy.*

Loren D. Lybarger is associate professor of classics and world religions at Ohio University. He specializes in the ethnographic analysis of religion and identity among Palestinians in the Middle East and North America. He is author of *Identity and Religion in Palestine: The Struggle between Islamism and Secularism in the Occupied Territories* and is a member of the board of directors of the Palestinian American Research Center based in Ramallah and Washington, DC.

Saree Makdisi is professor of English and comparative literature at the University of California, Los Angeles. He is author of *Romantic Imperialism: Universal Empire and the Culture of Modernity, William Blake and the Impossible History of the 1790s,* and *Palestine Inside Out: An Everyday Occupation,* and is coeditor (with Felicity Nussbaum) of *The Arabian Nights in Historical Context: Between East and West.* His articles on contemporary events have appeared in the *Los Angeles Times, The Nation,* the *London Review of Books,* and other publications.

Gabriel Piterberg is professor of Near East history at the University of California, Los Angeles. Born in Buenos Aires, Argentina, he grew up in Israel and studied Middle East and European history at Tel Aviv University and the University of Oxford. His books include *An Ottoman Tragedy: History and Historiography at Play* and *The Returns of Zionism: Myths, Politics and Scholarship in Israel.* He also writes for the *New Left Review* and the *London Review of Books.*

Sara Roy is a senior research scholar at the Center for Middle Eastern Studies at Harvard University. Trained as a political economist, her research in the Gaza Strip and West Bank has dealt with economic, social, and political development and U.S. foreign aid to the region. Her books include *Hamas and Civil Society in Gaza: Engaging the Islamist Social Sector, Failing Peace: Gaza and the Palestinian-Israeli Conflict,* and *The Gaza Strip: The Political Economy of De-development* (3rd edition forthcoming, 2013).

Index